CLAUDE SIMON

THE INTERTEXTUAL DIMENSION

MARY ORR

UNIVERSITY OF GLASGOW FRENCH & GERMAN PUBLICATIONS
1993

University of Glasgow French and German Publications

Series Editors: Mark G. Ward (German)
Geoff Woollen (French)

Consultant Editors: Colin Smethurst
Kenneth Varty

Modern Languages Building, University of Glasgow,
Glasgow G12 8QL, Scotland.

First published 1993.

Printed by Castle Cary Press, Somerset BA7 7AN.

ISBN 0 85261 372 5

Contents

Abbreviations and Conventions		v
Acknowledgments		vi
Introduction		1
Chapter One	The Classics and Renaissance literature	9
	Simon and Montaigne	10
	Sub-version and the intertext as literary authority	15
	The intertext as literary translation	18
	The intertext as source, influence and alternative version	25
Chapter Two	Seventeenth-century literature	35
	Seventeenth-century French theatre	38
	Shakespeare	44
	Spanish Golden Age drama	51
	Theatre as structure	54
Chapter Three	Eighteenth-century literature	59
	The Encyclopedia	60
	The History	65
	Simon and Rousseau	72

Chapter Four	Nineteenth-century literature	80
	Simon and Baudelaire	83
	Simon and Dostoyevsky	84
	Simon and Stendhal	88
	Simon and Balzac	93
	Simon and Flaubert	97
Chapter Five	Simon and Proust	106
Chapter Six	Twentieth-century literature	138
	Revolutionaries of the novel	140
	Simon and Faulkner	140
	Simon and Joyce	148
	Revolutions in the novel	152
	Simon and Reed	153
	Simon and Orwell	161
Chapter Seven	Simon quoting Simon	175
	Intra-textuality as regenerative strategy	176
	The intra-text as autobiographeme	185
Conclusion		192
Bibliography		204

Abbreviations and Conventions

To avoid the clutter of footnotes, references to all other articles and critical works cited are incorporated into the text and operate on the author-date system. The select bibliography contains all details of these references and of other works of importance in Simon criticism. The following abbreviations for Simon's works are used throughout, all references being to their first edition.

Trich	*Le Tricheur* (1945)
CR	*La Corde raide* (1947)
Gull	*Gulliver* (1952)
SP	*Le Sacre du printemps* (1954)
V	*Le Vent* (1957)
H	*L'Herbe* (1958)
RF	*La Route des Flandres* (1960)
P	*Le Palace* (1962)
F	*Femmes* (1966)
Hist	*Histoire* (1967)
BP	*La Bataille de Pharsale* (1969)
OA	*Orion aveugle* (1970)
CC	*Les Corps conducteurs* (1971)
Trip	*Triptyque* (1973)
LC	*Leçon de choses* (1976)
G	*Les Géorgiques* (1981)
Disc	*Discours de Stockholm* (1986)
I	*L'Invitation* (1987)
Album	*Album d'un amateur* (1988)
A	*L'Acacia* (1989)

Acknowledgements

I should like to express my thanks to everyone who offered me academic support in the publication of this book from its earliest stages as a thesis. My especial thanks go to Claude Simon, for his willingness to be interviewed and for his ongoing interest and correspondence. The largest debt of gratitude I owe is to my friends, whose helpful conversations and comments have been most valuable, and to my late father for his constant encouragement and support.

I would also like to acknowledge the support of the University of St Andrews, for grants towards travel and research costs for the final chapter and completion of the project as a book, and the Carnegie Trust for the Universities of Scotland, who provided a financial guarantee that greatly facilitated its publication.

Mary Orr St Andrews, November 1992

Introduction

For a writer whose novels were largely unknown to the general public even in France before he received the 1985 Nobel Prize for Literature, Claude Simon had already provoked much specialist response: several monographs and single issues of literary journals were devoted to him, not to mention a mass of reviews and articles, theses and essays, amply documented by the select bibliography to this study. Since 1985, critical output has increased both within France and among francophiles, focus shifting somewhat from thematic to generic and opus-centred analyses.

Influences on Simon and his use of previous literature have always been topics of critical interest, especially since the Nobel: Bertrand, Evans, and most recently Reitsma La-Brujeere have produced monographs on the subject, thus complementing the vast range of articles and essay studies. They are all unsatisfactory for various reasons. Either they sweep broadly over the whole opus without considering intertextual mechanisms in depth or they focus on only one text (Reitsma La-Brujeere, 1992) or a cycle within the opus (Evans, 1987 and Bertrand, 1987). Another blind spot has been the adherence to mainly twentieth-century influences. Important as these undoubtedly are, Simon's intertextual range is much wider. In order to show the breadth of Simon's uses of intertexts and how he uses them, this book adopts an approach different from others before it. Whereas these examine a Simon novel, or novels in the order of their place in his opus, my method of categorising is the chronological order of the intertexts and writers whom Simon has variously 'used' (in interviews as well as novels). Starting with the sixteenth century and moving forward to the present, my study will conclude with a consideration of Simon's uses of his own previous work. While focus throughout my book remains largely the place of French literature in Simon's work, his range of intertexts from other literary traditions (read mostly in translation) will also be taken into account, for various crucial turning points in Simon's stylistic development can only be mapped via such investigations. At a more general level, this book also explores the term 'intertextuality', and responds to a challenge from Sykes, who sees this term as 'the most fruitful terrain for the immediate future: the development of theories of reading' (Duncan, 1985, p. 150).

First, though, space needs to be cleared amid the work which has already been done, in order to delineate the scope and material to be covered by this different approach. Early monographs, most notably those by Loubère and Sykes, discussed Simon's relationship to Proust (Loubère, 1975, p. 40 and Sykes, 1979, pp. 131, 142, 176); Faulkner (Loubère, pp. 101, 240, Sykes, p. 83); Joyce (Loubère, pp. 240-1 and Sykes, p. 106); and also mention Dostoyevsky, Stendhal, Flaubert, Conrad, Chekhov, Malraux and Beckett. Their analyses, however, are representative of the relatively narrow focus to be found in almost all the books, monographs, theses and articles which discuss intertextuality in Simon. They do not include a wide-ranging survey of intertextuality in Simon: nor do they consider the variety of modes in which he uses it. They have preferred to describe literary influence simply in terms of the unqualified identification of an intertext, or have chosen to comment on a particular precursor in the context of one, or at most two, of Simon's novels. Moreover, most efforts have concentrated on the role of twentieth-century writers in Simon's writing—Proust, Faulkner, Joyce, and Orwell. The rare exceptions are the following: Apeldoorn (1981), who examines links between Simon and Balzac; Birn (1980), who studies some eighteenth-century influences on Simon; Carroll (1982), who mentions parallels with *Hamlet*; and Hollenbeck (1982), who refers to baroque theatre in Simon. These will be discussed more fully in the relevant chapters. Articles have often produced the most satisfactory and detailed discussion of intertexts in Simon, and concentrate on one of the major twentieth-century precursors already mentioned: they provide a useful foundation for any expanded study of all of Simon's writing, and I shall be taking up the views of the key article analyses where relevant. It is also true to say that most studies tend not to refer their thematic and stylistic comparisons to wider questions of intertextuality as writing practice. Again, my study aims not only to relate Proustian, Faulknerian, Joycean and other intertexts to the whole of Simon's writing, but also, incidentally, to suggest how they may enhance an understanding of deeper principles and processes involved in writers' use of intertexts to enrich textual referentiality.

Having established the place for a wide-ranging study of intertextuality in Simon, what is meant by the term 'intertextuality', which has been used rather loosely so far in this introduction? First, let us define what intertextuality is not. It is not the subjective response of a given reader who parallels one text with another. Fletcher (1975) exemplifies the dangers of such an approach, where highly tenuous thematic comparisons are forged between Simon's novels and the works of other novelists. The present study demands that there be evidence within Simon's *œuvre* of his *own* reading of a specific text, and 'unsignposted' passages will be considered only if they occur in conjunction with sufficient proof that Simon is influenced extensively by that text elsewhere in his work. Let us, for example, take the case of *Histoire*. Intertexts from Proust are not clearly marked, but Proustian names and other similarities to Proust's work furnish enough grounds for locating specific comparisons and these, backed up by Simon's interview articles, allow us to read *Histoire* 'through' Proust, to gain valid and rewarding insights into the workings of intertextuality.

In its broadest sense, then, intertextuality is the reference to works of art from the past remodelled in the present; it spans all languages, types of discourse and media. Intertexts from music or the visual arts within literature, as in the *Gesamtkunstwerk* of German Romanticism or in Proust, do exist in Simon's writing, but space is too limited here to explore them. Work in this area has already begun and full-scale investigation is merited. 'Intertextuality' is confined in this book to its written manifestations.

Intertextual investigations often make the distinction between the quotation from others' writings and *intra*textuality or the process of self-quotation. As Britton rightly remarks:

> One important version of [quotation and intertextual reference] is of course Simon's quotation of himself. The intertextual dimension of the corpus is... extremely marked; an extensive network of allusions, overlaps and permutations of textual material is gradually built up and modified with each successive text, so that the experience of reading Simon involves a mixture of recognition and displacement. (1987, p. 105)

Simon is indisputably a major exponent of intratextual refabrication. Indeed, all his early fragments appear in some form or other in a later novel. Duffy (Duncan, 1985, pp. 30-49) and more recently Sardonak (March 1992) have made the most substantial study to date of Simon's reusage of his own fragments. As the precursor is an early and unquestionable version of himself, the later figuration will embody the language of the earlier works. *L'Acacia* is paradigmatic here and will be discussed as a prime example of an intratext in the final chapter. To re-use one's earlier works may at first sight suggest a paucity of invention, but in fact a greater poetic and associative density of language may be the result in the hands of a skilful practitioner. As is the case with intertextuality (the borrowing from another), self-borrowing indicates the regenerative function of quotation. Previous words, themes and forms are revitalized by other components and combinations, so that new reverberations will occur from these old materials.

The theoretical parameters of this book need also to be defined from its outset. Criticism devoted to intertextuality in literature has mainly been limited to particular viewpoints. For example, the question of imitation is explored by way of a relatively traditional approach to influence illustrated by Meyer (1968). Structuralist approaches are adopted and elucidated by Barthes (1972), Culler (1976), and Kristeva (1969); Bakhtin (1978) offers a sociological and Marxist perspective on intertextuality; while Bloom (1973) outlines a psychoanalytical approach to the subject. Intertextuality has also been seen as 'mise en abyme' between specific texts by Dällenbach (1976) and as self-reflexivity in more general terms by Jenny (1976). Genette (1982) considers references within an 'architexte' , the sum of all codes of writing. However, no major book covering all aspects of intertextuality exists. How then is the term to be defined in order for it to become and remain throughout this book a useful working tool? The answer lies, I think, in keeping this general term separate from its usage by any one particular critic, and to see it as containing these various theories. The word 'intertextuality', then, refers to a specific critical viewpoint in a section or chapter until that of a succeeding section or chapter displaces it. None of the patterns contradicts another. Instead, each is complementary in the construction of an open definition of intertextuality. My claim in adopting this approach is to allow the term to encompass and explore a wide variety of writing structures. Ultimately, then, I shall show that to view the intertextual in Simon is to examine his *literary usage* of the composition from the decomposed texts of others, and to understand that Simon's writing projects its own decomposition within the composition of a future writing.

Because Simon's novels, particularly *Histoire, La Bataille de Pharsale* and *Les Géorgiques,* are so intertextually rich, individual analyses of these have offered one obvious method of exploring the relationships between the host and guest discourses. However, study of particular intertexts or their usage in a single novel (Reitsma La-Brujeere, 1992) or in a novel-by-novel study (Bertrand, 1987 and Evans, 1987) comes up against problems of repetitiveness and fragmentariness. Moreover, an attempt to catalogue all the different intertexts found in every novel, while perhaps scholarly, presents a rather dull and disjointed reading of Simon as exponent of intertextuality, and of his increasing skill in using previous literature as his work matures. This approach also ignores, to a large extent, the place of references in Simon's interviews, as well as the breadth of his sources.

To bridge the gap between the in-depth and the overview approaches, the method I have chosen to adopt, namely the non-chronological study of Simon's works, also has its pitfalls. Certain works will receive little attention. However, this has been the case anyway, even in the 'standard' novel-by-novel monographs. My method is nevertheless chronological, for the subject of intertextuality is treated by categorizing Simon's use of previous literature according to the century in which it was written. The major advantage of this approach is that it highlights Simon's knowledge and reworking of the earlier literature of the sixteenth, seventeenth and eighteenth centuries. None of these has been studied to any great extent before. The stress previously laid on the wealth of material from nineteenth- and twentieth-century writers is thus put in perspective, and a new approach to reading Simon is the corollary of dislocating his opus. The specifically century-by-century framework of this method is modified only in the fifth chapter, which deals exclusively with Proust, but is fitted between the nineteenth- and twentieth-century groupings of intertexts to show his key place in Simon's literary development.

While my survey of intertexts in Simon aims to be as comprehensive as possible and to highlight quotations and allusions which have hitherto been ignored, it cannot be complete. First, space is limited; second, even the most assiduous reader will miss references; third and most important, exhaustive cataloguing of less weighty references takes away from the interest of more major ones. Hence, figures in almost every century, while mentioned by Simon, have had to be excluded, for example quotation from Pascal and La Fontaine in the seventeenth-century chapter, Rimbaud, Mallarmé and Maupassant in the nineteenth-century chapter and Borges, Conrad and Camus in the penultimate one. In the twentieth-century chapter, reference could also be made to the influence, and the critical writings of Ricardou on Simon and the latter's subsequent rejection of them, together with the collective theories and practices of the Nouveau Roman. Again, in order to streamline this study, these have been discarded, because they belong to a sub-category of intertexts: critical theory. This area is again a potential, and important, subject for further investigation into Simon's writing practices.

Each chapter, while structured according to century, has an additional organising principle: a particular theoretical standpoint on intertextuality is used as a kind of Ariadne's thread. Thus, in my first chapter, which deals with Simon's use of Classical Latin and Renaissance texts, the 'traditional' approach to intertextuality, that is influence and source-hunting, is the guiding principle. Analysis of the wider issue of the role of imitation and vernacular translation is central to, and opens out, the argument of this aspect of intertextuality.

Chapter Two discusses Simon's borrowings from seventeenth-century drama. It uses the very different Structuralist approach to intertextuality as expounded by Culler and Barthes. This provides another key: intertextuality is seen as a dialogue of systems of discourse. It is this idea which is then elucidated by the drama of Simon's writing which embodies intertexts from French, English and Spanish plays. The consideration of dramatic structure in Simon's novels will also be examined here, as many have three or five 'acts' which underpin their textual constructions.

The third chapter explores Simon's uses of Enlightenment texts, and in particular the Encyclopedia and the History, which are exploited in *Les Corps conducteurs* and *Histoire* respectively. The concept which links these larger intertexts is classification of heterogeneous materials. Kristeva's work on intertextuality offers a theoretical parallel and springboard for this chapter. It was she who coined the word 'intertextuality' and began to categorize its manifestations. The nexus of codes and referential potential of language as History or Encyclopedia is thus highlighted in the use Simon makes of such heterogenous materials, and how he controls and shapes the proliferations which these genres entail.

Chapter Four then looks at Simon's use of nineteenth-century writers with specific reference to the genre of the novel in its Russian and French variations. Dostoyevsky's novels played an important part in shaping Simon's early work, while Simon's knowledge of French novelist precursors determines, to a large degree, his prejudices and criteria in prose creation. It is Bakhtin's theory of literary evolution with its apotheosis in the novel which forms the setting for this chapter. Here, emphasis is more on literary developments established by nineteenth-century novelists and Simon's stated views (and misreadings) of them than on direct references to their work in Simon's novels. Hence, where his work runs counter to the tradition of 'realism' in the novel will become entirely apparent, helped by the focus of the chapter. It is devoted primarily to Simon's interviews, an area largely unexplored by previous critics.

The interview materials and the nineteenth-century novel context then give shape, position and definition to Simon's particular development of the French novel as dominated by Proust. As previously indicated, chapter five breaks with the overtly historical frame to concentrate on the influence of Proust on Simon's writing, throughout his whole *œuvre*. Proust is for Simon the quintessential literary 'father'. This concept and the concomitant need to reject the progenitor signals Bloom's theory of intertextuality, the 'anxiety of influence', which provides a further pattern of intertextual relationships in this book.

The sixth chapter looks at twentieth-century writing collected together by Genette's label for intertextuality, the 'architexte'. This theory potentially draws upon the preceding five models from the earlier chapters in a way which lends a certain circular structure to our study as a whole. Two aspects of this circular revolution through intertexts are examined in this chapter. First, there is Simon's reaction to the major twentieth-century revolutionaries of literature, Joyce and Faulkner. Second, there is Simon's response to revolutionary literature in the political sense of the word: here, study focusses on intertexts from Reed and Orwell. Examination of the latter opens up the question of the overlap between narrating subject and autobiographer. The final chapter takes *L'Acacia* as epitome to distinguish the two. Reflexivity and self-reflection are questioned in terms of the extensive use of 'mise en abyme' and intratextuality in Simon's latest novel. Its proliferations and branchings and inversions as family tree close and open up the considerations of the whole book; Simon's part in and against his literary and cultural heritage.

The conclusion then evaluates these chronological groupings of intertexts found in Simon's works to establish the breadth of his use of references, allusions and quotations from other writers. If Simon's reputation as a major exponent of intertextuality can thus be established, then the development and importance of relationships at different times in Simon's own career (in its historical unfolding) may also be clarified. The conclusion also offers a synthesis of the types of Simon's intertextual usage which emerge from the findings of each chapter. From these comments on the particular use of intertexts, it is then possible to make some more general observations on the importance of intertextuality as a narrative strategy in Simon, and its function relative to some other narrative problems in particular works. While many aspects of Simon's work will remain relatively unexplored, this book does attempt to take up Sykes's challenge to Simonists to focus on the relationships between Proust's descriptive writing and Simon's as 'the beginnings of an even more fertile examination of Simon's own ideas' (Sykes in Duncan, 1985, p. 153). By meeting that challenge as one of its major goals in chapter five, this book goes further, and investigates literary relationships other than that with Proust which have shaped or merely impinged on Simon's writing. Ultimately, and most importantly, by pinpointing uses of intertexts in Simon, this book is a catalyst to further discussion of intertextuality in Simon and as a post-modern rhetorical device, leaving both fields open for the further work of future critics.

Chapter One

The Classics and Renaissance Literature

The study of influences on a given writer and the analysis of the 'sources' to be found in his/her writings have always been part of what is considered a 'traditional' approach in literary criticism. Source-hunting is usually associated with the idea of authority: the quotations or echoes are used as touchstones, points of reference by which the new writer may orient his/her work as well as a means of transferring the prestige of the precursor to the disciple. The terms 'influence', 'source' and 'authorities' have acquired something of a stigma, and are now often considered to be outmoded in critical methodology; nevertheless these concepts still play an important part in any study of intertextuality. Hermerén observes that 'influence statements provide us with causal explanations; they indicate *why* works of art have certain qualities' (1975, p. 122 [his emphasis]).

All writers practise on previous writing in order to create independently. Indeed, the use of quotations and the reusage of works of previous writers can be indicators of greater or lesser literary merit, separating the plagiarist from the imitator proper. For the former, the autonomy of the original remains intact, while for the latter, the model imitated is subordinated to the needs of the new context. Imitation of sources is therefore seen by many critics as essential in the development of a writer. Cave, for example, writes:

> the establishing of sources has usually been the prelude to a definition of the originality of an author as the residue which remains when the source-materials have been subtracted from his text. Any such residue is thus seen as having its source or origin in the author's mind, as being produced by an act of creation (virtually ex nihilo). Imitation theory is more complex in that it recognises the extent to which the production of any discourse is conditioned by pre-existing instances of discourse, the writer is always a re-writer, the problem then being to differentiate and authenticate the re-writing. This is executed not by the addition of something wholly new, but by the dismembering and reconstruction of what has already been written (1979, p. 76).

It is by studying Simon's uses of the Classics as both source and influence that his place as a 'rewriter', dismembering and reconstructing elements from a deeply engrained French literary and educational tradition, may be better understood. As Van Tieghem has put it: 'quel que soit l'apport étranger, l'Antiquité classique est toujours à la base de la formation esthétique de nos écrivains (1967, p. 4). Simon's formation as imitator, not copyist, will also become apparent in this chapter through analysis of the medium of translation as intertextual training ground, and the ways Classics and Renaissance texts are employed in his works. No critic has taken the trouble to investigate the particularly 'Renaissance' qualities of Simon's writing or study in detail his borrowings from and influence by the Classics. Karen Gould has indeed focussed attention on Simon's uses of Classical mythology, highlighting for example Greek and Roman mythic patterns of the archetypal feminine and the symbolic journey in his novels (1979, passim). However, her investigation of Simon's use of specific intertexts is a minor concern, and it is this area that I wish to explore, not in the context of Antiquity as such, but within the framework of French Renaissance practices of writing, which challenged Latin as the language of authority. Moreover, by imitating Renaissance texts as well, Simon exploits intertextual potential to a double degree. As is well known, too, the invention of printing led to the rediscovery in the sixteenth century of hitherto forgotten Greek and Latin texts which, through translation, acquired an increased readership, provoked a circulation of ideas and challenged source authorities. The copying of the content of these in translation produced a surge of vernacular imitations. 'Writing' as topic was no longer confined to theoretical treatises on poetics: it became valid subject-matter within creative works, which explored their own production. Quotations thus also acquired an important function: that of marking a separation between the old and new discourses, which 'draws attention to the mode of operation rather than to the product of the writing system' (Cave, 1979, p. 182). Discovery of Simon's style *as against* the Classics, his vernacular translations and imitations of Latin texts, his use of Renaissance texts to mark and undermine his literary authorities and heritage will thus be the foci of the chapter.

Simon and Montaigne

The borrowing, dismembering and reconstruction of quotations from the Classics and contemporaries, together with the self-exploration that can entail, is central to Renaissance writers like

Montaigne. He is the archetypal 'bricoleur'; he uses Latin and translated quotations; he imitates and distorts the writings of precursors by means of parody, pastiche, satire, irony and vulgarization. In similar ways, Simon interacts with other authors to form a 'bricolage' of languages and previous writing (including his Renaissance forebears). The comparison of his practice with that of Montaigne is the starting point for establishing Simon's place in this tradition. Both Montaigne and Simon acknowledge the importance of intertexts in shaping perception:

> Nous sommes à la fois formés par le monde des textes et par le monde lui-même; nous percevons d'une façon à la fois directe et médiatisé (Grivel, 1979, p. 106).

Simon's remark is reminiscent of Montaigne's description of integrating various materials into experience. He likens this process to bees gathering pollen from many kinds of flowers to make honey:

> Les abeilles pillotent deçà delà les fleurs, mais elles en font après le miel, qui est tout leur; ce n'est plus thin ny marjolaine: ainsi les pièces empruntées d'autruy, il les transformera et confondera, pour en faire un ouvrage tout sien, à sçavour son jugement. Son institution, son travail et estude ne vise qu'à le *former* (*Essais,* Bk. 1, p. 199 [my emphasis]).

Montaigne and Simon also write about writing within their writing, and express their ideas in remarkably similar ways. Montaigne describes involvement in his writing production thus:

> Me peignant pour autruy, je me suis peint en moy de couleurs plus nettes que n'estoyent les miennes premieres. *Je n'ay pas plus faict mon livre que mon livre m'a faict*, livre consubstantiel à son autheur, d'une occupation propre... estrangere comme tous autres livres (*Essais*, Bk. 2, p. 326 [my emphasis].

Simon formulates such creative processes at work in his novels as follows: 'Le roman se fait, je le fais et il me fait' (Duranteau, 1967, p. 3). It is only the greater degree of self-generation in Simon's writing (which we will discuss more fully in the final chapter), which distinguishes him from his sixteenth-century counterpart. Both claim that their creation impinges upon them, thereby eschewing the position of omniscient authors who control and direct their writing. Montaigne, indeed, makes the distinction within the *Essais*:

> Les sçavans partent et notent leurs fantasies plus specifiquement, et par le menu. Moy, qui n'y voy qu'autant que l'usage m'en informe, sans regle, presente generalement les miennes, et *à tastons* (Bk. 3, p. 287 [my emphasis]).

This comment on writing as constant and tentative process comes from Montaigne's very last essay. As a mature writer, Montaigne understands the motor of his *Essais*, this interaction of writing, the written and the writer, who is still open to the new directions the text might suggest. This definition appears strangely modern: Simon reiterates it within his own fiction in the preface to *Orion aveugle,* even using the same image:

> cette toute autre histoire qu'est l'adventure singulière du narrateur qui ne cesse de chercher, découvrant *à tâtons* le monde dans et par l'écriture [my emphasis].

For Montaigne and Simon, theories of writing are seen to be inseparable from textual production, just as the writer and narrator are inseparable and yet, paradoxically, not the same entity. The 'moy' of Montaigne's *Essais* is thus not Montaigne: the *Essais* are not his autobiography. Empirical facts may be used as raw materials, but they are fictionalized and the writer becomes other by his/her writing. Such questions as intratextuality, autobiography and the self-in-narrative will be addressed in more detail with reference to *L'Acacia* in the final chapter.

Attitudes to other kinds of mental process (reflection as thought process) are shared by Simon and Montaigne. Neither considers himself a great thinker—Montaigne said 'Je ne suis pas philosophe', the identical words repeated by Simon on numerous occasions in interviews (*Essais,* Bk. 3, p. 164; and, for example, Ricardou, 1975, p. 405: 'Je ne suis ni philosophe ni sociologue'). Philosophical questions about life, however, are valid concerns of fiction, as Simon recognizes in his one direct reference to Montaigne. Indeed, his Renaissance precursor furnishes the thematic and philosophical sub-structure for the whole of the *Route des Flandres* cycle, which is

> une constante et perpetuelle contestation... le 'Que sais-je' de Montaigne... Il me semble que c'est là... la démarche créatrice de l'esprit elle-même (Juin, 1960, p. 5).

Simon's opus contains a constant questioning of its own existence, which is the essence of Montaigne's momentous interrogation. For

Montaigne, this existential thunderbolt comes when he is thrown from his horse and glimpses death. Simon refictionalizes this experience in his very first novel, *Le Tricheur*. He updates the mode of transport to a bicycle from which Gautier falls to confront death in a similar way (*Essais,* Bk. 2, p. 44 and *Trich,* p. 88). This isolated episode is developed much more fully in *La Route des Flandres*, where the key motif is the horse, prompter of the questioning, as in Montaigne, of what is knowable. Simon takes the topos and develops the implications a stage further, for the existence of the horse itself is not fully verifiable (*RF,* pp. 26-7). The horse is passed on three separate occasions in Simon's novel, and each time provokes unresolved, existential reflection in Georges, for whom the uncertainties of his past will never be clear. He adopts Montaigne's question with choric intensity as the novel nears its end: 'mais comment savoir?' (*RF,* pp. 295, 302, 306). The formal aspects of the text mirror and stress these themes of questioning and unknowability, for in *La Route des Flandres* there are a flow of unanswered questions and a propensity to parentheses, which provide alternative versions (*RF,* pp. 183-9 for numerous examples). Any linear development is interrupted by a new bracket, allowing the writing to multiply and proliferate, which, again, inhibits the discovery of meanlng, whether this be the solution to the mysterious death of Georges's ancestor or the truth about the dubious fidelity of Corinne.

Reflection is closely linked to memory. It is well known that Montaigne complains of a bad memory, his inability to represent a previous event. Georges, in *La Route des Flandres,* is the fictional representation in Simon of the workings and failings of memory, unable to reconstruct what actually happened or assess his feelings. This novel, *Le Palace,* and *Histoire* are dominated by memory and its inability to recapture the past with any certainty. Both bad memory and the 'Que sais-je?' negate empirical certitudes, but they generate the fictional existence of things and create new writing born out of possibilities.

Confrontation with the dead horse also makes Georges aware of the flux of life around him, the silent decay, the unseen destruction and the repeating patterns of History. Montaigne's *Essais* bear witness to these preoccupations, to the processes of invisible change and fluidity (*Essais,* Bk. 2, p. 266 and *RF,* p. 30). Concern with decay as theme is reflected in the mode of presentation, which incorporates break-up of simple narration through inconsistencies, fragmentation by intruding texts (quotations, other languages) and digressions. Writing is associative rather than causal. Simon stresses this in the Preface to *Orion aveugle*: 'Chaque mot en suscite (ou en commande) plusieurs autres, non seulement par la force des images qu'il attire à lui...'. Montaigne's writing is the sixteenth-century parallel:

> J'ayme l'alleure poetique, à sauts et à gambades... C'est l'indiligent lecteur qui pert mon subject, non pas moy; il s'en trouvera tousjours en un coing quelque mot qui ne laisse pas d'estre bastant, quoy qu'il soit serré... Mon stile et mon esprit vont vagabondant de mesmes (*Essais*, Bk. 3, p. 208).

Reader-involvement is thus essential in the reconstruction of 'story' which is constantly interrupted by digressions. The corollary of highly associative writing, which denies one 'correct' reading, is openness to further development: this process is evident in Montaigne's essays, and, in the same way, the seemingly unrelated associations in Simon's *Orion aveugle* cohere into the new composition which is *Les Corps conducteurs*. Thus the birth of a new cycle in Simon's fiction once more illustrates the principles of generation in Montaigne:

> Nostre discours est capable d'estoffer cent autres mondes et d'en trouver les principes et la contexture. Il ne luy faut ny matiere, ny baze; laissez le courre: il bastit aussi bien sur le vuide que sur le plain, et de l'inanité que de matiere (*Essais*, Bk. 3, p. 238).

The open-endedness and intertextual embedding which distinguish the works of both writers form the technique of 'mémoire textuelle'. New writing is grafted upon the closed and finished structure of the 'déjà écrit'. Montaigne may plead a bad memory, but he never repeats a quotation, even if he borrows extensively from one Classical source and intercalates its fragments in all three books of the *Essais*. Pugh notes the same practice in Simon, and also the variety of his source materials:

> On l'a déjà noté, 'la bataille de la phrase' comporte une invasion de citations. Or il est évident que le travail de l'écriture chez Simon comporte une activité mnémonique considérable, mais on a insisté depuis trop longtemps sur cette activité au niveau de l'usage visuelle, c'est-à-dire des référents extratextuels, et au niveau de la transformation créatrice de souvenirs personnels (Pugh, 1976, p. 139).

In both Montaigne and Simon, therefore, intertextual activity relies heavily on a literary memory in the new practitioner, and also in their readers.

Sub-version and the intertext as literary authority

The properly 'Montaignian' and mature intertextual strategies which rework and are regenerated from previous literatures are key writng strategies Simon adopts in his middle and mature novels. They are notably absent from his early novels. A reason may be that Simon needed to go through the stage of copying both character and form from his novelistic heritage before he could develop from under the influence and authority of this tradition. The product is then a sub-version in two senses; it is the lesser text and it recasts it without destroying its ultimate authority. The Renaissance writers took their Greek and Latin heritage and borrowed its elements to provide material for their own vernacular alternatives. From the epic and dramatic forms issued the early development of the novel, a natural step in the transition of language, according to Josipovici:

> We use the words 'novel' and 'roman' without giving them much thought. But those words tell us more about the form than many a scholarly disquisition... Opposed to Latin is *roman*, the romance language, the vernacular. The term soon came to apply to a literary form, but it was a long time before it lost its old meaning (Josipovici, 1982, p. 69 [his emphasis]).

Opposition is not the only means by which the autonomy and authority of previous writing are punctured: vulgarization (in both the linguistic and technical senses) is another important form of subversion. Both aspects of 'vulgarization' are evident in Rabelais, who subverted Church Latin by transposing it into the vernacular: the episode of the 'écolier limousin' is an obvious example (*Pantagruel,* chapter 6 and *Hist,* pp. 43, 45). Simon uses the same vulgarizing subversion of language in *Histoire,* where the Latin mass is repeated in a lower key by Lambert. Note that this mouthpiece of mockery is also a *schoolboy,* friend of the boy-translator. Both react against the language of adult authority and social hierarchy, and Lambert turns the Latin mass into an overtly crude discourse on sex. The sacred becomes profane, not only through a challenge of the content, but also by a distortion of the fixed litany form, and comedy ensues because of the juxtaposition of normally different linguistic levels, the 'official' and the 'carnavalesque', to adumbrate Bakhtin's definition of this opposition (1978, p. 121).

Rabelais revelled in mocking erudite intertexts, his comedy relying on the techniques of digression, exaggeration, puns, anagrams and wordplay, to deflate and deform previous text, while simultaneously commenting on its operations. Ricardou emphasizes the textual importance of these figures in Simon, but insularizes them within the context of the Nouveau Roman, omitting to link them to their literary tradition. Simon specifically acknowleges his debt to these features in Rabelais: '...le roman se donnant et se dénonçant comme texte et *fiction en procès*... (par exemple [ceux] de Rabelais et de Sterne)' (Haroche, 1981, p. 15 [Simon's emphasis]). Simon thus lays claim to be a follower in Rabelais's and Sterne's footsteps. For all three, plot, character and theme serve as pretexts and vehicles to enable language play to operate: 'Le produit de l'activité de l'écrivain apparaît dès lors comme un objet spécifique, le "fait littéraire" qui n'a d'existence que dans le poème ou le roman et qui est viable indépendamment de toute référence à un modèle réel. Il importe peu désormais que *Pantagruel* réponde ou non à une quelconque "vérité psychologique"' (Rieben, 1971, p. 57).

There are only two specific references to Rabelais in Simon's novels. In *Le Palace*, the adjective 'pantagruélique' conjures up the gigantic, the corporeal and the earthy:

> comme, aurait-on dit, la viscérale exhalaison d'un organisme, de tripes pantagruéliques à l'intérieur desquelles eux-mêmes se seraient trouvés (*P*, p. 14).

As in *Gargantua* and *Pantagruel*, bodily functions are a metaphor for the excreta of writing itself, something expelled after ingestion from various sources and digestion by the writer. For Rabelais, however, writing is a positive creation, giving birth to wonderful possibilities. An example which springs to mind is the account of Gargamelle's pregnancy, in which she eats vast quantities of tripe and gives birth to Gargantua by the ear. Simon abandons the fun-poking fantasy of his precursor by focussing on the negative aspects of his writing excretions. By substituting Rabelais's birth of a progeny of fictional possibility (Gargantua) with a still-born child in *Le Palace,* the asphyxiating side of this language is also underscored:

> une puante momie enveloppée et étranglée par le cordon ombilical de kilomètres de phrases enthousiastes tapées sur ruban à machine par l'enthousiaste armée des correspondants étrangers de la presse libérale (*P*, p. 17).

The city itself is described as if in the throes of a giant birth, but the baby is malformed, not a giant, but a monster: 'quelque petit monstre macrocéphale' (*P*, p.230).

The ludic and clownish sides of Rabelais emerge explicitly again in *La Corde raide*, where the opus of the Renaissance writer is in dialogue with the new writing:

> —Je retiens que vous avouez la farce—je pensais bien
> que c'était quelque chose comme ça.
> Avez-vous lu Rabelais?
> —Tout le monde reconnaît que c'est très bien écrit.
> —Les farces de Picasso sont encore mieux peintes.
> —Mais ce n'est pas drôle!
> —Et trouvez-vous que le monde soit drôle? (*CR*, p. 180).

This conversation makes possible the direct comparison of two worlds. Rabelais's epicurean clowning is transposed by Simon into black humour. The grotesque provokes not laughter, but disgust: the carnivalesque quality in Rabelais becomes a danse macabre in Simon. Where parody is positive in Rabelais, changing and renewing the text with humanistic zeal, it is negative in Simon, destroying any illusion of hope and fragmenting the writing. Picasso and the decay and aborted writing of *Le Palace* are supposedly more relevant to the modern world than Rabelais.

Subversive and 'vulgar' intertextuality in Simon also occurs in his borrowing from the Latin Classic, Apuleius's *The Golden Ass*, which makes an intertextual appearance in both *Histoire* and *La Bataille de Pharsale*. However, unlike Rabelais, who remains a cypher for a type of writing Simon cannot imitate, Apuleius's text does appear in fragmented form, and thus impinges more directly on the generation of the novels in which it appears. In its capacity as *fictional* Classic, it acts, in *Histoire* as a foil for the non-fictional Latin passages from the dry histories the boy is forced to translate. It also acts as a trigger for his fertile erotic imagination, contrasting with his boredom with his translations. The exaggeration of sexual fantasy present in Apuleius is matched and devalued by Simon's transformation of its original context. The coupling of the donkey and the woman in *The Golden Ass* was to be part of a fairground pornographic peep-show. In *La Bataille de Pharsale*, this peep-show becomes its contemporary visual equivalent, a pornographic film-strip. Thus, the passage chosen from the intertext attests a lineage of Simon's rather explicit descriptions of the sexual act (*BP*, pp. 92-3 and *The Golden Ass*, pp. 215-6): yet within this tradition, the Apuleius intertext is more than merely an exemplum of 'pornographic' writing reset in a contemporary context. Simon implants it as a literary counterbalance to his own descriptions, the exaggeration and grotesqueness of the coupling of woman and ass in Apuleius being reused as a foil for his own flat, clinical accounts of lovemaking. The metamorphosis of man turned ass, which releases the erotic in the Classic through transformations of shape and size, is absent in Simon, as too is the mythical dimension, the interference of the gods (despite Gould's enumerations of the 'mythic' in Simon). At another level, however, the intertext is used to express, and comment indirectly on, the manner in which previous literature stimulates developing writing. The metamorphosis which is the subject of *The Golden Ass*, itself a parody of Ovid's *Metamorphoses*, becomes structural process in Simon's writing which 'ânonnai[s] le mot à mot' (*BP*, p. 17). This pun on 'âne' and 'ânonner' links the two directly through word-play. Moreover, the coupling which is action in Apuleius forms a metaphor in *La Bataille de Pharsale* for the coupling of intertexts with Simon's writing, so that new fiction is engendered from previous literature.

The intertext as literary translation

Like his Renaissance precursors, Montaigne and Rabelais, Simon employs translations and imitations of previous Classical texts in his novels. He is also fully aware (as above) of the vulgarising potential and/or colourful play of language itself, particularly if two registers or translations are placed side by side by the medium of quotation. I have written elsewhere on the generative power of translation in Simon, the role of the intertext as doubling procedure and the potential for the translator to be an interpreter or mask of meanings (Orr, 1989). What I wish to stress here is that the Latin raises questions that the transfer from one *vernacular* language to another does not; the literariness and not the orality is paramount in Simon's use of Latin and hence, as dead, written, language, its *fixity* of form. Few critics have noted and commented on the importance of the

Latin translation in Simon apart from Loubère, who asserts that the movement from the '...august Latin to the vulgar French is also a passage from a dead spiritual state to a vigorous, if crude, physical one, in which, through the inventiveness of procreation, the word becomes flesh and recreates the word' (in Birn, 1980, p. 191). Again, the function as stimuli to erotic fantasy, rather than on their motivation of text is commented on. I shall be concentrating, rather, on the Latin and its translation as central to an understanding of Simon's writing production.

Intertextuality as translation presents the same semantic block as two experiences of writing, the original and the other, juxtaposed. These two versions break the authority and uniqueness of the quotation and denote the finite, past expression of the original words.

> Le Latin se meurt, il se fige, se momifie en citations; quand la langue latine n'est plus génératrice d'énoncées nouveaux, elle devient le champ privilégié de la répétition. La citation est toujours la survivance d'une langue morte, ne serait-ce que d'un idéolecte (Compagnon, 1979, p. 243).

In *La Bataille de Pharsale,* the Latin quotations serve to underline three different time layers: the text itself, uncle Charles with his established adult values and ability to translate the 'dead' Latin correctly into vernacular prose, and the boy translating in the present and distorting both the Latin and uncle Charles's translation by his own clumsy, incomplete rendering.

> Versions latines dont j'ânonnais [the boy] le mot à mot comme une écœurante bouillie jusqu'à ce que de guerre lasse il [l'oncle Charles] finisse par me prendre le livre des mains et traduire lui-même
> César la Guerre des Gaules la Guerre Civile ---> s'enfonçant dans la bouche ouverte clouant la langue de ce. Latin langue morte (*BP,* pp. 17-18).

This introduction is important in that it underlines not only the protagonists, but also the battles which will ensue. First, there is the boy translator battling with the linguistic difficulties of the Latin words themselves. Second, there is his battle with the authority and language of oncle Charles who is the paragon translator. Third, there is the battle between 'dead' language and the vernacular which will translate it into creative text, *La Bataille de Pharsale.* Literary humour is also evident, in that Simon chooses Caesar's *Guerre des Gaules* and *Guerre Civile.* Uncle Charles and the boy are preoccupied, not occupied, by Caesar, but their private battle is far from 'civile'.

On page 43, the Latin reappears, aligned with its French equivalent:

> commemoravit : il rappela
> uti posse : pouvoir prendre (qu'il pouvait prendre)
> testibus se militibus : à témoin ses soldats
> quanto studio : avec combien d'ardeur (de l'ardeur avec laquelle)
> pacem petisset : il avait demandé la paix

However, the juxtaposition creates an uneasy relationship: for the vernacular provides an alternative in brackets, a typographical representation of the possibilities waiting to be released; whereas the Latin words stand alone, given, complete, unchangeable, *dead* language. When alignment also includes the proximity of the Latin and French words, the battle between translation competence is highlighted (for example *BP,* pp. 51-3). Confrontation is the essence here, for although uncle Charles mocks the boy's literalisms by his comments and his own polished version, the whole section is prefaced by '[son] regard me dévisageant derrière les lunettes *d'un air las vaincu d'avance*' (*BP,* p. 51 [my emphasis]). The passage ends with the boy's meaningless 'translation' being rejected by uncle Charles, who juxtaposes it with his correct one, which he tells the boy to copy:

> bon si ton professeur te demande le mot à mot tu te débrouilleras tu lui expliqueras que le quidam est tombé dans la rivière aux bords obstacles c'était sans doute un jockey qu'en penses-tu?... écris Une rivière aux rives escarpées protégeait son aile droite (*BPm* p. 53).

The boy confronts not only the Latin but uncle Charles's final draft, a model of a *finished* piece of writing, which is ironically as dead and uncreative as the Latin. New text proliferates precisely because the boy is a *bad* translator, making mistakes when the Latin and French words appear identical, but are 'faux amis'. Thus he translates 'cornu' as 'corne' , not 'aile' (*BP,* p. 52). The accurate, fluent translator is redundant as creative writer, because only repeated copies of fixed language can be produced. Charles's energies remain locked in bellettrism, the polished surfaces of meaning, whose form is closed to further question.

The autonomy of the translator begins to be undermined as uncle Charles's function as correct decoder declines with the increasing competence of the boy. Uncle Charles corrects register, not meaning:

> omnesque conversi : et que tous faisant demi-tour
> tournant bride, dit-il : il s'agit de cavaliers (*BP*, p. 80).

This devaluation of uncle Charles is matched by the boy's challenge to the autonomy of the text itself. This occurs through a visible battle of typescripts, the Latin and its translation in roman type being disrupted by the boy's independent thought, in italics, to mark the difference, '*Je ne savais pas encore...*'(*BP*, p. 80). This ellipsis signals the open nature of the creative writing and contrasts once more with the closed fixity of the Latin and of the translator/reflector, both of which the boy sees as meaningless:

> De nouveau je le regardai. Mais ce n'étaient rien que des mots, des *images* dans des livres,
> Il attendait, patient ou plutôt résigné... les verres de ses lunettes... *comme deux lunes reflétant* le désordre des papiers sur son bureau... (*BP*, pp. 81 and 82 respectively [my emphasis]).

Separation from the authority of both the Latin and uncle Charles's version occurs when the boy becomes independent, the translator 'O' in the third part of the novel. Uncle Charles is not even named: he is merely a presence, invisible behind his reflector glasses (*BP*, p. 221). His redundancy leads to his disappearance from the text where O sits *alone* at his desk and translates the story of Crastinus who promises to honour Caesar in 'le dernier combat qui nous reste'(*BP*, p. 233). This last battle is a metaphor for O's combat with previous writing and authority, a direct confrontation between the Latin and his own discourse. Taking up the word 'cornu', whose mistranslation previously provoked ridicule from the now textually 'dead' translator uncle Charles, O translates the Latin correctly, but this re-version is not simply a rhetorical exercise. The authority of the Latin text recedes into itself because it is embedded in the French of O's narrative. O can repeat the same Latin words concerning Crastinus—killed in battle by a sword piercing his mouth—posited at the beginning (*BP*, p. 18, the words 'la bouche ouverte clouant la langue'), but they are now under his control, instead of controlling him. The 'mot à mot' mechanical use of language has become a dynamic in the writing process. The fixed, dead Latin is subjugated by the remainder of *La Bataille de Pharsale,* which issues from topoi within the Latin, but is independent of its previous form. The Latin tongue has indeed been transfixed as Crastinus's was by the sword: its authority has been silenced, but its components have generated new narrative, not copies of old forms. Rhetorical exercise has been left behind. The boy had to submit to Latin exercises in order to exorcise the authority and control of both the text and oncle Charles to create his own writing. His development as writer offers a paradigm of intertextual activity. Writing has to be mistranslated to allow new practice to occur. From a breakdown of literary language through the rewriting and translation of its phonemes comes the deflation of the whole pursuit of translation as literary process in *La Bataille de Pharsale.* This is presented through the banality of the petrol station sign, given in Greek, then French through the medium of Roman characters (*BP,* p. 32). The petrol-station sign is just as important a place to re-charge language for the continuation of the textual journey, as are the literary intertexts. Translation is reduced to utility: 'mot à mot' juxtaposition again occurs, but the materiality and fictional potential of these alternatives are stressed. It is O's new text, in uninterrupted roman type in part three, which emerges as the dominant version of writing not least by the defeat of italic intrusions from other intertexts.

Simon thus draws some attention to the *material* aspects of intertextuality, and the materialization of his own text. Materiality is particularly evident in the concluding pages of *La Bataille de Pharsale.* The previous Latin intertexts from Caesar all find their refiguration as banal objects surrounding O, and yet all are tools of fictional generation. There is the closed *Petit Larousse,* a compilation of all of the French language, which has displaced the Latin dictionary the boy was using. The packet of Gauloises is another comic intertextual repetition: through punning, it is linked to Caesar's 'Guerre des *Gaules*'. This parallel is enlarged in the text:

> Sur son enveloppe bleue est dessiné un casque pourvu d'ailes. Le casque fait penser à des bruits de métal entrechoqué, de batailles, à Vercingétorix, à de longues moustaches pendantes, à Jules César. Les ailes évoquent des images d'oiseaux de *plumes*, de flèches empennées (*BP*, p. 257 [my emphasis]).

Nearby are Italian banknotes (Caesar reduced to money and material of exchange) and 'une boîte de trombones en carton mi-partie rouge et jaune comme un costume de page *Renaissance*' [my emphasis]. It is only now that O writes his first words, the beginning of the text *La Bataille de Pharsale*, because the intertexts and versions of writing conventions have all been interiorized as *materials* in the production of new writing. Through punning, the 'plumes' and the 'page Renaissance' become the pen and paper forming the new text. The Classics, the Renaissance debt to them, and the Renaissance itself, form the palimpsest for O's writing, the page on which it can appear.

Simon uses Latin texts not merely to query literary authority, but also to subvert any belief in historical authority. As early as *La Corde raide,* the authority of Latin histories suffers deflation:

> il reçut sous forme de vers dodécasyllabiques, de citations et de discours Latins, l'héritage de successives et énigmatiques civilisations, dont combats, clameurs, ambitions, agonies lui étaient transmis, soigneusement ordonnés, catalogués dans les nécropoles du temps, ces outrageantes conclusions de toute tentative humaine que sont les textes choisis et les manuels aux ternes couvertures grises (*CR,* p. 109).

In *Histoire,* the subject matter for translation is from the Latin historians Suetonius and Tacitus. The boy has to learn to question these presenters of authenticated 'facts', and understand that the events described are as unverifiable as heroic tales. However, he also has to realize that the re-writing of fiction takes place within the framework of History, understood as both the chronicle of events and as well-wrought literary story. Kristeller sees such processes as hallmarks of Renaissance quotation: 'In a period in which the emphasis is on authority and tradition, originality will assert itself in the adaptation and interpretation... of the tradition [as well as] in the choice of quotations' (1961, p. 138).

These lessons are most fully developed, however, in *La Bataille de Pharsale,* where the very historicity of Pharsalus is questioned by the writing itself. Caesar triumphed over the Roman nobility at Pharsalus in 49 B.C. Accounts of the event thus record the victory of order over anarchy; they map a chronicle of events out of the chaotic choice of viewpoints and descriptions. The narrator of *La Bataille de Pharsale* tries, unsuccessfully, to find the site of the battle through these texts. This is the surface manifestation of the deeper 'story' of intertextual investigation of textual fragments as artefacts. Quotation from the past, employed as an authority or order to be cited for purposes of identification and authentication, is vain. Accounts of the battle from Plutarch, Lucan and Livy are juxtaposed and purport to record the same event: the fact that they are all Histories highlights their inadequacy as truth-bearing materials. The subjective element cannot be removed. Thus, it is impossible for textual fragments to state unquestionable, verifiable fact, although they attempt to by quoting chapter and verse and acknowledging their sources.

The first historical Latin intertext in *La Bataille de Pharsale* is from Plutarch (*BP,* p. 29). Its autonomy is, first, undermined by fragmentation as it is both cut up by, and enveloped in, Simon's text. Second, although quasi-scientific exactitude of detail constitutes much of the original material (numbers of cohorts, horsemen, distances, geographical location), these 'facts' display their contradictions through the narrator's experience, the visit he makes to the site. The topographical descriptions given in the Classics, in fact, furnish insufficient evidence to identify the actual battle site. Place names like Larissa are clues that Pharsalus is in the vicinity, but only delineate an approximate zone of possibility. Contradiction also occurs through various literary experiences of the event. Plutarch's account uses material from the other Classics, cross-references from other historical authorities on the subject, used to reinforce the accuracy of his account: 'avec 110 cohortes (117 d'après César)' (*BP,* p. 27). Yet the juxtaposition of these conflicting details and chronologies, inconsistencies and inaccuracies, completely disintegrates their vèracity; and History as the written, ordered, objective reconstruction of events in the past is deflated. These intertexts are reduced to fictions within the new fiction, artefacts demonstrating their temporal 'pastness', but nothing more. They are signposts towards an interpretation, a means of orientation in cultural space and time, but do not, and cannot, present definitive Authority. Just as there is no direct correlation between words in one language and those in another, so there is no epistemological link between descriptions and facts, the signifier and the signified. Employment of intertexts as proof texts is fallacious; they perpetuate their own fictionality, and when multiple 'authorities' are embedded, their inter-referentiality forms a closed and introverted fictional space where creativity is stifled. Their meaningfulness in communicating fact is subordinated in Simon's novel by the treatment of their tropes as a lode of non-Historical associations which are most apparent in the third, almost intertext-free, section of the novel.

The historical reports given by the various Classical texts, and the experiences of the present visitor, are interspersed with a layer of accounts from intermediary historians, who interpreted the same artefacts. These play an 'oncle Charles' function in that they embody scholarship and learning from a previous generation. They display a pedantic adherence to detail, and reconsider and cross-reference what others have said on the subject: yet no new light is shed on the problem (*BP,* p. 26). The historical data are even re-checked for mistakes in the Latin translation (*BP,* p. 90-1). Despite this laudable empirical methodology, the doubt as to the reality of the event the words describe cannot be removed. These historians are no more able to construct a definitive report than their ancestors, and their utterances are empty repetitions.

The intertext as source, influence and alternative version

Where the intertext maintains its authority, as we have seen, the new working is tantamount to a copy or plagiarism. It is only when the new host text begins to work on and fragment the power of the intertext that the properly literary dynamic of intertextual usage occurs. Mockery of the intertext goes further, for it implies homage to the precursor, whose writing is seen to be of sufficient weight to merit it, before subjection of it to a radical reorientation and end. This reworking highlights the virtuosity of the new practitioner as he/she uses parody, pastiche, antithesis, exaggeration or vulgarization of the source text. Of all the Classics, it is in Simon's imitation of Virgil's *Georgics* that the interplay of these highly intertextual elements is most visible. As early as *Histoire,* exploitation of *The Georgics* as anti-model occurs, showing Simon's knowledge of E. de Saint-Denis's 1956 translation of the text, which I append to the quotation:

> tendu et arc-bouté (le marteau non pas levé au-dessus de sa tête comme celui du géorgique forgeron dont les coups tombaient réguliers et paisibles sur l'acier tintant, mais un peu en arrière de son corps et sur le côté, entraîné, semblait-il, dans un tourbillon désordonné par le bras frappant non de haut en bas mais sous tous les angles dans une avalanche une frénésie de coups furieux)...(*Hist* , pp. 211-12 and Virgil Bk. 4, ll. 170-5).
>
> 'Ainsi que les Cyclopes hâtent de forger les foudres avec des blocs de métal amollis, les uns avec leurs soufflets en peau de taureau, aspirent l'air et le refoulent, les autres trempent dans un bassin de bronze qui siffle; leur caverne gémit sous les coups frappant les enclumes; rivalisant de force ils lèvent leurs bras en cadence et tournent et retournent le fer avec la tenaille mordante'.

Simon's most systematic and complete reworking of an intertext in any of his novels is his version of Virgil's *Georgics* in the novel *Les Géorgiques*, which draws on its themes and topoi. Contrary to the suggestion of several critics, who have seen *The Georgics* as merely a vague model of seasonal change (for example, Calle-Gruber, 1981, p. 111; Duncan, 1983, p. 93; and Reitsma-La Brujeere, 1984, p. 232), I contend that it forms an important substructure to the new version. Simon's close imitation of Virgil shows both admiration for, and distance from, his precursor. The repetition of the title illustrates this at the most simple level. Direct adoption of Virgil's title reveals literary kinship, but at the same time the plural form, the 's' of *Les Géorgiques,* can be interpreted as positing two (or more) Georgics, the ancient and the modern, which, when superimposed, permit comparison and contrast. Distance is also inherent in the pun contained in the name Les GEORGiques and Georges, its major protagonist in Simon's version.

Although Simon does not quote directly from Virgil, there are close linguistic echoes to be found in *Les Géorgiques.* In Virgil, Book 3 an exhausted racehorse dies of disease (ll. 498-508). In Simon's text, this topos is transposed into a mare, which, exhausted from the forced retreat, falls and dies. More generally, Virgil's paean to Caesar's exploits is embodied in LSM's military campaigns during the Napoleonic Wars and O's experiences in the Spanish Civil War, which take place in the same locations as Caesar's conquests. The subjects of farming crops, vine-dressing and rearing horses in Virgil are all incorporated into *Les Géorgiques* as LSM writes letters to his steward and mistress, Batti, instructing her in the management of his estates and telling her when to undertake certain tasks in the farming year. The historical general, Caesar, and the fictional farmer in Virgil become amalgamated in LSM in Simon's text, his factual (historical) and imaginary lives existing in juxtaposition. Simon used historical records of LSM, both personal, family documents and Michelet's *Histoire de la Révolution française* to form his fictional character.

Simon also adopts essential structures from *The Georgics.* For instance, his text also has a Proem, although it is the rather surreal canvas of an unfinished painting of a general, and only becomes comprehensible as a cameo of the writing in progress with textual hindsight. Just as Virgil balanced Books 1 and 3 against Books 2 and 4, using contrast to heighten the implications of each, so Simon employs the same 'chevauchement' technique. Parts One, Three and Five deal with LSM and O, their two time strands being differentiated by the use of Roman or italic script. These are separated by Parts Two and Four, which focus on O and twentieth-century society. Virgil, the poet at work within his text, is mirrored by O, quietly sitting at his table in tranquil England, recalling his war experiences and trying to record them. Another example of shared techniques is the superimposition of myth and levels of narration. Virgil effects such embedding in the Bugonia legend; Bugonia is defined in *The Georgics* as the 'spontaneous generation (of bees) from the carcass of an ox' (p. 121). Similarly, Simon overlays the lives of LSM, O and oncle Charles, who shows LSM's register to the boy descendant. The common denominator is a literary reference to Virgil.

> Au cours d'une de ses tournées d'inspection il admire à Mantoue la statue de Virgile...
>
> J'en partis à la pointe du jour pour me rendre à Mantoue qui vous doit la place Virgiliane.
>
> *Avec le 'Contrat social et Virgile il semble que ç'ait été une de ses passions* (*G,* pp. 26, 64, 446-7 respectively).

These similarities, striking though they are, afford only a starting point for comparison. Let us look at the more fundamental ways in which Simon forges his new Georgics. He takes a topos from the Latin poet, recognizably borrows its components, but changes the emphasis to produce a twentieth-century parody. The result is a direct antithesis to Virgil, which creates literary humour for the reader familiar with both.

Simon's reworking of Virgil in fact ironises, or implicitly criticizes, elements from all sections of the original poem. In Book 1, winter is described as a time for planning ahead, indoor work and communal feasting (ll. 381-2). In Simon, it is a time of pain, hardship and suffering for the soldiers faced with frozen rations, misery and intense cold (*G,* pp. 79-80). There is no place for a civilizing picture of winter in Simon, only a confrontation with the brute facts of nature. He borrows another seasonal reference, this time a description of spring, but deletes the idyllic overtones of Virgil, Book 2, which contains a large section praising and welcoming it as a season of new fertility, of nature reproducing, couched in terms of human marriage. Spring, in *The Georgics,* is also the mid-point between the extremes of winter cold and the heat of summer, but in Simon it is a season scarcely featuring on the calendar, and of no consequence for the generals in their overheated offices, an environment artificially outside the rhythm of seasonal temperature variation (Virgil Bk. 2, ll. 323-35 and *G,* p. 105). For the soldiers, spring is ironically the time for a new batch of pornographic literature to arrive, the non-creative sexual act taking precedence over the creative, fertile Mother Nature images in the Latin text (*G,* p. 216).

In Virgil, Book 1, the plough is revered and given prime place in the process of cultivation. With Simon, it is relegated to an equal place with other incongruous articles LSM sends to Batti (*G,* p. 188). For Virgil it is an implement of peace. In Book 1, a farmer ploughing uncovers the old battlefield of Philippi and the giant bones of bygone heroes. War is subordinated to cultivation, the growing of new crops covering over past battles. By contrast, the layers of ancestors in the family tomb in Simon's novel rot away completely. The grave of LSM's first wife is revisited in the twentieth century by a stranger who meets the last of the family line, an idiot, who deciphers the half-eroded inscription. Later, the family has been completely annihilated by time and degeneration until the very tomb itself is demolished by the bulldozer, a parodic twentieth-century plough, destructive rather than constructive in its use (Virgil Bk. 1, ll. 493-7, and *G,* p. 168). The heroes' cemetery is levelled to a common burial ground in Simon as death itself shows no favouritism.

The other major paean in Virgil is to Italy, a land of temperate climate and fertile soils where eulogies are made about its archetypal heroes and ideals (Virgil Bk. 2, ll. 173-6). By contrast LSM finds discontent and uncultivated fields on his Italian campaign: 'J'ai perçu dans toute l'Italie un état de mécontentement et un air morose...'(*G,* p. 73). Italy is also to Virgil the land where an abundant variety of grapes is grown (Bk.2, ll. 89-103). Simon imitates this by reducing the kinds of grape to an inventory of *French* wines in LSM's cellars: '[LSM] dresse l'inventaire de sa cave en vin blanc, vin noir, vin de Cahors, Malvoisie, vin du Roussillon et eau-de-vie' (*G,* p. 70). The praise poetry of Virgil is transformed into the most mundane kind of prose, enumeration. Both writers also address the topic of vines. Virgil gives detailed instruction on vine-dressing and how to care for the crop, with gentle warnings, lyrically expressed, on what kind of conditions to avoid (Bk. 2, ll. 298-304). Similar instructions occur in

Simon's text, as LSM writes to Batti, his estate-manager: however, vine-dressing details are interspersed with orders about linen and hedges. The anxiety and obsession, both of which are absent in the poetry of Virgil, shown by LSM in *Les Géorgiques* are underlined by the repetition of the word 'Muscat' (*G*, pp. 166-7). The universalizing and didactic tone of Virgil's text is particularized in Simon into the orders of one absentee gentleman farmer to his estate manager. The frequent use of imperatives in Simon's text again highlights an obsessive fear in LSM which becomes gross displeasure when his commands fall on deaf ears. LSM's increasing authoritarianism stems from insecurity of position as he grows older, whereas Virgil's text maintains a quiet equilibrium of authority throughout. In addition, imperative usage in Simon ironically undermines the dominance of the speaker, emphasizing his need always to command and give orders, which frequently are disobeyed, especially at the end of the novel.

Book 3 of Virgil's *Georgics* deals with animals. The poet invests the humble subject of horse-breeding with greater importance by using a cluster of mythological references to gods who changed into horses, or who owned famous ones. The horse is ennobled by the terminology of human marriage and much stress is laid on lineage, pure breeding and the careful selection of stock (Bk. 3, ll. 79-106). In Simon's novel, LSM devotes many letters to the care of his horses, especially to the breeding from his thoroughbred stallion, Mustapha (*G*, pp. 240-1, and pp. 464-7 for example). At various stages in his advancing military and political career LSM buys horses for his stables, but with declining years his stables also empty, until Mustapha, effectively his alter ego, dies, at which point LSM also dies. Again, what was fertile and bucolic in Virgil becomes decayed and infertile in Simon. In fact, Simon literalizes Virgil's horses by turning LSM into the stud stallion itself. The general is described as: 'lui, sa crinière, ses deux cents livres d'os et de viande de *cheval* ballottés dans l'entrepont d'un navire' (*G*, p. 245 [my emphasis]). and LSM's Dutch wife is 'engrossée par un étalon' (*G*, p. 169). Like Virgil's horse, LSM is full of boundless energy and has only to scent the rumour of war to be off on a new campaign. Simon also lays stress on LSM's declining potency and increasing old age (*G*, p. 66). But, contrary to the maintaining of stud selection in Virgil, the noble stock of LSM's family becomes bastardized. Former glory attached to the name is ridiculed and debased into a cheap consumer product, a low-quality aperitif. Thus, ironically, all LSM's worries about good quality in his vineyards have been fulfilled.

Virgil lyricizes horse-breeding by endowing it with the language of human marriage; and virility, associated with stallions, is presented as a noble attribute. Simon turns this image on its head by reworking the comparison. He describes the sexual relationships of his human protagonists in terms of animal breeding, thereby deflating the institution of marriage and any suppositions as to the superiority of the human species over other animals. LSM is the synthesized bull-stallion sparring with his brother over Batti, the heifer-filly. Actual animal rivalry in Virgil (Bk. 3, ll. 215-28) is transposed by Simon into that of the two human brothers. The civilizing veneer of clothing and pomp is only superficial, and does not hide the human animal underneath. LSM is 'le lointain étalon... *non pas revêtu de son uniforme de général aux pesantes dorures* mais les épaules drapées d'une toge à l'antique d'où sortait, nu, le cou de *taureau*' (*G*, p. 196 [my emphasis]). Batti, too, is dehumanized 'avec cette tête de jument, de mule ou de chèvre' (*G*, p. 420). She is a mule, not even a thoroughbred, infertile, because she is the *mistress* not the wife, of LSM and his half-brother, and does not come from 'pure' stock. To complete his ironic adaptation of Virgil, Simon takes the motif of Saturn's progeny, the centaur, and de-mythologizes it in the jockey, who is seen as a kind of cross-breed: 'les quelques jockeys qui n'ont pas été pris comme ordonnances par les officiers supérieurs faisant en quelque sorte office de charnière entre les deux groupes sociaux' (*G*, p. 81). One is reminded here of the jockey Iglésia in *La Route des Flandres,* who fills a similar intermediary position.

The sparring of the bulls over a mate in Virgil, Book 3, echoes an earlier incident in Book 2, where brothers fight each other and one is ousted from the family home. This unrest leads into a picture of the archetypal paterfamilias, his agrarian lifestyle and his contentment with rustic simplicity, the very model of what family life should be (Bk. 2, ll. 510-31). The emphasis Simon gives to the theme of the family is quite different. He adopts the topos of fratricide, but expands it to the internal strifes and jealousies within LSM's family. The disputes on the family level mirror the wars on the national level. LSM signs the edict for his half-brother's execution, and, unlike the Virgilian model of the ideal farmer who only leaves his land briefly to fight, remains far from the family home during his military campaigns and political career. He returns to his estates only when too old to continue fighting, and decays alone, except for his mistress Batti. Instead of loving children around him (as in Virgil) LSM leaves his son, second wife and mistress intriguing over his property and dividing it up. He never enjoys satisfaction from his land, whereas Virgil's farmer rejoices in the fruits of his labour. LSM dies an obsolete patriarch, his family heading for decline and annihilation, and an obsolete general, unlike Caesar, who, in Virgil, has not yet reached the zenith of his career.

In his agrarian descriptions, Virgil often uses the imagery of battle to depict points of order and form, and in doing so, indirectly praises the Roman army. The vine rows in Virgil are compared to cohorts in battle formation in serried ranks (Bk. 2, ll. 277-84). Simon takes the simile and inverts it. As in his earlier novels, he underlines the disarray and disorder of the troops in the field and the chaos of war. This is the reality of modern warfare, not the theoretical form of the rows of pins stuck in the battle maps at army headquarters (*G*, p. 44).

Battle imagery reappears in Virgil, Book 4, in the 'civil war' between the two beehives. The dispute is allayed by the beekeeper's sprinkling of a handful of dust. Virgil advises the death of the lesser bee, so that the better strain, the one with the *golden* markings, may rule uninterrupted. Simon parodies Virgil's bees by dressing LSM in a uniform with gold trimmings. LSM overcomes his brother, but not by the intervention of any deus ex machina beekeeper. LSM is also denied the loyalty and support which the Virgilian bees give the victorious leader. Within his family he finds only rejection and discord, for there is never any definitive solution to the quarrel.

Just as Virgil painted the family idyll round the farmer-patriarch as a microcosmic pattern for a new Golden Age, so he uses the social structure within the beehive as a paradigm for the macrocosm of society (Bk. 4, ll. 153-68). However, the utopian nature of the Latin text is deflated totally in Simon's ironic treatment of an 'ideal' society in *Les Géorgiques* (p 122). Family order disintegrates round LSM and society falls to pieces with the advent of the Revolution and wars. In the Virgilian bee society, lazy drones are expelled, their corpulence being a sign of their inactivity and lack of usefulness in the community. Simon's novel describes a society peopled with drones in the guise of plump bureaucrats and armchair soldiers in their comfortable offices (Virgil Bk. 4, ll. 93-4, and *G*, p. 127). Within Virgil's utopian hive, all sleep at ease after a hard day's labour, safe in tranquil surroundings. Simon appropriates this idyll in Part Four of his novel (pp. 312-13), where he paints twentieth-century England. Motifs of sleep, peace in little cottages and food in plenty echo Virgil, but these similarities are employed to reveal the blandness of England and serve only to heighten its political insularism at the time of the Spanish Civil War. The society of reserved, unemotional people in greyish surroundings acts as a foil for the poverty, war, degradation and disease O (Orwell) finds in Spain. Barcelona is a city of degeneration, described in terms of crippling sexual disease leading to death, a far cry from the bugonic reproduction and continuity in Virgil's bee society.

The exemplary bee society which includes Bugonia in Virgil, Book 4 contains a lesson on the destructive power of lust. The moral emerges through the Orpheus/Eurydice myth retold by Proteus as a parallel model on a different, but applicable plane. Simon's novel also incorporates this tale of tragic love to set up reverberations and parallels, but with the force of an anti-model. First, the myth is transposed to the medium of Gluck's opera, *Orfeo ed Euridice*. In a way, Simon copies the *mise en abyme* technique found in Virgil, as the opera is an accepted convention of unreality like the world of myth, but has relevance to the outer 'real' world. However, the focus in Simon is neither the story of the lovers, nor its retelling. It becomes a pretext for the presence of the lovers, LSM and his future wife, at the Opera House at Besançon. The attention of the audience is not on the unfolding of the account of love on stage, but on the other members of the audience: so, the real theatre is within the space of the building, not merely the stage. Second, the Orpheus myth is de-mythologized in that it is re-enacted by mortals playing roles. A further artificiality is introduced by the operatic genre itself and the unreal stage set. This devaluation of the times of past antique glory is doubled by the striking resemblance between the stage set and the state of decay of LSM's ancestral home (*G,* pp. 144-6). Third, unlike Virgil, Simon does not keep the Orpheus myth as a single entity within his text. The opera appears in fragments not only in the experience of LSM, but also in the twentieth-century strand of the novel, where the old woman takes her grandchild, LSM's progeny, to see the same opera. It also appears in the third thread of Simon's text, wherein O and the soldiers hear snatches of the opera broadcast on radio. The myth was totally appropriate to the Bugonia of Virgil, but its parodic reappearance as opera is totally inappropriate to the context in Simon, war. The powerful Orphic song which, in the Classical myth, caused the jealous and lustful

Thracian women to kill the singer (as they were unable to extinguish it in any other way), is again parodied by Simon. The singing is either lost in the orchestral accompaniment at the opera (p. 74) or drowned by interference during the radio broadcast. Furthermore, the medium of radio, by its very nature, disembodies song from singer. Lastly, it is the text of *Les Géorgiques* itself which causes the final extinction of the referential voice, because the fragments of the Italian words are lost amid the other layers of typescript and thematic intrusion. Virgil concludes his *Georgics* on an optimistic note: Simon's text ends with mortality and disillusionment as LSM's letter fades out.

Undoubtedly, the appropriated Classic remains the greater work of art, not only for its striking subject matter, but also for the innovation in its approach to expressing it. It is a poem of rich reverberation and tight structure. It is perhaps in acknowledgement of these *inimitable* attributes that Simon entitles his own novel *Les Géorgiques* to allow the precursor text to retain its superiority in being juxtaposed with a studied, but more digressive and lesser version. What Simon takes from the original can be seen to be a tribute to the model, a recognition of the origins and source of a genre and the influence of a Classic on future generations of writers. However, Simon's re-writing is at the same time a highly personalized imitation of Virgil outside the limitations of classical imitation proper. His own literary preoccupations, and rejection of textual authorities, are embodied in the proximity to, and paradoxical distance from, Virgil. By over-writing the Latin, the epic and the source of universal experiences through contemporary vernacular and novel form, Simon translates not just a small intertextual fragment, but a complete intertext. The relationship between the two *Georgics* then is not so much metaphorical or synechdocal, but metyonymic. Parallels, associations and intertextual reverberation are shown to be controlled in the mature Simon. And, counter to the purposes of pastiche, the two versions guard their stylistic individuality. The tribute to Virgil lies in how Simon owns up to the originality of the intertext, but disowns its over-riding influence.

*****

My discussion of the aspects of intertextuality as translation and literary alternative has shown how skilfully Simon remodels his source material by reshaping literary and vernacular languages. The way these sources are exploited may be said to exemplify the dual meaning of the French word 'version'—variant form and translation into one's native vernacular. The *bricolage* discussed above which results in Simon's novels is a highly crafted, conscious reworking of materials, which, while still identifiable as to their origins, are lent new and recognizably Simonian features which continue to individuate and regenerate his prose.

Chapter Two

Seventeenth-Century Literature

The previous chapter investigated the intertext at the level of authority and source. This chapter takes the altogether different perspective of the intertext as a rhetorical utterance which provides a linguistic structure for the later text. Language is seen to be culturally free property at the disposal of any user, and not, as is the case with an authority, the possession of a hierarchy of persons. As language then, in our new model, is without originator, influence is seen not as a person-to-person relationship, but as the reverberation between structures. Thus, for structuralists, such as Barthes and Culler:

> [T]he notion of intertextuality names the paradox of linguistic and discursive systems; that utterances or texts are *never moments of origin* because they depend on the prior existence of *codes and conventions*, and it is the nature of codes to be always already in existence, to have lost origins... Intertextuality is less a name for a work's relation to particular prior texts, than an *assertion of a work's participation in a discursive space and its relation to codes which are the potential formalizations of that space*... The study of intertextuality is not the investigation of sources and influences, as traditionally conceived; it casts its net wider to include the anonymous discursive practices, codes whose origins are lost and which are the conditions of possibility of later texts. Indeed Barthes has specifically warned against confusing study of the intertext with source hunting: 'les citations dont est fait un texte sont anonymes, irréparables et cependant *déjà lues*' Culler, 1976, p. 1382 ([my emphasis, apart from the final italicization, which is Barthes's]).

Discursive space being anonymous has further implications, for it shifts interest away from ordering texts and intertexts according to 'greatness' and focuses attention on relationships between structures which have equal importance within their respective systems. The mode of judging the efficacity of the re-utterance is its performance against the rules governing it. For the structuralists:

> The cultural meaning of any particular act or object is determined by a whole *system of constitutive rules*: rules which do not regulate behaviour so much as create the possibility of particular *forms* of behaviour... Culture is composed of a *set of systems*... The object is itself *structured* and is defined by its place in the structure of the system (Culler, 1975, p. 5 [my emphasis]).

Barthes and Culler see the verbal construct in terms of a linguistic model: the grammar of language, and the intertext within it, operate according to rules, paradigms and functions, against which new utterance may be compared. On the scale of literary utterances, generic models also act as performative touchstones against which a new work can be assessed and its borrowings or adumbrations from other genres or its own may be judged. Hence the intertext in this chapter engages specifically with its rhetoricity. According to Culler,

> [intertextuality] leads one to think of a text as a dialogue with other texts, an act of absorption, parody or criticism, rather than as autonomous artifact which harmoniously reconciles the possible attitudes towards a given problem; it alerts one to the artifice of literature, the special conventions and interpretative operations on which it is based and it makes one particularly sensitive to the special referentiality of literary works (Culler, 1976, p. 1383).

The notion of the intertext and the host text being in dialogue is not unique to Structuralists, such as Culler and Barthes. We shall be returning to Bakhtin's very different formulation of 'le principe dialogique' in the fourth chapter. What interests us here is the structuralists' emphasis not on lineage of intertexts but their synchronic dialogicity afforded by the juxtaposition of codes and systems across space and time. What delineates these codes and structures is the systematized nature of the parameters governing them. Just such parameters concerning rhetoric were set by Malherbe in seventeenth-century France .

The intertextual dialogue as 'act of absorption, parody or criticism' within the artifice and artifiality of its re-enactment also underlines the mood of the reworking. Tone and emphasis are highlighted as they are in any verbal communication or its written genre, drama. In the study of intertextuality, drama is the paradigm of the totally quoted form. Past utterance receives a new body in which it is a voice or collection of voices. Talk, on the stage, then, is not only the theme, but also the material and structuring device of the play. By extension, the intertext, as recognizably different speech-act, speaks and shows its otherness by being placed in literal or metaphorical speech-marks, made present by its staging in the new discursive space. Performance is of the essence. This privileged position of theatre is stressed by Barthes:

> Toute représentation est un acte sémantique extrêmement dense: rapport du code au jeu (c'est-à-dire de la langue et de la parole), nature... du signe théâtral, variations signifiantes de ce signe, contraintes d'enchaînement, dénotation et connotation du message, tous ces problèmes fondamentaux de la sémiologie sont présents dans le théâtre; on peut même dire que le théâtre constitue un objet sémiologique privilégié, puisque son système est apparemment original (polyphonique) par rapport à celui de la langue (qui est linéaire) (Barthes, 1964, p. 259).

Language is thus perceived in embodied form on the stage. The actor remakes the play by voicing the given words with his/her *own* accentuation and hence interpretation. Comparable to this is the writer's reusage of an intertext, which 'speaks' in a new way because of its different context. In addition, just as the actor uses his/her memory to reconstruct the lines, the reader does the same to build up the text in his/her mind and form it as a whole. Repetition of the words is therefore essential to the re-enactment of the intertext. Such doubling of discourse(s), and the text-within-the-text structure, are functions which the intertext performs in ways similar to plays. Dramatists frequently employ repetition or doubling techniques for structural effect: for example, the fool may repeat his master's words in a different language register. The play-within-a-play, or the doubling of main and sub-plots (for example in *Hamlet*), constitutes dramatic commentary on the very mechanisms and structures of theatre, both as particular play and as system of writing.

Within the dramatic system, the theatre as genre *per se* (and, by extension, the intertextual play of texts), are three important sub-systems: character, plot and theme. Seventeenth-century dramatists exploited these strictly using stock characters, plots and themes; their skill was then demonstrated in the remodelling and recombination of these materials within the constraints of the comic or tragic forms. It was also the time when the very rules governing Classical drama were fixed: the three unities of time, place and action. Intertexts operate similarly: potentially clichéd references, stock figures or 'plots' are revived in the new structure. The grammatical equivalents of subject, verb, 'signifié' become other in the new enactment of the utterance.

The most fitting illustration of the *dramatic* qualities of intertextuality in Simon is, in fact, his references to seventeenth-century theatre—French, English and Spanish. Critics have touched on the Spanish theatre in the consideration of Simon as a 'baroque' writer (as Hollenbeck, 1982, pp. 17-34) but no full study has been made of these three separate pinnacles of European drama. This chapter seeks to rectify this omission by looking first at these particular theatres to show the intertextual exploitation and new performance of 'stock' characters and plots and themes in Simon. Where this form of intertextual usage takes place within his *œuvre* will also be assessed. Second, the very theatricality of Simon's later novels will be demonstrated, with specific reference to their dramatic form.

Seventeenth-century French theatre

In his early novels, Simon borrows stock characters from seventeenth-century French drama, and these borrowings can be classified as adjectival in function.

> Le sème... est un connotateur de personnes, de lieux, d'objets, dont le signifié est un *caractère*. Le caractère est un adjectif, un attribut, un prédicat... Bien que la connotation soit évidente, la nomination de son signifié est incertaine, approximative, instable: arrêter le nom de se signifié dépend en grande partie de la pertinence critique à laquelle on se place: le sème n'est qu'un *départ*, une avenue du sens' (Barthes, 1970b, p. 196 [his emphasis]).

In *Gulliver*, for example, Bert's face is described as

> un de ces comédiens au menton bleu, encore jeune mais usé, au facies sculpté par les quinquets de la rampe enavant du fond obscur et poussérieux des décors, à la fois désolé et sarcastique, capable d'incarner, selon les besoins, des personnages aussi divers que le Cid, Sganarelle ou Tartufe (p. 71).

The diversity of this enumeration is secondary to the cultural recognizability of these names, which provide an implicit means of comparison for Simon's characters within French literary tradition. Bert is no hero of the magnitude of Corneille's protagonist: however, he is a character in conflict with the world and with history around him, fighting the pressure of society and its mores. In this sense, Bert stands as a kind of anti-heroic shadow of his Cornelian model. The other two allusions to Molière's plays suggest a span of heroic enactment, from the fool/foil (Sganarelle) to the arch-villain Tartuffe. As neither of these cultural referents is applicable to Bert, their force as anti-models is further underlined and then, through the combination of alternative theatrical impostures offered, cancelled out.

More complex re-modelling of such common figures from French theatre occurs in *Le Vent.* Montès is compared to Don Juan (p. 57), but the qualifying sentences underline the irony of the comparison. Montès is no seducer, but the seduced. The woman in question is neither noble nor rustic virgin, but the inverse, a prostitute. The 'conquest' is re-couched in terms of mock-heroics. Furthermore, Montès is no treacherous villain but the object of villainy from society. This reference is a good example of how Simon takes a stock character (with all its cultural connotations) and re-uses it as a foil for his own protagonist, the original model being parodied and de-mythologized in the process. The role of the reader is also made evident in such 'stock-taking' of cultural referents, for without the necessary recognition of the standard form, the intertextual/adjectival usage, fails to come into play.

References to seventeenth-century French drama not only deflate Simon's characters as heroes, but also puncture their values. The very fact that one of Simon's protagonists is called Sabine, after the character in Corneille's *Horace,* provides a further demonstration of this ambivalent intertextuality, and raises many questions about similarity and contrast. Simon's Sabine recounts the story of her ancestor, de Reixach, his portrait, hanging in the family home, being the trigger for the incident:

> on l'avait portraituré ensanglanté par le coup de feu qui avait mis fin à ses jours, se tenant là, impassible, chevalin et bienséant... Sabine... ne sachant sans doute au juste elle-même si, en rapportant ces histoires scandaleuses, ou ridicules, ou infamantes, ou cornéliennes, elle désirait déprécier cette noblesse, ce titre... (p. 57).

The adjective 'cornélienne' in the second half of the parenthesis gives the account more prestige and underscores the place of family honour and the forces of ancestry, both of which are intrinsic to the tragic dilemmas of Corneille's protagonists. That de Reixach may have committed suicide to avoid family dishonour places him in the lineage of one of Corneille's tragic heroes. Simon does not, however, make the heroic version a certainty. The unheroic and scandalous version is also presented as a viable alternative. The adjective 'cornélienne' therefore becomes invested with a rhetorical irony, de Reixach then being the antithesis of his model. By placing his cultural reference in the position of climax at the end of the series of adjectives, Simon highlights it. It becomes the pivot of two alternative readings, literal and ironic, the 'titre' of the literary reference itself deflated as well as Sabine's allusion to rank, and her own implicit literary lineage.

In *Les Géorgiques*, the word 'cornélienne' plays a similar role in highlighting ambiguities of interpretation. The scene is again the ancestral home, and in the shadow of the huge marble of the illustrious ancestor (LSM) various family relics are listed. They are guarded by an old lady, the last of the line, who conserves everything 'dans le même esprit de cornélienne piété filiale' (p. 174). Again Simon uses the adjective in the sense of 'reinforcement of duty', but, as before, he undercuts its aura and shows that this kind of emotion is at best anachronistic, at worst laughable, for the old lady is the daughter of the 'fils du rénégat', that is from the dishonourable side of the family. Her family reverence becomes grotesque exaggeration in that she guards a family honour and unity which are only a myth. The living, 'bad' branch extant in herself is ironically preserving the dead 'good' branch of the family. Secondly, the whole exercise is in any case worthless because she is a quasi-vestal virgin 'chargée d'entretenir non pas une flamme mais quelque chose d'éteint, oublié depuis longtemps' (p. 175). So the full force of the discrepancy between filial piety and the setting of decay and extinction in the house—appearance and reality—is made very clear, thanks to the reference to Corneille. We, as readers, can thus map Simon's increased craftsmanship in reworking such referents, and bringing out their ironies.

Simon uses references to Racine in a similar manner, as a means of ironic, tongue-in-cheek comment on his own protagonists. In *L'Herbe,* contrast is the main force behind the adjective 'racinienne':

> (Sabine et Pierre) sous l'aspect de ces redoutables et sacrés personnages hollywoodiens, cousins de ceux de la tragédie grecque ou racinienne, le plus insignifiant de leurs gestes empreint de cette majestueuse solennité... (p. 191).

For Racine, destructive forces were seen not so much in man's struggle with the cosmos or society, but as operating through the passions within himself. Passions were concentrated to a supra normal degree, accentuated by a close-knit web of relationships set within a stylized time and place, so that no extraneous minor detail could impair the full impact of the tragedy. The impact of the artificiality of this staged world is effected by conjoining this world with its modern setting, Hollywood. Similarly, Simon uses *Phèdre* as a literary synonym for passion and incestuous love in literature and as a comparative anti-structure of the relationship between Sabine and Pierre in *L'Herbe* (p. 190). It is quite clear from Simon's novel that here at least the world of classical theatre is an anachronism. Is Simon, in fact, emphasizing the unreality of all spectacle by juxtaposing such oppositions? A particular and harsh irony is created by the application of Racine to Sabine and Pierre. Sabine's 'reality' is that Pierre is a passionate lover, deceiving her with many mistresses. She dresses up to appear seductive and erotic. Outside her theatrical illusion, Pierre is in fact an impotent mountain of flesh. The mirror shows Sabine's dyed hair and exaggerated make-up for all their grotesqueness: she is an aging alcoholic. The mirror as object in the text is echoed by the literary mirror of the Racine referent in showing the discrepancies of fact and fiction. Pierre and Sabine, while each has aspirations above actuality, are less than human,

> de cette inhumanité propre aux créatures de théâtre et de passion, le dialogue, les paroles échangées... empruntant elles aussi à cette irréalité comme une sorte de passionnelle grandeur (*H*, p. 192).

Not only is the drama of their life deflated by reference to Racine, but Racinian language is also punctured. Instead of magnificent rhetoric in alexandrines, the final outpouring is a banal interchange of words.

Simon also appropriates the climactic image of one of the key speeches in Racine's *Athalie*, and reworks it in *La Route des Flandres*:

> Mais je n'ai plus trouvé qu'un horrible mélange
> D'os et de chairs meurtris et traînés dans la fange,
> Des lambeaux pleins de sang et de membres affreux
> Que des chiens dévorants se disputaient entre eux...
>
> Wack... disant Les chiens ont mangé la boue, je n'avais jamais entendu l'expression, il me semblait voir les chiens, des sortes de créatures infernales mythiques leurs gueules bordées de rose leurs dents froides et blanches de loups mâchant la boue noire dans les ténèbres de la nuit, peut-être un souvenir, les chiens dévorants nettoyant faisant place nette. (*Athalie*, II:5, ll. 503-6 and *RF*, p. 9).

In Racine's play, salvation does overturn this scene of chaos and disorder. In Simon's novel, on the other hand, this image of Cerberus-like dogs, mud, night and broken bodies is the preparatory cameo for what is to follow in the rest of the text. Simon forces the reader to focus on this image (it is on the opening page of *La Route des Flandres*) by drawing attention to its singularity—the 'je' has never heard the expression before: and the 'peut-être un souvenir' signals the alert reader to seek a literary parallel. By drawing attention to these words at the very beginning, this veiled Racine quotation operates to show the subliminal levels of cultural connection at work to enrich Simon's writing. Simon is in fact copying Racine's own tactics. This phrase, as he himself points out, was far from the audience's expectations of noble language associated with the *bienséances* of seventeenth-century tragedy: 'nous ne sommes pas au Grand Siècle où il y avait des sujets (et un vocabulaire) "nobles" au point que l'on a sévèrement reproché à Racine ses "chiens dévorants"' (Poirson, 1977, p. 32).

In *La Route des Flandres,* Simon also makes considerable use of Molière. Blum reconstructs a possible series of events for Georges's ancestor by embroidering, recasting and changing *L'École des Femmes*. Molière's play provides a skeleton structure for this episode in *La Route des Flandres* which borrows its characterization, themes and action for ironic and comic effect. The difference from the Corneille and Racine references, however, is the degree of exaggeration and re-modelling of *L'École*. Irony and parody are therefore heightened and intensified and rely heavily on the cultural familiarity of (French) readers with Molière's play, because the intertext does not underwrite the whole novel, but only a part.

Simon recasts all the main characters from the precursor text. Arnolphe is remodelled as de Reixach:

> Arnolphe philanthrope jacobin et guerroyeur, renonçant définitivement à perfectionner l'espèce humaine (ce qui explique sans doute que, fort de ce souvenir et plus sage...) (p. 96).

Arnolphe's ludicrous philosophizing on love and marriage is repeated, but with variations:

> En sage philosophe on m'a vu, vingt années,
> Contempler des maris les tristes destinées,
> Et m'instruire avec soin de tous les accidents
> Qui font dans le malheur tomber les plus prudents;
> Des disgrâces d'autrui profitant dans mon âme,
> J'ai cherché les moyens, voulant prendre une femme,
> De pouvoir garantir mon front de tous affronts,

> ...le fidèle jockey ou plutôt étalon dont l'infidèle Agnès avait fourbi... en elle... l'instinct, la ruse qui n'a pas besoin d'avoir été apprise... (*L'École des Femmes,* IV:7, ll. 1188-95 which takes up the *Maximes du mariage* from III:2, and *RF,* p. 197).

The elevation of sex through the institution of marriage in Molière, which is a deliberate gilding of its animal side, is totally inverted in Simon. The retelling issues from the mouth of the salacious Blum, his imaginary reconstruction reinforcing the animality of mating, with marriage being couched in terms of horse-breeding. His words, moreover, are placed in parentheses, this reinforcing the double degree of parody (the original passage is itself highly ironic), achieved by superimposing two contrasting and exaggerated language registers.

Agnès is metamorphosed by Simon into Corinne in the description 'la virginale Agnès'. This is completely inappropriate in view of Corinne's many lovers. Where Molière only permits Agnès a few kisses from Horace, Corinne's ardour and physical expression of love are described explicitly. This is partly due, again, to the way Blum's imagination works, but the corollary is that Corinne is, as it were, Molière's Agnès defrosted from the *bienséances* of the seventeenth century. The original play makes it clear that Agnès's nature is very passionate: at the same time, Corinne literalizes the intertext by pretending to play the innocent Agnès. Corinne's explanation for locking the door to her husband is 'par crainte des voleurs'. The excuse of protection in Molière becomes an excuse for licence in *La Route des Flandres.*

De Reixach returns to find a lover has come between him and his wife, just as Horace appeared during Arnolphe's absence. The lover is put in a convenient cupboard in both cases:

> Qu'elle a sur les degrés entendu son jaloux;
Et tout ce qu'elle a pu dans un tel accessoire,
C'est de me renfermer dans une grande armoire.

> vers l'inévitable et providentiel placard ou cabinet des vaudevilles et des tragédies... dontl'ouverture pourra provoquer... aussi bien une explosion de rire qu'un frisson d'horreur parce que le vaudeville n'est jamais que de la tragédie avortée et la tragédie une farce sans humour (*L'École des Femmes,* IV:6, ll. 1151-3 and *RF,* p. 198).

The repetition of situation and action through Blum's retelling leads not only to mockery of the particular situation, but to mockery of the cupboard convention itself. Its fortuitousness is emphasized to question again the division between 'real life' and make-believe. Of course, the double irony is that Blum's words do not reconstruct 'reality' either. The play on character allusions and literary comparisons is therefore highlighted ('Tu mélanges tout... Tu confonds avec...'). The intertext remains recognizably Molière's, since its main components are transcribed, but is also recognizably Simon's, due to the transformations occurring in their transposition Simon's use of stock cultural refrences, then, mirrors the restagings of stock dramatic texts in the seventeenth century as Bray puts it: 'L'art classique n'est nullement un art réaliste... On repousse l'imitation servile pour se tenir à une imitation libérale. On s'attache aux modèles, mais on les embellit. On imite la nature, mais en l'imitant, on l'ordonne, on la stylise, parfois même on la trahit' (1951, p. 158). Furthermore, we might add that Molière's play is used for not only comic, but also black comic effect in Simon's novel; for Blum's words act as a slapstick scene, a point of light relief amid the war passages in *La Route des Flandres*.

Shakespeare

Simon draws on Shakespeare for character models to 'comment' on differing historical contexts, and in order again to add cultural acceptability and credibility to his own. In *Le Vent,* for example, Hélène is described as 'semblable à quelque personnage shakespearien' (p. 163). But, if the pre-text lends literary status to its new model, it also suffers depersonalization in the process as literary stereotypes are perpetrated and clichés re-enacted:

> la fonction cognitive... dépend... surtout d'une référence au déjà dit, ou plutôt à un dire déjà monumentalisé—clichés, formes stéréotypées, formes conventionnelles d'un style ou d'une rhétorique, bref des textes ou fragments de textes anonymes, ou au contraire les textes signés qui forment le corpus d'une culture (Riffaterre, 1980, p. 4).

Examples of this are to be found as early as *Le Tricheur*:

> Il émane des indications des mouvements de scène, dans Shakespeare, une sobre puissance dramatique... la rue nocturne éclairée de loin en loin par son chapelet de réverbères (p. 108).

Gautier, on a bicycle ride, meets a gypsy, which triggers off another Shakespeare character reference, Othello (p. 99). Simon uses these merely as tools to highlight irony in the text. The allusion to Othello is reduced to a kind of rhetorical ornament, mere name-dropping, a cultural intrusion which is quickly forgotten. As a single occurrence, it marks incomplete literary competence (excusable perhaps in a first novel) because it has no links elsewhere in the text.

Hamlet is the only Shakespeare play from which Simon has borrowed a direct quotation, spoken by Louis, chief protagonist of his first novel: 'chacun à ses affaires, à ses plaisirs, ceci, cela, et moi pour ma part...'(p. 221 and *Hamlet,* 1:5, ll. 136-8). The words reflect Louis' increasing awareness of existential questions of life and death. Up to this point, he has had discussions on the existence of God, and it is noteworthy that he leaves Hamlet's sentence unfinished. He does not 'go pray', but is in a gunsmith's, to purchase a weapon to commit his 'acte gratuit'. Louis sees himself in the tragic and heroic role of Hamlet, with revenge to exact and the possibility of his own death as the price. However, through the borrowing of the person of Hamlet and impersonation of his words, the reader sees the ironic and inflated notions of self-importance which Louis has. All his acts to date have turned out to be rather ordinary. The incongruity between the heroic and anti-heroic levels is thus presented indirectly and economically by means of the allusion to Hamlet.

Most of Simon's references to Shakespeare are concentrated in *Le Sacre du printemps,* and his own literary development is evident here, because the *Hamlet* references are not simply character prototypes, but have a stylistic function in the text as well. Simon takes stock forms to create instant 'working' definitions, as exemplified in the comparison of Hamlet to Bernard. Apart from Kanters (1954, p. 121), critics focus on Faulkner, not Shakespeare, as the main literary referent of *Le Sacre du printemps.* Carroll (1978, p. 56) indeed, treats the Hamlet comparison as confirmation of a Freudian reading of the Oedipal complex. His psychoanalytical approach, however, misses the irony in the text (p. 78), which counters such analyses.

In each direct reference to *Hamlet* in *Le Sacre du printemps,* Bernard's behaviour echoes similar traits in his Shakespearian precursor. Bernard is deliberately provocative and waspish, answering back rudely by repeating his interlocutor's words in an attitude of defiance. Hamlet reacts similarly, but in conversation with his mother (*Hamlet,* III:4, ll. 8-15). Both Bernard and Hamlet share the same hurt—their mother's remarriage—but the difference is that

Hamlet is more calculating in his responses, intending to hurt his mother, while Bernard blusters, his adolescent impetuosity uppermost (*Hamlet,* III:2, ll. 386-7, and *SP,* pp. 13, 70-2.

Through the next Hamlet reference is revealed the crux of Bernard's antagonism—his inability to accept his mother's sexuality: 'Comme il a dit, je n'avais pas à jouer les Hamlet. Certainement elle avait le droit de se remarier' (p. 20). Indeed, as his father was killed after being a prisoner of war, his mother is morally more free to remarry than Hamlet's. Hamlet's antagonism, on the other hand, is caused less by his mother's sexual activeness, which he finds distasteful at her age (III:4, ll. 68-9) than by her incestuous marriage with his uncle. She is breaking civil and natural laws (III:4, ll. 91-4).

The pluralization, 'les Hamlet', however shows a concomitant generalization and devaluation of the intertext. By the third explicit reference to *Hamlet*, the comparison is even less applicable. The issue is a discussion of fathers, the Shakespearian spectre being used to connect Hamlet's experience to Bernard's. Bernard takes the anterior text and makes it his own by the shift of personal pronoun: '...du roi *son* père, le roi *mon* père' (p. 31 [my emphasis]). Hamlet contrasts his god-like father with his uncle, using language which idealizes him. His father's marital relations are imbued with a model virtue and purity, which find their antithesis in his uncle's behaviour (*Hamlet,* III:4, ll. 55-65). In a similar vein, Bernard compares his brilliant engineer father to his new step-father who has no profession and who smuggled guns during the Spanish Civil War. However, just as Bernard is no Hamlet in terms of heroic stature and complexity of character, his excessive idealization of his father is equally belittled because it compares ridiculously with its literary antecedent. The adjective 'piètre' which qualifies 'roi' in Bernard's own mouth also helps to produce this effect. Shakespeare might indeed be described here as a 'ghost' intertext, because its connection to the new context is so tenuous.

The fourth quotation, 'espèce d'Hamlet en carton pâte' (p. 67) highlights Bernard's tantrums and behaviour as increasingly ridiculous, a false pose, when compared to Hamlet's actions. At the same time, Shakespeare's play is reduced to an anachronism. In the episode where Bernard is trying to sell the stolen ring at the Golden Gloves bar, there is an organized duel (p. 110). Hamlet's fatal and tragic fencing match with Laertes, which concludes the play on a peak of dramatic intensity, is transcribed by Simon and debunked to the level of organized sport. The whole is larded with mock chivalric terminology. This is a far cry from the ends of revenge and honour which are at stake in *Hamlet*. Thus, in this Simon novel, high tragedy is reduced to a kind of farce. Bernard is a cardboard Hamlet, or a paper one on the page of Simon's text; and his Ophelia, the virgin who dies of a broken heart, is Edith, a prostitute.

Simon uses the textual voice of *Hamlet* not only to form his character, Bernard, but also to shape the structure of the novel. All the specific allusions to the precursor play fall in the first section of the novel. There are none in the stepfather's account of his political initiation in the second part of *Le Sacre du printemps,* or in the last portion of the novel. This is because by Part Three Bernard has grown up sufficiently to be more reconciled to his stepfather, and thus is no longer in any way comparable to Hamlet. This is paralleled by the increasingly ironic position of the *Hamlet* allusions as the novel unfolds. *Le Sacre du printemps,* in fact, rejects *Hamlet* as an overall structural paradigm because it is not a tragedy. There is conflict: that is where the references to Shakespeare occur. Once these conflicts are resolved, the potential outcome of tragedy is circumvented. A tragic ending being therefore totally inappropriate, the Shakespeare references disappear completely.

By *La Route des Flandres,* Simon's uses of Shakespeare are even more refined and better integrated into his own text, although allusions to Shakespeare are still vehicles of parody, and a means to inflate minor characters. Blum, who loves to exaggerate, offers alternative stories to help Georges reconstruct what might have happened to de Reixach, the incongruity and exaggerated reusage of the Shakespeare references being totally in keeping with their speaker: 'Cet adjoint avec son parapluie et ses bottes à rustines! Le Roméo du village!' and: 'tu ne l'as jamais vu qu'en peinture... comme l'autre Othello bancal de village' (pp. 127 and 282 respectively). Othello and Romeo, placed thus in village surroundings, become anti-heroes. That archetypal lovers or generals are consistently dislocated from their heroic contexts gives Simon's novels a sophisticated, literary humour. The effect of this is, again, the demythification of both Simon's and Shakespeare's protagonists.

Similar treatment is meted out to Shakespearean heroines. In *Histoire,* references are superimposed so that, instead of concentration or intensification of associations, there is a levelling out and dissipation of focus:

> les balustrades les galeries entassées sculptées superposées peuplées de fantômes plaintifs poignardés ou décapités d'éternelles Juliette d'éternelles Boleyn (p. 256).

The balustrades and balconies are not for love-scenes but belong to a bank. The Juliets and Ann Boleyns are past history, 'fantômes', anachronisms in the world of cars and business.

The use of Shakespeare as alternative voice develops as Simon refines him to an echo in *La Bataille de Pharsale,* in the segment entitled 'César':

> la tête de Jules César... apparue à la façon d'un spectre blafard et shakespearien, comme le fantôme, le négative pour ainsi dire, de ce pondérable et sévère personnage qui contemplait le champ de bataille de Pharsale... (p. 127).

This intertext voices, in the *dramatic* key, the intersection of other historical and fictional portrayals of Caesar, including Plutarch's *Lives,* which was also a major source for Shakespeare's play. Juxtaposition of voices from these multiple discourses deflates the common subject matter: Caesar is no longer privileged as hero of war, as historiographer or writer, or even as central protagonist in Shakespeare's play or Simon's novel. This accumulation of cultural associations is further pricked by the rematerialization of Caesar simply as a figure on a banknote, common currency.

References from Shakespeare also provide Simon with ready-made plots for his novels; and in this respect he stands directly in the tradition of seventeenth-century theatre. Playwrights frequently borrowed the material of their contemporaries, the same basic story-lines generating a mass of different plays. For example, Calderón reshaped many of Lope de Vega's plays. The intertext illustrating these processes in Simon comes from the central section of *Le Palace*, 'Les Funérailles de Patrocle':

> L'Américain... disant que ça faisait encore trop de drapeaux, trop de couleurs différentes, qu'il n'aimait pas ça: trop de pleureuses derrière le cercueil: comme dans Shakespeare quand le jeune héritier du trône, l'enfant-roi aux cheveux coupés en frange, a été égorgé malgré les aboiements affolés du petit épagneul entendant approcher les pas des meurtriers, et que les sept oncles qui avaient juré devant Dieu, les Saintes Huiles et tout le saint frusquin de le protéger et veiller sur lui font de nouveau serment tous ensemble de venger la victime et châtier le lâche coupable (le serpent, le reptile), appelant sur lui toutes les malédictions du ciel et de la terre, les sept mains droites unies dans un indéfectible nœud pour sceller la nouvelle et sainte alliance, les sept

> paires d'yeux se regardant de travers et les sept mains gauches prudemment posées derrière les dos sur les manches artistiquement ouvragés de sept poignards italiens. 'Et il y a naturellement dans le nombre le bon et le mauvais oncle, mais ici quel est le bon?'(p. 109)

On first reading, the reference forms a coherent whole. However, no Shakespeare play incorporates all these elements. The major interest and difficulty of the passage lie precisely in the fact that it is the outline of not one dramatic plot, but two, intertwined. The young heir-apparent is Edward, son of Edward the Fourth, strangled by order of his uncle, Richard the Third (*Richard III,* IV:3, ll. 17-19). the little prince's Protector, the 'good' bad uncle (*Richard III,* II:3, ll. 16-22 and III:1, ll. 4-14). In Shakespeare's play, much emphasis is placed on swearing oaths and cursing members of the family, the 'indéfectible nœud pour sceller la nouvelle et sainte alliance' finding its parallel in Shakespeare (*Richard III,* III:3, ll. 5-6). The rhetorical question concluding the passage in *Le Palace* emphasizes once more the centrality of distinguishing the good/bad uncle. The problem is that Edward did not have seven uncles, only three: Clarence, Richard and his mother's brother. Richard is the only one alive at the time of Edward's death because he has disposed of all his brothers who blocked his access to the throne. The specific mention of the spaniel barking as the murderers approach is also a problem. The only reference to a dog in Shakespeare's text is the metaphor applied to Richard himself at various points in the play. (For example, by Margaret, I:3, ll. 289-91.) Although Richard is asked by his nephew, the Prince of York, to give him his dagger—which Richard deliberately reinterprets as a synonym for stabbing the little prince—both princes are in fact strangled, not stabbed: two murders are committed, not one as Simon's text suggests. The mystery of the single death intended for 'le lâche coupable' (certainly not the apt description for the *innocent* children, *Richard III,* IV:3, ll. 17-19) and the *seven* murderers with seven Italian daggers is solved if we look at Shakespeare's *Julius Caesar*. Caesar's arrogance and tyranny are seen as motive enough for the coup by the seven conspirators listed by Mark Antony after the crime in the third act (1, ll. 183-9). The emphasis Simon puts on 'les sept mains droites' and 'les sept mains gauches' picks up the motif of hands which is a recurrent topos in *Julius Caesar* (III:1, ll. 103-10). Furthermore, Brutus likens Caesar to a serpent in the egg (III:1, ll. 32-4). On a structural level, the killing of Caesar takes place in the third act of Shakespeare's play, and in the third of five sections in Simon's novel, at the point of dramatic climax. Each element of the Shakespeare reference in *Le Palace* is now accounted for. However, mere identification is not sufficient. The question is why Simon interlaced these two scenarios, and what their specific purpose is in *Le Palace*?

The idea for such intertwining may have been implanted by *Richard III* itself. In the section concerning the little princes, still alive at this point, Prince Edward mentions Julius Caesar to his good/bad uncle Richard, as it was the Roman who had the tower built in which the princes are to be imprisoned (*Richard III,* III:1, ll. 68-9, 84-5). Therefore, Simon copies Shakespeare by embedding a reference to *Julius Caesar* within his own writing. More importantly, however, he is applying a series of historical associations to the given situation in his own text. Shakespeare's plays are based on two historical assassinations, which changed the course of history in Italy and England. For dramatic effect and tension, the order and historical accuracy of the events were changed, to produce not an historically factual documentary, but an exciting and intense historical drama. This poetic licence, then, is an accepted part of the dramatist's craft. It is precisely this historical, and at the same time dramatized, portrayal of events that inspires Simon here. Just as his precursor changed his material to suit the needs of his play, so Simon takes Shakespeare's plays and repeats the same process, choosing and changing elements to mould them into a new form. In the novels prior to *Le Palace,* character is a more predominant concern. Hence it is most fitting that in these we find character links to some of Shakespeare's non-historical plays, *Hamlet, Othello,* and *Romeo and Juliet.* However, in *Le Palace,* where the concern for history, and for associations between events of various epochs and civilizations, is central, it comes as no surprise that Simon should insert references to Shakespeare's historical tragedies and use them as dramatic historico-fictional examples in collusion with 'real' present history (for example, the funeral of the anarchist Durruti during the Spanish Civil War). In one of the very few intertextual references in *L'Invitation,* Simon reiterates this historical use of Shakespearian drama to underline the 'staged' quality of political assassination in the Soviet Union:

> peu après la mort du bandit séminariste ils... avaient rouvert la porte de la salle du Conseil où ils s'étaient réunis et, sans un mot, d'un simple mouvement de tête, montré aux gardes stupéfaits le corps étendu sur le plancher de celui qu'ils venaient d'assassiner: quelque chose (l'épisode-ou comment l'appeler? : le drame, la scène shakespearienne, le meurtre,

> l'exécution? le pugilat?...) relevant non pas même alors des balbutiements de l'Histoire, de ses bégaiements, mais de ses vagissements...' (p. 43).

The essential point to note is that Simon mentions *no names*. We identify the inferred plays by literary detective work, just as Durruti in *Le Palace* may only be named by turning to a history book. The Shakespearian history is in fact weighted equally with both contemporary history and the mythical story contained in the title of the third section of *Le Palace,* the funeral of Patroclus, a solemn event arranged by Achilles. The overall effect of these various intersecting references is to underline the process of retelling which automatically fictionalizes what has happened in the past. It is abundantly clear that Simon also wants to stress the temporal nature of any event and give pre-eminence to death, the only unchanged element in all three referential layers (*P,* pp. 125-6). Simon even applies the theme of death to language itself by using Shakespearean inferences, for example in *Le Palace*: 'proclamation... comme un cadavre blanchâtre, inapaisé, et inapaisable, le fantôme même, menaçant et berné, d'un cri, de la révolte et de l'indignation' (p. 106). In both *Julius Caesar* and *Richard III,* the ghosts of those assassinated return to haunt the living, and have more force than when they were themselves living characters. In Simon, intertextual fragments are similarly given space to haunt the present text, but as disembodied and past discourses their power recedes, because of the dominant voice of their new context.

Spanish Golden Age drama

Simon also takes stock figures and plots from Spanish Golden Age drama. His *Le Vent* is a particularly 'Spanish' novel, and, not surprisingly, it contains references to such major dramatists as Lope de Vega and Calderón. However, no critic has noticed that Simon has inserted an unusually long reference to Calderón's *La Dévotion à la Croix*, or rather a plot synopsis fashioned to suit the needs of *Le Vent*:

> et au premier acte la scène représenterait une place avec, à gauche, le lourd porche tarabiscoté d'une de ces cathédrales baroques, et à droite la maison de Don Eusébio, le riche veuf, et entrant d'abord le notaire, tout de noir vêtu, l'air vaguement d'un ecclésiastique, demandant à parler d'urgence au veuf pour une affaire... d'argent... un héritage, et... puis

> apparaît le cousin pauvre ou plutôt riche puisque c'est lui qui vient d'hériter, ce qui en fait le principal sujet des conversations... non seulement du riche veuf... mais encore d'un certain nombre d'autres personnages se rencontrant, ou manquant de se rencontrer, ou s'évitant, ou se recherchant dans une suite d'actes, de scènes, de chassés-croisés, de quiproquos, sans oublier même l'épisode bouffon, salace, vert et même scabreux, plus élisabethain... que castillan, plus digne de Ben Johnson [sic] que de Calderon.

This passage plays a role similar to that of the résumé of Shakespeare's tragedies, *Richard III* and *Julius Caesar*, in *Le Palace*. Calderón's play, however, is a comedy, but because of the religious element it is like the *Auto,* a theatrical form peculiar to Spain. The *Auto Sacramental* was a dramatic homage paid to the Eucharist at the feast of Corpus Christi, a symbolic representation which may deal with the Eucharist itself or with biblical or hagiographical themes. By choosing Calderón's religious comedy as a parallel, Simon couples the serious with the comic, the saintly with the profane. Therefore, instead of asking whether Montès is a saint or an idiot, as critics have done, it is possible to see him as both in the light of the literary reference. Montès can *act* the saint and *be* the inverse at the same time.

In *La Dévotion* the central figure, Eusebio, is born under the sign of the cross and experiences divine protection. Not knowing who his real father is, he becomes the heir of a rich man. The quasi-saintly side is partnered by unsaintly features. He falls in love with his sister Julia, the daughter of Don Curcio, a rich widower, who wants to save money on her dowry by placing her in a convent. Eusebio kills his half-brother in a challenge over Julia, and is forced to become a bandit, losing all his inheritance. Similarly, Montès inherits from a father whom he has not known, falls in love, this time with a prostitute, Rose, and loses both her and his lands. As with Eusebio, suggestions of Christ-like attitudes are written into his nature, an example being his ease with children and social outcasts. Montès also gets involved with a band of gypsies, the equivalent social group to the robbers in Calderón. However, Simon accentuates and changes elements to show the approximate nature of the parallel. By making details of Montès' biography like Eusebio's, the parodic and caricatural force is accentuated. The strongly religious message in the Spanish play is reduced in Simon to mere hints: in fact it is hard to justify a 'religious' reading of *Le Vent* at all. Curcio's individual avarice and materialism are transformed into the norm of society around Montès, who is not a materialist. He is a misfit, and although he stands out as different, it is not by any supra-human power, like Eusebio's, but by his inherent being. Eusebio acts upon society: Montès is acted upon by it.

Much is 'raconté' in *Le Vent,* yet in spite of so many speeches, the language used is powerless as a vehicle to reconstruct past events. Dialogue in the text even mirrors the seventeenth-century device of stichomythia, but the recognizable rhetorical form only contains incomplete utterances and unfinished fragments (p. 166, for example). 'Meaning' is denied, whereas the goal of seventeenth-century plays is to tie many loose ends together in the dramatic climax. By refusing to close his protagonists' lines, Simon opens up the possibilities and proliferations of meaning, making the lawyer's attempt to reconstruct the chronological order of events in *Le Vent* a Sisyphean task. This mocks the lawyer's credentials to produce 'reliable' facts. His speech is not of a superior category, and his efforts are further lampooned by his 'Sozie', the comic lawyer in Calderón's play.

In the seventeenth century, the stage was seen as a metaphor for the real world. For example, Calderón's *El gran theatro del mundo,* and Shakespeare's *As you like it* ('All the world's a stage...'). In Simon, the opposite is the case: the reader of *Le Vent* is actually given warning from the outset that the novel will not proceed according to the dramatic model, 'comme leurs propres héros, leurs propres acteurs... et tout cela vague, plein de trous, de vides' (p. 9). It is ironically the theatre vocabulary in *Le Vent* which serves to highlight the artificiality of representations, which can never capture the real:

> Comme... une sorte de petit théâtre lumineux au sein de la nuit, avec ses personnages *muets*, dessinés et coloriés avec cette absurde et minutieuse précision des détails qui contribuait à les rendre irréels, privés d'atmosphère, ciselés (p. 9 [my emphasis]).

Language is not only seen as insufficient for communication: it is denied, or made equivalent to silence.

This fits with the penultimate section of the novel, which breaks completely from the drama of Calderón and Lope and the seventeenth century: 'Non. Ni Lope de Vega, ni Calderon. Rien que le décor' 'comme si tout cela était inutile, bon tout au plus pour des habitants de Vérone...' (pp. 215-16). A new play centring on the personae of wind and death is made present in the old decor. The action-packed, tightly-structured theatre of the seventeenth century, with its dramatic tension and psychological concentration, becomes what could almost be the open theatrical space of Beckett's *En attendant Godot*

> et pas d'acteurs bavards venant sur le devant de la scène raconter leurs secrets, leurs souffrances, mais quelque chose de muet, d'aussi muet que le décor... même pas une pantomime avec des gestes expressifs... et les acteurs apparaissant, traversant la scène sans s'attarder... avec ce même masque muet, impersonnel, muré, une simple suite d'allées et venues, inexplicables, inexpliquées, la scène restant de longs moments vide, seulement occupée par le vent, entre deux apparitions, deux passages silencieux (tout au plus les acteurs allant jusqu'à parler du temps qu'il fait, de riens, du repas qu'ils ont pris...) (p. 215).

This 'synopsis' in the third panel of the novel recasts the elements of religious questioning and farce present in Calderón and in Montès as an alternative dramatic voice. Such recasting is possible because the audience accepts a familiar pattern, this then being the basis of comparison, whereby the old forms depending on rules and dramatic unities are replaced by intertextual *Verfremdungseffekte.*

Theatre as structure

There is an important turning-point in Simon's *œuvre* which has escaped critical scrutiny. It occurs in its *centre*, after *Le Palace* and *before Histoire,* and coincides with his one literary 'failure', *La Séparation,* a play which dramatizes *L'Herbe,* and which was presented at the Théâtre de Lutèce in March 1963. According to the critics, Simon was unable to construct a play which unfolded by its own voices alone (Lemarchand, 1963, p. 20 and Abirached, 1963, p. 234). The procedure for writing a novel, especially the simultaneity which can be produced by juxtaposing voices from previous and present discourses, evidently did not work on stage. We have already noted the decline in emphasis on characterization in Simon up to this point, seen through the references to past theatre applied to his own protagonists. With his interest shifting to historical parallelism and cultural association it is not surprising that his play was not a success. Furthermore, it is after *La Séparation* that Simon's use in his novels of direct speech, delineated by quotation marks, declines.

Simon's 'failure' has been forgotten, but he evidently learnt something from it: the importance of structuring voices. Interest, for Simon, is not on one speaker, or the development of relationships, but on *forms* of narrative voice itself, be this shifts of narrative perspective ('il' to 'je') or time shifts, achieved by the juxtaposition of various intertextual voices. Consequently, Simon's later novels are heavily indebted to dramatic structure, the formal aspect of Classical theatre, with its artificial conventions, being the model for textual concentration. *Le Vent* neatly expresses this:

> qui, de même que la maladie, peut être somme toute considéré comme le dernier acte, le vestibule, la salle d'attente avant la fin ou, si l'on le préfère, le passage à un autre mode d'existence: en quelque sorte comme une de ces tragédies classiques au type invariable, à la construction invariable, aux étapes, à l'acheminement invariables,... en ce sens que si le dénouement (la mort du héros) en est par avance connu, il ne peut toutefois se produire que dans le respect de certaines formes, c'est-à-dire qu'après qu'un cérémonial rituel ait été observé, un certain nombre d'actes, de tirades déclamées, de beaux cris, de sorte qu'à tout moment un spectateur survenant peut s'informer auprès de ceux qui sont arrivés avant lui, la question n'étant pas: 'De quoi s'agit-il? Que s'est-il passé?', mais simplement: 'Où en est-on?', sachant immédiatement ce qu'il lui reste encore à voir' (p. 180).

The model of Classical tragedy, with its five acts, intensifies the action of the *dénouement* because the mechanisms leading to it have been set in motion in the centre, the third act. This stress on the *centre* as structuring device is iterated by Culler:

> The study of structure is in this sense governed by 'a move which consists of giving it a centre, of referring it to a moment of 'presence' or a definite origin'. This centre founds and organizes the structure, permitting certain combinations of elements and excluding others: 'the centre closes the play which it inaugurates and makes possible... The concept of a centred structure is in fact that of limited or founded play' (1975, p. 244. The quotations are Derrida's, from *Écriture et la différence*, pp. 409-10).

The centres of Simon's novels are therefore made the focus of attention because of their structures. It seems no accident that the Calderón synopsis is in the centre of *Le Vent,* just as centre-stage in *Le Palace* we find the Shakespeare résumé. Focalization occurs in the former because it is the middle act of a three-act play, the centre 'panel' of the reredos structure of the novel.

Simon is extremely aware of the reflexive and self-referential potential of the retable or reredos as model for the interconnections, associations and thematic unity available to the artist in the combination of three panels but one subject. There is another aspect of the retable which has escaped critical comment, the specifically theatrical meaning of the Spanish word 'retablo' which Shergold defines:

> These altar-pieces often had carved wooden figures as part of their decoration and the term in due course came to be transferred to a religious scene, or play, represented by wooden puppets or automata. From this, it became a general term for 'puppet show' (1967, p. 562).

In his mock synopsis above, Simon underlined heavily the stereotypical elements of Calderón's play, Eusebio being like one of these stock, automaton figures. By interlacing his life with Montès', Simon replaces the saint with the idiot, and Montès comments on himself within his own play, a 'caricature étirée et grotesque' (*V,* p. 128). It is no accident that Montès is seen in theatrical conditions: 'éclairé par en-dessous comme un acteur par les feux de la rampe, avec ce côté *clownesque* insolite, cette figure sans âge, désolée...'(*V,* p. 128 [my emphasis]). This 'dramatic' presentation not only undermines Montès' sainthood, but also reduces stock characters still further, to the level of buffoons. The scenes, too, unfold mechanically, as if programmed. The recipe is no longer a play but a 'truc', full of 'épisodes burlesques ou macaroniques' (*V,* p. 112). The religious implications of Calderón's play, and the *Auto* as genre, are thus mocked through this secularization in *Le Vent*. Religious or heroic characters are made intertextual puppets in Simon's hands.

Usually, critics classify Simon's works as belonging to three distinct periods, early, middle and mature. In the case of theatre intertexts, the delineation and codification cannot be so neatly drawn, for 'retablo' features in *Le Vent* occur again in *Triptyque*. Certainly Bacon's painting of the same name influenced the visual aspect of the novel, but the 'retablo' draws attention to itself as structure *per se*. The title *Triptych* evokes altar-pieces, and leads the reader to expect religious material (as in *Le Vent*). This expectation is totally deflated through the clown as *anti-establishment* figure; his appearance in all three 'panels' of the text parodies the repetition of saints within the reredos structure. As overpainted clown, a kind of puppet-human, made to react within strict conventions, parody and mechanical humour are introduced in physical form, for the clown's exaggerated and grotesque actions repeat and comment on those of the other characters. The clown's gross make-up, for example, scarcely differs from that of the made-up film stars, and his antics parody the positions of the lovers. Thus the clown acts as a subversive link man between all three 'serious' thematic levels in the novel, playing the games of each and underlining their absurdity. The whole novel is thus totally dependent on its programmed structure to prevent the vertiginous effects created by the multiple *mises en abyme* from overpowering the text and so keep it from dissolving into chaos. The final irony is that this is what happens in controlled form when the anonymous man deliberately knocks all the interlocking puzzle pieces off the table. Textually, this ensures that the patterns are once more open to new permutations and structures, and thus circumvents the emergence of a single meaning in the novel, or the intertextual typecasting structuring merely a rigid, mechanical, virtuoso game of representation.

Similarly, the rigidly balanced structure of *Le Palace,* where Parts One and Five, and Two and Four are equally weighted to heighten the import of the middle section, is also remodelled in a later novel, *Leçon de choses.* Where the historical and referential climax, a dominant voice in each 'act', the physical and lasting presence of the palace as concrete structure overshadowed the earlier novel, *Leçon de choses* is a five-act 'play' of referentiality itself. The language of theatre is actually employed in the section headings 'générique' and 'divertissement'. Parts One and Five, and Two and Four are again balanced to illuminate the central section (encircled by the two divertissements), entitled 'Leçon de choses', a *mise en abyme* for the whole novel. The school manual describes the construction and destruction of material structures. Its precise, authoritative voice as school book dialogues with, and then is engulfed by, the often incoherent fiction which is its host, the Beckettian babel, slang and colloquial language of the *divertissements.* The whole novel then comprises anonymous (therefore non-authoritative) intertextual voices talking in continuous prose, with not one single punctuation mark except the final full-stop. The *structure* of theatre is therefore intrinsic to the control of the novel. The staging of their discourses is what gives them speech matter and form—the section headings channel the flow of speech-acts which are changed and differentiated only because *Leçon de choses* is the stage which allows its own fictionality to speak and converse with itself. It is a play of languages, mocking play itself, and the convention of the play-within-a-play is nowhere better exemplified than in its central section.

*****

References to seventeenth-century drama in Simon's fiction can be seen therefore to act as markers of his stylistic development. The early novels have *dramatis personæ* belonging to old structures and unities of character construction. What has not been noted is the concurrence of allusions to the Golden Age theatres in Spain, England and France in these early works, all working to the same end. They trigger the shift to Simon's later, analogical and associational 'characters' like Georges, O and 'il' which occurs through the intertextual play on stock characters to create anti-models. Once this stage is complete (when the *character* references from plays disappear), the structures which constitute Simon's own particular fictional voice can begin. The divide can be drawn where the particularly simonian restructuration of materials and compositional techniques (in the mode of his seventeenth-century precursors) take place: with *La Séparation*. Thereafter, Simon demonstrates his greater technical skill to handle, rework and incorporate many 'voices' on the 'stage' of his own fiction. What Simon desires above all is for the voice of writing itself to emerge, its formal drama to become visible:

> à partir du moment où un romancier ne dissimule plus que la continuité et la 'réalite' font pour lui un problème, qu'elles lui échappent, qu'il ne prétend plus les représenter, il attire *ipso facto* l'attention du lecteur sur le phénomène de l'écriture *en soi*, ce qui revient à mettre en question son discours... Il est ainsi rappelé au lecteur qu'il se trouve en présence d'un *texte* (de même que dans la tragédie classique dont les personnages ne parlent pas de façon réaliste, mais en alexandrins (interview in Poirson, 1982, p. 37).

To this end, theatrical allusions as/and structures emerge as key speakers in his novels (as seen in the various plot synopses we have analysed), in order that they can dialogue with other materials, systems and sub-systems. Intertextuality in this chapter then may thus be summed up by the word 'représentation'. Not only is the intertext made present within the new structure: it is visible in its new 'performance'. It is not without irony that Simon refers to himself as the 'M. Jourdain du Nouveau Roman' (Paulhan, 1984, p. 45). Like his illustrious precursor, he mocks pretensions of rhetoric, by deliberate repetition and misrepresentation of fixed forms; and the 'dramatic' nature of the intertext structures such mockery, to ensure that 'Tout ce qui est prose, n'est point vers; et tout ce qui n'est point vers, n'est point prose' (*Le Bourgeois Gentilhomme,* III:3, ll. 83-5).

Chapter Three

Eighteenth-Century Literature

In this chapter, the structuralist definitions of intertextuality are incorporated in a larger system than in the previous one. Focus is shifted away from specifically 'literary' intertexts, and the generic systems such as drama to which they belong, to include other 'codes' at the writer's disposal. Kristeva offers a useful definition of this global aspect of intertextuality, which serves as the theoretical base of our discussions in this chapter:

> Le signifié poétique renvoie à des signifiés discursifs autres, de sorte que dans l'énoncé poétique plusieurs autres discours sont lisibles. Il se crée, ainsi, autour du signifié poétique, un espace textuel multiple dont les éléments sont susceptibles d'être appliqués dans le texte poétique concret. Nous appellerons cet espace *intertextuel*. Pris dans l'intertextualité, l'énoncé poétique est un sous-ensemble d'un ensemble plus grand qui est l'espace des textes appliqués dans notre ensemble.
> Dans cette perspective, il est clair que le signifié poétique ne peut pas être considéré comme relevant d'un code unique. Il est le lieu de croisement de plusieurs codes (au moins deux) qui se trouvent en relation de négation l'un par rapport à l'autre (Kristeva, 1969, p. 194 [her emphasis]).

Thus any text is part of the system 'Text', and may draw on intertexts from any other subset within it. These include not just literary codes, but other discourses more usually classified as non-literary, such as history, science, philosophy and politics, all of which found their parameters being established during the Enlightenment. Hence, having studied the drama of Simon's usage of 'baroque' intertexts as somewhat gongoresque embellishments of his early characters, this chapter will engage with the 'rococo' materiality of his later works, which have embedded within them surprisingly consistent reference to eighteenth-century writing.

The Enlightenment saw an eruption of scientific exploration in all fields of knowledge and a search for a new definition of Truth outside the bounds of the accepted Authorities (the Church, the Monarch, the Classics). Classification of the world was a chief concern particularly of men of letters, many of whom wrote fictional as well as non-fictional texts: Diderot worked on the *Encyclopédie*, Voltaire on histories of the Far East, Rousseau on models of society. It is precisely this overlapping of non-fictional with fictional discourses by eighteenth-century writers which is reflected in Kristeva's theory of intertextuality. Indeed, it was she who coined the term, and thus, to a large extent, classified it. Simon, like his eighteenth-century precursors, engages with non-literary discourses. This chapter will consider how his use of 'intertexts' in this wider application of the word regenerates and redefines what might be deemed 'fictional' or 'literary'. Through his reusage of non-literary codes of writing and his allusion to eighteenth-century writers, the interdisciplinary aspects of Simon's intertextuality are made visible. The Encyclopedia and the History are the two codes I have chosen to investigate as they play a major part in his later novels. Although these are singularly lacking in eighteenth-century literary quotations, and I shall explore the few there are at the end of the chapter. The point I wish to make here is that these novels are no less intertextual, in Kristeva's wider sense. Indeed, one might even argue that Simon's mature novels are underpinned by a 'rococo' intertextual framework, this adjective itself appearing not infrequently in such novels as *Histoire* (pp. 147, 244, 249, 348) and *Les Corps conducteurs* (pp. 42, 45, 100, 140).

The Encyclopedia

The Enlightenment saw an upsurge in the compilation of compendia: Diderot's *Encylopédie* collected definitions and categorized heterogeneous matter for the first time. The epigraph to *Le Palace* is from the Larousse dictionary and this acts as a definition for the whole novel as well as for Simon's subsequent *œuvre*: 'Révolution: Mouvement d'un mobile qui, parcourant une courbe fermée, repasse successivement par les mêmes points'. The encompassing structural frame of the novel mirrors any encyclopedia's ordering and classification of heterogeneous entries; 'Inventaire' and 'Le Bureau des objets perdus' frame and generate the material of *Le Palace*. Within the text, the student holds a dictionary with its 'colonnes de minuscules caractères' on his lap within the text, which opens at an encyclopedia entry for Santa Cruz, outlining a brief history, geography and list of industries (pp. 88-9). The 'révolution' through the same items, but with different results can be seen clearly in the columns of names, enumerations and lists which appear in *Leçon de choses,* for example the saints' names on page 26 which include Santa Cruz. It is the 'Leçons de Choses' section, the *mise en abyme* in the centre of the novel, which operates the shift of emphasis. In didactic, oversimplified school textbook language, this section highlights 'knowledge made easy' learning which contrasts with the disorder, confusion and chaos of the fiction which surrounds it. Omni*science* and authority converse with fiction which is tentative and non-logical, a *process* of learning to encounter and make sense of the world rather than a product of 'fact' or 'truth'. Hence, the narrative counter-lesson, the novel *Leçon de choses*, ironically deflates and questions any rigid codifying of meaning, scientific or indeed literary, by bursting the classificatory confines of definition itself.

The same process occurs in the structure and form of the novels lying midway between the poles of *Le Palace* and *Leçon de Choses, Orion aveugle and Les Corps conducteurs*. Here, scientific and cultural codifications are interconnected through the Anatomy and the Museum Catalogue, both of which gather together and order heterogenous components. Both compendia have their roots in eighteenth-century interests: the field of scientific investigation of the body and the mania for collecting and exhibiting. Simon's *Orion aveugle* is an Anatomy in the double sense in that it reproduces and incorporates plates which illustrate the written text. Two are notably *eighteenth-century* plates: 'Tronc de femme disséqué—document tiré de l'"Exposition Anatomique de la Structure du Corps Humain" de Jacques Gautier d'Agoty, Marseille 1759', and 'Tête d'homme—document tiré de "Mythologie complète en couleurs et grandeur naturelle" de Jacques Gautier d'Agoty, Paris 1746' (pp. 115 and 145 respectively). The link between a scientific and a mythical universe is precisely the hinge Simon exploits in the constant double movement of this text which straddles the divides of many genres. The summation is the twentieth-century counterpart to the above mentioned plates, the 'planche anatomique—document tiré du "Larousse Classique Illustré", Paris 1928' (an illustrated encyclopedia, a compendium of compendia) at the beginning of *Orion aveugle*.

However, any hinging or doubling of discourse also opens up the place of ambiguity or paradox. One such is underlined in the preface to this text, where Simon underlines the fundamental importance of the *visual* representations as textual generators. They are intrinsic to the shaping of both the content and the form, yet 'work' in a text calling attention in its title to *blindness*. Therefore the anatomical plates, in that they are a structural motif and punctuate the text at regular intervals, act, I contend, as a central metaphor for the text itself. Image and word collide but do not coincide. Critics have considered Poussin's 'Paysage avec Orion aveugle' as the key metaphorical expression of the text, of the writer's blind, searching journey as he composes. Axiomatic as this painting (and metaphorical reading) may be, it is only a partial synecdoche for the text: the whole is not reproduced. In fact, Simon pinpoints only the torso of Orion on the cover detail, so that the 'Paysage avec...' is ignored. Similarly, the full title of Poussin's work is also curtailed, the remainder stressing the giant's body and sightlessness, not the landscape, which is of secondary importance, and which Orion cannot see:

> Un de ses *bras* étendu en avant *tâtonnant* dans le vide, Orion, le géant aveugle, avance sur un chemin en direction du soleil levant, guidé dans sa marche par la voix et les indications d'un petit personnage juché sur ses épaules musculeuses (p. 19 [my emphasis]).

The focus is on the groping, outstretched arm, the *anatomical* detail, and the insignificant, nameless figure on the giant's shoulder who is the one giving directions and controlling the giant's course. Simon seems to be deliberately demythologizing Orion by visibly shrinking his stature in the novel to a fragment. The preface states clearly that the novel 'ne racontera pas l'histoire exemplaire de quelque héros ou héroïne'. Orion is not the hero of the text: the text itself is the chief subject, evolving from a detail which is coupled with the reproduction of a *fraction* of Poussin's painting. Mythic or artistic associations are reduced to Orion as body and as constellation of planetary bodies. This cosmological aspect is reinforced by a reproduction of another eighteenth-century plate inset midway in the text, 'Signes du Zodiaque—document tiré de "Harmonia Macrocosmica", *Atlas Universalis* d'Andrea Cellari, Amsterdam 1708' (pp. 92-3). Orion as figure is then only mentioned on the last two pages of Simon's text, but the continuity of description here is disrupted by the reproduction of a third anatomical plate. The Orion reference is only a 'mock' frame to the text, for what emerges is that, as with the constellation, he disappears completely in the sunlight. The final focus is not Orion, but the head *dissected* to reveal its constituent parts:

> Une coupe longitudinale de la tête de profil permet de voir les principaux organes, la masse ivoire du cerveau injecté de sang dont les

> circonvolutions compliquées battent à chaque afflux, la langue violette, les dents, les os poreux et la boule exorbitée de l'œil, livide, enserrée par ses racines rouges, avec son iris, son cristallin, son corps vitreux, et la mince membrane de sa rétine sur laquelle *les images du monde viennent se plaquer, glisser, l'une prenant la place de l'autre* (p. 146 [my emphasis]).

Orion has titular status, but only a secondary function in the generation of the text. The final irony of *Orion aveugle* is that the organ of *sight* is central, not Orion's blindness. The reader's insight is therefore fully engaged, not least in the paradoxes of this textual anatomy.

The reproduced anatomies furthermore illustrate binaries and serve to oppose and confuse masculine and feminine, the head and the body, the mental, visual and the physical, in other words all kinds of contrasts which comprise the human form. These contrasts are reiterated in twentieth-century art plates. In J. Dubuffet's 'Caballero' (p. 124), the figure consists of a jigsaw of interlocking shapes and colours, thus emphasizing the parts rather than the whole. Picasso's 'eau-forte no. 308' (pp. 96-7) merges male and female bodies in visual form. In the same way, Simon uses fragments of writing, units which are broken off for formal, not semantic reasons, to underline the important structuring principles of repetition and difference. The punctuation of *Orion aveugle* at intervals by the anatomical plates therefore signals the text as body for dissection, and corpus able to proliferate.

In *Les Corps conducteurs*, a repetition and expansion of *Orion aveugle*, the anatomical (and other) plates are omitted, but the body is highlighted by being the focus of the new title. Originally entitled 'Propriétés de quelques figures géométriques ou non', the emphasis was on the form, the frames and structure, not the dynamic processes of the parts. The choice of *Les Corps conducteurs* emphasises 'Corps' which is no longer associated only with anatomical plate: it equals 'mot', an atom of the anatomy and locus of diverging semic paths. *Les Corps conducteurs* is thus the embodiment of kinds of writing, and exemplifies intertexts as codes. This novel practises what Kristeva outlines in her theory of intertextuality:

> Le texte se présente alors comme un *corps* résonnant à registre multiple, et chacun de ses éléments obtient une pluridimensionalité qui, renvoyant à des langues et des discours absents ou présents, leur donne une portée hiéroglyphique (Kristeva, 1969, p. 224 [my emphasis]).

Les Corps conducteurs is built up around dissections and cross-sections, with both the body and the aeroplane cut open, but more important are the cross-sections of language from all fields of human endeavour, crossed by one narrator's journey through a city and a text. The novel is a compendium of citations (as opposed to quotations from literary sources). These paraliterary codes encompass the specific metatextual discourses of medical textbooks (pp. 17, 24-5, 47, 154, 162, 165, 183-4, 206-7), astronomy and geography books (pp. 55, 57, 122), travelogues (pp. 128, 132, 137, 164, 184), ornithologies (pp. 174, 185, 212, 215-17), political oratory (the Latin-American Writers' Conference), dictionary and encyclopedia entries (pp. 19, 23, 97, 149), and the most non-literary form of prose, enumeration of heterogeneous names—a list of shops is given on page 211. Associative generations and expansions ensue. The word 'serpent' has been discussed to illustrate this (Duffy, 1983-4, pp. 8-10). The body words, I suggest, are even more interesting, given the novel's title.

'Jambe' is the first anatomical part mentioned in the text. Not only is it the major theme; it is also the text's mode of locomotion. The text progresses in step with the wanderings of the sick man, Orion's groping advance towards the dawn, the explorers pushing their way into the jungle. The legs of the opening sentence are static, but are word pictures for the text 'mis en marche' (p. 7). The badge on the negro's cap (p. 15) picks up the colour and the angle of the foot (p. 20) echoes the alignment. On page 27, the reflection of the row of legs 'dont les cuisses se superposent aux photos d'acteurs, à celle des gratte-ciel émergeant de la brume et à la suite d'images où la femme en rose rampe sur l'arrière de la voiture' illustrates the structural composition of the text, its various parts superimposed in different contexts. The simile of the dancers is embodied by the dancing-girls (pp. 65-6). The disembodied nature of the legs in the incipit is transposed to what the viewer in the bar can see in the window (p. 98)—the passers-by as far as the knee. The metaphor 'bataillon' in the opening sentence is incorporated into the text when the soldiers' legs are the object of focus (p. 123). The sexual connotations are developed on page 147: the frozen immobility of the legs is staged on page 212 and transferred to the sick man at the *end* of the text, 'à quatre pattes' (p. 225), but unable to use his legs any longer, just as in the same way the fiction is drawing to a stopping point.

The second body word which proliferates the text is 'tuyau', taken from the description of the first anatomical plate of the male torso:

> A peu près en son milieu il y a une poche vert olive clair, collée à la paroi, arrondie en un petit dôme sur le haut, et dont la partie inférieure s'amincissant finit en un fin tuyau *qui se divise en fourche* dont les branches disparaissent dans les replis des lobes rougeâtres. Un second tuyau, mais celui-ci d'une couleur mauve et d'une section plus large, s'entrelace avec le premier et ses ramifications (pp. 9-10 [my emphasis]).

Textual ramifications are developed precisely by means of these forking pipes which send the fiction off in new directions from the metonymic bifurcation. The first analogous object is the hydrant on which the sick man sits to survey his surroundings (p. 11). A snake in the fork of a tree is then likened to 'un gros tuyau' (p. 19) and the animate tube becomes inanimate, but no less generative, the 'corps conducteurs' of the central-heating system (p. 31). The topos of undulating lines reappears in the crests which decorate the conference room (pp. 34-5). Elsewhere, reiteration of 'tuyau' links the telephone to the snake and to the human body, the telephone being the locus of transmitted words: speech disembodied from the speaker (p. 79). Rivers (p. 86) and the metro (p. 161) are systems which echo the anatomical model, so that the small and the large in nature, the human and non-human, are all inter-referentially presented in this one fictional body of words; and at one key point, an apparently flat descriptive image of, again, anatomical tubes (p. 68), becomes a cameo for the text itself, throbbing as its parts intertwine and subdivide.

The History

While Simon's novels of the seventies are a high point of the encyclopedic dimensions of Simon's citational universe from non-literary codes, they sprang from, and are subsumed in importance by, the quintessentially human-centred code of the History, which has, in fact, gained in importance since *Leçon de choses*. *Histoire*, much earlier, is the root connecting through its title the two branches of fact and fiction. It is worth remembering that it was again during the eighteenth century that the two were segregated and that the notion of historiography itself was drastically reviewed. Brumfitt sums this up neatly: '[if writers] were often lacking in historical imagination, they nevertheless brought about a profound revolution in historical thought. They created a new type of social history, interesting themselves in laws and constitutions, in economic progress, in the arts and the sciences. They strove to separate history from legend and to make the past appear as rational as the present' (1970, p. 1). Voltaire was very much the central figure in historiographical writing, his scepticism and concern for detail and accuracy being a reaction against the seventeenth-century taste for moral instruction encased in an embroidered tale of some national figure. Despite his Western European prejudices, Voltaire was also a cosmopolitan historian, concerned with the histories of China, India and the Far East; he thus displaced Christian European history as the centre of study. His interest, though popularized and propagandist rather than profound and philosophically consistent, propelled History toward the study of civilizations and societies and away from that of individual heroes. In his article 'Histoire' of the *Dictionnaire Philosophique,* history is defined as 'Le récit des faits donnés pour vrais au contraire de la fable, qui est le récit des faits donnés pour faux'. Voltaire defines history not so much as the events of the past themselves, but as the narrative connecting them.

Parallels between Simon and Voltaire are therefore evident in their interest in the telling and reconstruction of past events, H/histoire in both forms. The focus is not so much on the individual or a dynasty, as on European and other societies as economic groups. It is Simon's *Histoire* which explores most fully the possible combinations and facets of 'H/histoire' and includes an allusion to Voltaire (pp. 202-3). The economic and satirical thrust of the novel is almost condensed here, for the writer Voltaire figures on a banknote, paper used in the form of exchange.

To illustrate what '(Hi)story' is, Simon's *Histoire* dovetails elements taken from discourses on all points on the scale between 'Histoire' and 'histoire'. The category closest to the latter is the genre of the fairy tale or 'conte'. This genre of the fabulous and the purely imaginary seems utterly contrary to Simon's concerns with fictionalised H/histoire. However, his use of *Gulliver's Travels* is extensive and comes as early as *Le Tricheur,* to furnish literary metaphors of size. Louis is described thus: 'Son corps était lourd, cloué par terre, immense, Gulliver' (p. 16). The reference is of course to the occasion when Gulliver wakes up to find that the Lilliputians have tied him down as he slept.

In *Gulliver*, the cover blurb positions the intertext against Simon's novel succinctly, for it: '...malgré son titre emprunté à Swift, n'est en rien un conte philosophique. L'auteur n'entend pas tirer des comportements et des faits quelque leçon que ce soit. Il s'attache à découvrir les êtres, sur le plan individuel et non pas social, derrière les images qui les dissimulent. Chacun est géant ou pygmée aux yeux d'autrui, suivant l'optique du voyageur'. Apart from Simon's adoption of the original's four part structure, there is no reworking of the precursor text; the travels are omitted both from the title and as a narrative vehicle. The only confluence point is the constant stress on the huge size of Loulou de Chevannes and his twin brother Jo (pp. 41, 53, 89, 93, 95, 109-11, 150, 199, 267, 276). The only allusion to Swift is on page 125, where the *giant* is replaced by another legendary one, Goliath. As was noted with the Shakespeare references in Simon's early novels, *Gulliver* seems to operate on the level of cultural name-dropping rather than on interiorized and revitalized reworkings of the pre-text. *Gulliver* cannot then be said to be a parody, a pastiche or even an 'anti-Gulliver'. Intertexts can also be treated as giants or pygmies within Simon's writing. Here, the literary giant overshadows Simon as pygmy text.

Where *Gulliver's Travels* envelops biting social and political satire within imaginary travel stories, Simon's borrowing in *Histoire* is quite different:

> quelque chose semblable aussi à un monstre mais à l'intérieur cette fois comme la mâchoire ouverte d'une baleine avec son palais nervuré livide des voûtes des ogives des dents des cavernes orifices d'œsophages de bronches au-dessus ou à travers lesquelles chemineraient quelques explorateurs *liliputiens* (*sic*) armés de bâtons de cordes écartelés enjambant les gouffres *Gullivers minuscules* dans le cadavre de saindoux graisseux où ils se fraient un chemin (p. 133 [my emphasis]).

The comparison here is not so much a thematic repetition, but a way of emphasizing the importance of different perspectives by which to review that which is familiar. Giants and pygmies are essentially the same in their form; it is their proportion which is the variant, with the world of the one a distortion of the other, and the size of the one the inverse of the other. Elsewhere in Simon, the word 'liliputien(ne)' occurs to imply smallness. In *Le Palace,* the speaker becomes 'une minuscule poupée costumée en singe, une lilliputienne et noire mandragore' (p. 221). In *Les Corps conducteurs*, perspective differences of *Histoire* are reinforced by this literary adjective:

> Du fait de l'absence de toute commune mesure de grandeur entre la taille des petites pastilles et celle des façades dont les sommets se perdent dans le couvercle de brume, on dirait la monotone errance de lilliputiennes multitudes condamnées à tourner sans fin (*CC*, p. 37).

The most consciously reworked instance of the Swiftian adjective comes in *La Bataille de Pharsale*. Little dolls on sale are described as 'liliputiennes, crapuleuses et commerciales réincarnations de Vénus' (p. 139) with the pun in lili*put(e)*ienne central to the inferences of the passage. Simon is thus using a literary allusion to his own fictional advantage, that of vulgarisation and deflation in ways parallel to the uses we explored in *The Golden Ass.* The last reference to Swift's character is in *Les Géorgiques,* and evokes the same episode as in *Le Tricheur,* but in order that the referent is transferred to the fixed, static and dead:

> statues couchées dans des berceaux, fixant le ciel de leurs yeux d'aveugles amarrées sur des coussinets et emmaillotées de cordes par une nuée de liliputiens au milieu d'échafaudages compliqués et de machines de levage (*G,* p. 243).

It is quite clear that the intertext is barely recognisable the more Simon transgresses from the 'conte' overtones of his early works and the more indirect, but no less biting, social comment preoccupy his fictions.

Moving farther on the scale from the point of pure 'histoire' as fabulation, Simon bevels fact / fable codes of 'Histoire' in *Histoire* with cognate *linguistic* terms. 'Histoire' is used euphemistically in the novel for underhand financial deals ('Sales histoires', p. 90), head-in-the-sand political idealisms ('Alors ne venez pas me raconter d'histoires', page 93), comic stories (p. 158) and finally as untruth or lie ('menteur comment peux-tu inventer des histoires par...', p. 242). There are references, too, in *Histoire* to 'unrealistic' accounts in the form of symbol—'famille des figures symbolisant travaux et vertus sous les aspects de personnages éternellement géorgiques, sommairement vêtus et optimistes' (p. 207); allegory—'les infatigables personnages allégoriques, optimistes et musculeux, condamnés à brandir sans repos parmi les rameaux d'olivier, les cornes d'abondance et les lauriers' (p. 247); and myth—references to Leda and Daphne (p. 270). In each case, the seriousness of the categories is deliberately mocked by the contemporary context which reinvests them with new critical overtones. The most sustained is a humorous remodelling of the Theseus myth. This provides, through indirect comment, biting criticism of Western capitalism and the power of money, the original components being translated into contemporary terms:

> pensant à quelque monstre qui serait tapi dans un coin caché au fond des couloirs de marbre (peut-être dans les sous-sols, comme la chaudière du calorifère): une sorte de ruminant impotent et obèse (mais pas les cornes, le front bouclé, les bras d'égorgeur: plutôt, comme le calorifère, des tubulures, des assises de fonte, des manomètres—pensant que si Thésée faisant irruption ce serait sous l'aspect d'un gringalet gominé et armé d'une mitraillette, et qu'il l'abandonnerait non pas sur une plage mais au bord d'une route, ou à la rigueur dans une chambre d'hôtel meublé, après l'avoir soulagée de sa dot constituée de titres de puits de pétrole et de mines d'étain), obèse, donc, vorace et végétarien, et qu'il faudrait nourrir sans arrêt de pâte à papier, de chèques et de bordereaux comme d'autres de feuilles de salade ou d'épluchures de légumes (p. 71).

All of these provide other landscapes by which Simon can compare, contrast and highlight the 'real' world settings in his novel. Yet such mythic and fabulous worlds are ironically close to their opposite pole, Ancient History and archaelogical reconstruction. In *Histoire,* History as History is fully represented—the Ancient World of Herculaneum or Pompeii (page 110), and Caesar's exploits (page 119); the Medieval World of Germany and Italy (pages 11-12), colonization (page 213), the Battle of Waterloo (page 101), the Russian Revolution (page 214), the Spanish Civil War (page 297), evocations of the Second World War and the concentration camps (page 148) and the decrepitude of modern cities (page 365). Contemporary History is also included as newspaper headlines. However, the 'sketchy' nature of such references makes them no different from their 'fabulous' counterparts, for it is their narrative reconstruction which is again questionable. Indeed, History as the written study of events, the 'manuel d'Histoire' used by the narrator (page 10), is intertextually present but it too turns into cliché, even caricature. Mockery of family trees, the unsystematic time progression and enumeration of the above Historical events, serve to underline the fact that Simon is not pretending to be an Historian, but is using History as just one of the materials for his novel. History textbooks are in fact derided (pp. 105-6). Forced into the confines of a textbook or arranged as exhibits in a museum, History as ordered chronology is undermined (pp. 109, 117, 379). Furthermore, the novel destroys the autonomy of individual Historical figures by demonstrating their disparateness and interchangeability: 'un de ces noms interchangeables aux creuses et poussiéreuses sonorités de plâtre César, Verrius, Charles, Laurent, Philippe, Law, Rothschild, Le Bref, Le Chauve, Le Bel, Le Magnifique'(p. 85). They are tantamount to fictional heroes.

Simon's strategies concerning the overlap of H/histoires indeed mirror Voltaire's *contes philosophiques, Candide* in particular, where real and imaginary lands (France and Eldorado) provide alternative milieux for social criticism. Similar juxtaposition of imaginary or exotic worlds is exploited in *Histoire* which contrasts European 'civilization' with the foreign lands of Henri's travels. It is then deeply ironic to find an allusion in *Histoire* to *Candide*, the name Cunégonde: 'Imbécile probablement qui envoyait aussi ces cartes postales signées Cunégonde ou Dévinez qui' (p. 51). In *Candide*, Cunégonde is the impelling force which moves the hero round the world. The quest for her is the unifying thread of the tale. In *Histoire*, it is the mysterious writer, Henri, who adopts Cunégonde as a pen-name, and it is his wife who remains static, mere recipient of the postcards. Yet, the itinerary of picture postcards in *Histoire* actually overplays the utopian dream of Henri's wife (the Candide figure by implication), their new life together (p. 18). She never does rejoin her husband (as do Cunégonde and Candide): she only receives cards from him. *Histoire* thus becomes an *anti-travelogue*, and mocks the genre of Travel writing.

Simon further mocks travel writing and literary journey-tales with their picaresque implications by the use of the postcard form itself. The central narrator of *Histoire* has the world compressed into his lap through the postcards sent to his mother from all parts of the world. By simple juxtaposition, East can meet West, or the exotic parts of the world can be skimmed in an instant (pp. 258, 132-4 for example). The images denote real places, but the supporting text rarely comments on them. Then the use of glaring colour and the frequent focus on elements which belie their geographical accuracy make the whole *unreal*. Criticism of European culture is nowhere stated directly by Simon: indirect comment is no less biting, however, due to the distancing effect of the postcards and the need for the narrator to interpret them. For example, furnishings from Europe are in evidence in their foreign setting (pp. 136-7). The postcards, as Carroll notes, act as 'a displaced Europe because

Europeans imposed their own image and customs on the colonized world' (1977, p. 815). The fact that exact place names are given with precise dates (p. 63) and even specific times of the day (pp. 260-1) has the paradoxical effect of making Henri's journeys *less* authentic and almost legendary in the mind of the boy narrator as he studies them. Near the end of the novel, the procedures of the whole textual composition by postcards are mocked when

> une des piles que j'avais posées à côté de la commode s'était écroulée et elles avaient glissé s'éparpillant sur le carrelage J'ai posé ma veste et le dossier sur le lit et me suis accroupi pour les ramasser (pp. 328-9).

Prefiguring the destroyed jigsaw puzzle in *Triptyque,* the list of place names continues in a new order for three pages, thus revitalizing the fictional possibilities and allowing new comment and connections between hitherto unjuxtaposed elements to occur (as do the generators in *Les Corps conducteurs*). As Riffaterre notes:

> The chief characteristic of a poetic text, as opposed to the purely cognitive use of language, is that while the text seems to progress from image to image, from episode to episode, it in fact keeps repeating the same information. The text progresses syntactically and lexically and it keeps adding meanings, but each step forward is actually a repetition of one significance. Each of these steps is only a transcodage of that significance from one means of expression to another. The significance, of course, is found in the structure first given by the text, with its network of binary oppositions and their transformations. Every subsequent transcodage is a variant of this structure (1973, p. 44).

Histoire does move from 'image to image' via the postcards but, due to their unique pictorial mode of presenting writing on one side and image on the other, they are the means par excellence of doubling fictional space, thereby condensing the 'binary oppositions' and ambiguities of description between the visual and the scriptural codes. As is the case with *Orion aveugle,* their significance is the impossibility of establishing the 'real', whether it be place, fact, History or order: they delineate a fictional space in visual form and a means of critical and cultural displacement.

Simon's novel, then, rejects the diachronic History for the synchronic 'histoire'. The genealogy of the History book is doubled in the narrator's attempts to reconstruct his family tree and solve the mystery of the missing links. Watching the tree as object outside his window, the narrator is aware that he is in the presence of 'l'Histoire en train de se faire' (*Hist,* p. 181), and imagines uncle Charles 'écrivant à son tour sa page d'Histoire—quoiqu'il fût trop bien élevé évidemment pour se laisser aller à ces sortes de pompeux commentaires' (p. 189). The task of diachronic reconstruction, however, is just as fruitless on the personal and family scales as on the national level. There is always uncertainty because of repeated redefinition, qualification, inexactitude, and accumulation of phrases such as 'peut-être' (as pp. 272-3). Speculation, supposition and approximation are all that can be achieved because the fragments of 'facts' are

> dans leur ordre monotone, mais d'une combinaison, d'un ombreux et fulgurant enchevêtrement de lumières et de lignes où les éléments éclatés, dissociés se regroupent selon le foisonnant et rigoureux désordre de la mémoire (p. 273).

Simon does not answer the question of what H / history is in this novel, but indicates and illustrates the multifaceted intermingling of 'fact' and 'fiction'. As Carroll sees it, the net result is that

> History must be read synchronically in order to undermine its assumed linearity, and space must be read diachronically in order to undermine its apparently closed nature (1977, p. 823).

Simon and Rousseau

Of all the eighteenth-century figures mentioned (rather than quoted) by Simon in his novels and interviews, it is Rousseau who receives special treatment. His place as the theorist of a workable society (*Le Contrat social*) rather than the inventor of imaginary ones like Swift or Voltaire is closely akin to the History-rooted orientation in Simon.

> Parmi les facteurs qui ont présidé à l'avènement de la bourgeoisie capitaliste, triomphant des entraves du monde féodal, qui peut faire la part entre le conflit des forces économiques, l'œuvre de J.J. Rousseau, celle des conventionels et des découvertes scientifiques de l'époque?... Il convient de mettre fin à une légende: jamais aucune œuvre d'art, aucune oeuvre littéraire n'a eu *dans l'immédiat* un poids quelconque sur le cours de l'Histoire. Si des monuments du langage qui en appelle à l'action tels que 'Les Tables de la Loi', 'Les Évangiles', 'Le Discours de la Méthode', 'Le Contrat Social' ou 'Le Manifeste Communiste' ont parallèlement à l'évolution des techniques et des conditions économiques, transformé les sociétés de façon spectaculaire... il n'est aucun exemple d'ouvrage *littéraire* (poème, roman) qui ait influé de cette façon (Simon, 1967, p. 12 [his emphasis]).

The only direct quotation from an eighteenth-century writer in Simon's novels is the epigraph to *Les Géorgiques* which is taken from Rousseau's *Les Confessions*:

> Les climats, les saisons, les sons, les couleurs, l'obscurité, la lumière, les éléments, les aliments, le bruit, le silence, le mouvement, le repos, tout agit sur notre machine et sur notre âme par conséquent.

This quotation epitomizes the overlap between the Encyclopedia and fiction, but adds the highly personal viewpoint which is typically Rousseauesque. Elsewhere in *Les Géorgiques,* Simon refers to *Le Contrat social* in connection with LSM, who was fully involved in the political upheavals of the French Revolution: 'Avec le "Contrat social" et Virgile il semble que ç'ait été une de ses passions' (pp. 446-7, referring to his horses). The allusion to Rousseau is historically in keeping with both the reconstruction of LSM's political career and the climate of eighteenth-century France after the Revolution. Moreover, due to the twentieth-century perspective in the novel, critical distance from Enlightenment idealisms is achieved: the French Revolution did not end all revolutions. The fictional disillusionment and personal failures of LSM also pinpoint this. Rousseau's Golden Age was the dream of attempting to return to original and natural man, a de-civilizing process, determined by the laws of abundance in nature. Man's relationships with the soil and his neighbour were to be in harmonious equilibrium. The patriarchal family was the paradigm of a larger social model. It is no accident, then, that the allusion to *Le Contrat social* is coupled with Virgil. Comparison of Simon and Virgil has already uncovered the failure of LSM to be the archetypal patriarch and the contented landowner desiring to cultivate his estates until death. Once again, by alluding indirectly to literary parallels, Simon stresses the *illusion* of utopian models, given the harshness of the Historical world of war, revolution and death. The same criticism of idealism is as it were popularized in the painting of Rousseau described in *Gulliver*:

> un Rousseau de plâtre colorié, la main appuyée sur une canne absente, promeneur élyséen à perruque friseé, pensif, affable, un mince sourire sur ses lèvres peintes, avançait solitaire dans un rêve genevois d'éternité idyllique et poupine (p. 70).

Rousseau the social idealist is also Rousseau the botanist and literary 'naturalist' (before Zola), and Simon pays homage to his eighteenth-century precursor's role in changing the shape of the novel:

> La description apparaît avec la littérature dite réaliste, comme si celle-ci cherchait à s'accréditer par l'accumulation des descriptions. Avant l'arrivée du réalisme, avant l'arrivée de Rousseau, la nature n'existe, pour ainsi dire, pas (Simon, 1978, p. 91).

Simon and the practitioners of the Nouveau Roman owe much not just to the nineteenth century but also to Rousseau as writer of descriptions. Rousseau's attitudes to nature ranged from the curiosity of the scientific botanist to a semi-mystic awareness of something beyond nature. His interest in the countryside and landscape was presented in lyrical prose, with visually forceful presentation, the familiar being seen with new eyes. Simon's own awareness of nature and the changes in the life cycle is exemplified in *L'Herbe*. The descriptions of the rotting pears, overripe and odorous, dropping outside Tante Marie's window from the tree, immediately spring to mind. Within this text, however, there are two very different world views: Georges's and Marie's, who see and experience the world directly, understanding its cruelty and natural processes; and Pierre's, who lives through the world of books and believes in their overriding authority and the conclusiveness of scientific facts. A family photo of Pierre presents him as a quasi-Rousseau:

> l'air... d'un jeune professeur ou plutôt d'un instituteur en vacances (et peut-être botaniste amateur, ayant passé la journée à herboriser, ou passionné d'entomologie, avec peut-être aussi dans le sac un livre de Rousseau, ou de Fourier) (pp. 232-3).

Pierre's unquestioning, rational, scientific approach to life is regarded by Georges as inappropriate and out-of-date. Scientific exactitude and reverence for past literature to lend 'vraisemblance' to novels are also, by implication, inauthentic for Simon.

Rousseau also brought much to the evolution of the autobiography, confessional novel and fictionalised autobiography by confessing openly to socially unacceptable inclinations in his character, such as his exhibitionism. Thus art for Rousseau became an important means of divulging truth and attaining reality, both personal and public: he considered self-description (autobiography) to be the most authoritative presentation of a person's life and milieu, and saw introspection as the best path to truth and self-knowledge. In *La Route des Flandres,* a novel which seeks 'truth' concerning the mystery surrounding Reixach, Rousseau is given prominence by existing as the full set of his writings belonging to this ancestor of Georges: 'un livre, peut-être l'un des vingt-trois tomes que remplissait l'œuvre complète de Rousseau' (*RF,* p. 83). Birn is the only critic who begins to uncover the significance of Rousseau in the novel, by mentioning Pierre's speech 'derived from Rousseau's notions in the Discourse on the Origin of Inequality 1755 of property as the source of trade and war' (Birn, 1980, pp. 90-1). Pierre (*RF,* p. 35) tries to explain war as a catalyst leading to an improved social state, a view consistent with his bookishness. Birn also notes that Pierre has become a hermit in a pavilion astonishingly similar to Rousseau's refuge at Ermenonville (p. 248). However, she disregards the other Rousseau references which to my mind are more pertinent to the adulation yet distance which is Simon's stance towards this teller of H/histoires. Simon mocks his precursor by superimposing de Reixach, the idealist ancestor reader of Rousseau, and Pierre, the modern reader. Both are commented upon by Georges and the literary parodist *par excellence,* Blum.

> [Georges] l'imaginant donc, le voyant en train de lire consciencieusement l'un après l'autre chacun des vingt-trois volumes de prose larmoyante, idyllique et fumeuse, ingurgitant pêle-mêle les filandreuses et genevoises leçons d'harmonie, de solfège, d'éducation, de niaiserie, d'effusions et de génie, cet incendiaire bavardage de vagabond touche-à-tout, musicien, exhibitionniste et pleurard qui, à la fin, lui ferait appliquer contre sa tempe la bouche sinistre et glacée de ce...(pp. 83-4).

Criticism of Rousseau's idealism, because this ideal world was not what Reixach experienced, comes through Georges, who posits his ancestor's *disillusionment* with his Enlightenment world, this then being the reason for his suicide.

Blum also negates Rousseau's *Confessions* by helping Georges 'reconstruct' Reixach's past. He mocks the literalism of imitation taken to extremes:

> que dans son imagination ou ses rêves il voyait sans doute déjà promue à cet état supérieur auquel, croyait-il, on pouvait accéder par la lecture indigeste de vingt-cinq tomes...', et Georges : 'Vingt-trois'(p. 194).

There is comic irony here because Georges corrects Blum's mistake concerning the number of the volumes, *not* their content. Later, Blum continues his hypothesis for Reixach's behaviour:

> Et Blum : 'Mais n'as-tu pas dit toi-même qu'ils l'avaient trouvé complètement nu? Comment l'expliquer, alors? A moins que ce ne fût l'effet de ses convictions naturistes? De ses émouvantes lectures genevoises? Est-ce qu'il—je veux dire ce Suisse mélomane, effusionniste et philosophe dont il avait appris par cœur l'œuvre complète—est-ce qu'il n'était pas aussi un petit peu exhibitionniste? Est-ce que ce n'était pas lui qui avait la douce manie de montrer son derrière aux jeunes f...' et Georges: 'Oh arrête! (p. 201).

Blum's reasons for Reixach's nakedness are of course unfounded. His salacious mind delights in picking up literary parallels and distorting them, removing literary reverence for them, and presenting them in crude, but comic terms. By dressing up his comments with the ironically tentative 'un petit peu' his wit becomes more incisive, his understatement as grotesque as his exaggerated descriptions of Rousseau. Now Georges has a new perspective on his ancestor thanks to Blum's interpretation, and sees the portrait anew.

> et Reixach, debout, là,... de ce que (non pas le pouvoir, les honneurs, la gloire, mais les idylliques ombrages, l'idyllique et larmoyant règne de la Raison et de la Vertu) ses lectures lui avaient fait entrevoir (p. 202).

Georges reacts less against Rousseauist morality than against his father, who still believes in the Enlightenment virtues, the chief being Reason. Georges has been shocked into seeing things in a new way: allusions to Rousseau are the means to this end. The final undermining of ideals comes at the end of the novel when Blum is dead:

> il faut croire aux larmoyantes homélies sur la fraternité universelle la déesse Raison la Vertu et qui l'attendaient embusqués derrière les chênes-lièges ou les oliviers je me demande quelle odeur quelle haleine avait alors la mort si comme aujourd'hui elle sentait non pas la poudre et la gloire comme *dans les poésies* mais ces écœurants nauséeux relents de soufre et d'huile brûlée les armes noires (p. 312 [my emphasis]).

Simon's view of human nature is revealed as the antithesis of Rousseau's—the belief that with education and training the intrinsically good and altruistic side of man may be developed and directed, aided by Reason.

The quotations from *La Route des Flandres* show an interesting shift from third to first person narrative, which raises important questions of narratorial perspective, and in particular its place in autobiography. Novels like this one, concerned with reconstructing the life of a person (de Reixach), or mock biographies like LSM's in *Les Géorgiques* (where the political and private life of an actual Historical personage is traced), have 'je' voices as part of their diegetical progression, and suggest autobiographical traits as well. Concerning autobiography in his novels, Simon has said openly: 'C'est vrai, je n'invente rien. Ce que l'on écrit est toujours autobiographique' (Senlis, 1960, p. 27). However, Simon makes clear distinctions about what he means by autobiography. The 'je' becomes a surrogate self, not the writer, but the 'other' (il) that he wishes to be:

> Nous ne pouvons imaginer que ce que nous avons vécu nous-mêmes: imaginer l'histoire des autres, c'est donc encore se souvenir de soi. Il y a un passage extraordinaire de Buffon, décrivant Adam tel qu'il vient de s'éveiller au monde. Buffon suppose qu'Adam regarde autour de lui, et tout ce qu'il voit, il croit d'abord que c'est lui-même. Ainsi le monde se réflète en nous (Duranteau, 1967, p. 3).

Georges demonstrates this in *La Route des Flandres*, and the multi-layered biographies in *Les Géorgiques* furnish many parallels for the Writer as persona. The imagination is essential in these juxtapositions of lives, and opens the door, naturally to discrepancies, inflations and distortions, in short the true stuff of fiction. In this respect, Simon's view of autobiography is different from Rousseau's. The latter used it as a vehicle to present the only real and authentic picture of himself to the world and to himself. Rousseau seemed unaware that any retelling becomes a variation. Simon is more than conscious of the fictional element in any Histoire. Indeed, asked if *Histoire* was an autobiography, Simon replied:

> Je ne crois pas, non. C'est un roman. Sans doute j'utilise mes souvenirs personnels comme premiers matériaux, mais la dynamique de l'écriture et de l'imaginaire les déforme. Il y a des choses que j'ai passées sous silence, d'autres qui ont grossi. Au bout du compte, le narrateur est moi et n'est plus moi (Simon, avril 1967, p. v)

Autobiography, then, impinges on the personal, so it is only in this broader sense of the word that Simon and Rousseau are interfaces, these 'autobiographical' characteristics being clearly illustrated in *Les Géorgiques*. I have considered these at greater length elsewhere (Orr, 1990). We shall be returning to the question of the self in history in the final chapter when *L'Acacia* will be under scrutiny as 'autobiography' and as intratext. The point to make here is Simon's debt to Rousseau, with the reminder from May that 'l'autobiographie tend vers la vérité sans pouvoir l'atteindre' (1979, p. 212). In his quest for the depiction of real self, Rousseau failed to see that his *Confessions* could never be complete and therefore authentic. Simon writes in the backlash to Enlightenment (and nineteenth-century) 'realism'. Through intertextual insertions from Rousseau, he reveals the artifice of eighteenth-century character autoportraits in literature (Beaujour's term, 1989, p. 8). The half-finished painting of LSM which is the prologue of *Les Géorgiques* is a palimpsest and model for the incomplete and incompletable (auto)biography, simply because the text is necessarily a fiction.

*****

In every case, encyclopedia and history references have been seen to cause digressions and developments which constantly supplement the verbal density of Simon's text. Each new proliferation becomes an 'histoire' in its own right, an episode which can then itself be mined for verbal materials. En route, Simon's later novels also explore eighteenth-century writing forms. *Histoire* may be viewed as a 'roman à tiroir', the label given to a novel whose practice is the insertion of minor narratives into the main story in an episodic form (Mylne, 1981, p. 59). However, the text is not just a collection of semic drawers—its total contents are contained in drawers:

> Le premier tiroir rempli de l'hétéroclite et habituel fouillis accumulé... le second tiroir basculant en avant sous le poids du linge... Le troisième tiroir occupé presque tout entier par les rangées parallèles feuilletées des cartes postales: quelquefois des paquets encore liés par des faveurs déteintes mais la plupart en vrac (sans doute primitivement groupées et enrubannées par dates, par années, puis peut-être ressorties, regardées plus tard et remises pêle-mêle), l'ensemble disposé en colonnes serrées perpendiculairement au tiroir, comme des cartes à jouer (*Hist*, pp. 248-50).

As was the case with the random order of Historical facts, the postcards provide an unclassified, unencyclopedic and unhistoric series of images and representations of codes which can be structured at will within the text: writing is itself a form which places groups of random letters in columns. It is this emphasis on the *narrative* construction in *Histoire,* through the narrator's frustrated attempts to impose the 'right' order on his family's past which lead him to pose the insoluble question 'Mais comment? suivant quel ordre?' (p. 271).

This is the chief question for the novelist, Simon, when dealing with a multiplicity of textual codes.

With *Les Géorgiques,* Simon comes closest to exploring the eighteenth-century vogue for epistolary novels, Laclos being their most dexterous exponent. The reason Simon's novel fails to become a letter-novel is twofold. First, letters are only one element in the collage of narrative materials, so the purity and condensation of form and viewpoint (to be found in Laclos's mastery of letters only) are sacrificed for breadth and reverberation between different media and perspectives. Second, it is only LSM who writes letters, although he reports correspondence with others. 'Il écrit' becomes a choric phrase in the novel, but always introduces LSM, so that it becomes obsessive, a marker of his frenetic activity into a void of response. Without epistolary dialogue, he is defeated and reduced to the complaining voice at the end of the text. This distortion of the letter-novel, the paradigm of the genre being Laclos's *Les Liaisons dangereuses,* is necessary to Simon's exploration of writing techniques. His aim is not a close psychological dissection of motivations and intrigues (as in Laclos); rather it is a search for analogies, a poetics of association, including the investigation of literary and stylistic codes.

I have tried, in this chapter, to investigate problems connected with classification, and to look at the variety of codes which can become the constituents of new textual 'bodies'. Simon's structures are, in a sense, the self-conscious 'embodiment' of intertexts: his fiction functions then as the ordering principle by which all the parts hang together and by which his own voice becomes more audible.

Chapter Four

Nineteenth-Century Literature

Having examined 'intertextuality' as the use of anonymous, self-sufficient, and 'non-literary' codes of language constituting the code-of-codes, Text, this chapter returns to specifically literary aspects of discourse. Its theoretical focus, already intimated in the second chapter, is Bakhtin's reply to structuralist formulations of intertextual dialogue which can only take place as subsets within the global structure, Text. Bakhtin summarises the limitations of this Formalist view as follows:

> The work of art is a closed-off unity, each element of which receives its meaning, *not in interaction with something outside the work (nature, reality, idea)*, but only within the structure of the whole, which has meaning in itself. This means that each element of the artistic work has primarily a purely constructive significance for the work as a closed-off, self-sufficient construction (1978, p. 45 [my emphasis]).

His own rather different theory of intertextual dialogue is dialectic in nature: a work enters into relationships with other works but also engages with the world(s) *outside* them. In other words, writing 'evolves' in relation to what has preceded it generically as well as historically. While careful not to equate directly the signifier with the signified, Bakhtin nonetheless allows some reciprocal equivalences and interrelationships to exist between them by calling on their necessary participation in any act of representation. Thus, the autonomy and anonymity of codes and structures of language are replaced in Bakhtin's 'dialogism' by his emphasis on named or namable interlocutors, that is, responsability of utterance to provide and change *cultural* meaning within a historico-linguistic context involving speakers. What interests him are:

> cet événement de rapports mutuels entre interlocuteurs... la position des autres participants... la valeur hiérarchique du personnage ou de l'événement qui forment le contenu de l'énoncé... leur degré de proximité avec l'auteur... l'interrelation de l'auditeur avec l'auteur, d'une part, avec le personnage, d'autre part. (in Todorov, 1981, pp. 75-6).

Bakhtin's emphasis is on the polyphony of utterance, its position in community, the values implicit in its speech act and historical context. Yet the individuality of the text within its culture and genre is paramount and can be gauged evaluatively. Focus then also returns to the role of the reader in this dialogue of realities, but without this position receiving the overriding attention given it by reader response theory. Consequently, it is the *context(s)* of an intertext which is important for Bakhtin, and for him, therefore, the genre most fitting to convey evolution and change in its development is the novel:

> The novel is non-canonical by nature. It is moldability [plastichnost;L. plasticus] itself. It is eternally researching itself and revising all its former forms. It can only be thus for a genre which is constructed in the zone of immediate contact with generating reality (1978, p. xxi).

Intertextual activity is thus at its most intense in the novel because it contains previous contexts and vestiges of their forms within itself:

> Tout roman est à un degré variable un système dialogique d'images, de 'langues', de styles, de consciences concrètes et inséparables du langage. Le langage, dans le roman, ne fait pas que représenter: il sert aussi lui-même d'objet de représentation. Le discours romanesque est toujours autocritique (in Todorov, 1981, pp. 103-4).

The novel therefore circumvents the limits of any self-sufficient system, school or epoch by its intertextual potential, whereas poetry does not:

> La prose qui est intertextuelle s'oppose à la poésie qui ne l'est pas... On pourrait peut-être voir les raisons de cette opposition dans le fait que le poème *est* un acte d'énonciation, alors que le roman en *représente* un (ibid. pp. 100-1 [Todorov's emphasis]).

The novel is thus seen by Bakhtin as *representational,* and without developing the social implications of Bakhtin's theories, some useful parallels may be drawn, by which Simon's development and evolution as a novelist, writing within the tradition of the novel, may be evaluated. Simon's works—as the previous chapter argued—are historically aware: his interest in the upheavals caused by revolution and war is a case in point. Therefore, there is obvious absorption of elements which are *external* to any self-sufficient literary structure in his novels. Second, the Bakhtinian focus on the centrality of prose, not poetry, is intrinsic to Simon, the novelist. It has not been noted that Simon draws largely on prose intertexts, not poetic ones. Perhaps one major reason for this may be found in the representational potential of the novel form, as Bakhtin suggests. As this chapter, then, focusses on Simon's evolution as a *novelist,* his borrowings from poetry, and in particular Baudelaire, will first be studied to show its relative unimportance, before attention is turned to the novel and the question of representation. Bakhtin saw the superlative form of this in the novel as genre in the work of Dostoyevsky. We shall consider briefly how Simon, as a developing novelist, also viewed Dostoyevsky as paradigm in this respect. The main focus of the chapter, however, will be Simon's familiarity with, and position within, the nineteenth-century French 'realist' tradition. To this end, Simon's borrowings of intertexts from Stendhal, Balzac and Flaubert will be examined.

Simon has produced no theoretical work on writing as has Robbe-Grillet: instead, he comments indirectly on writing techniques, mainly in his colloquia papers and interviews, by means of references to foregoing models. As I pointed out in my introduction, no critic to date has concentrated attention on Simon's writings other than his novels. This chapter seeks to redress this omission, especially as the interviews contain so many references to previous literature, particularly the novel. These references are thus signposts to the underlying criteria Simon sees as central to his own writing practice. Literary allusions are chosen because they have an affinity with his own pursuits, or because they crystallize a particular, paradigmatic element in the development of fiction, against which he may react. Furthermore, a study of Simon's interview statements provides fruitful evidence of his positive and negative literary confrontations and can counter merely personal intertextual readings of his novels which critics have often over-indulged in. When I interviewed Simon shortly after the publication of his prose poem *La Chevelure de Bérénice* (February 1984), my question was whether Baudelaire's 'La Chevelure' was an intertext within it. Simon's reply was that he was unfamiliar with this poem, but, reaching for a copy of *Les Fleurs du mal*, he read the poem and grew excited at the similarity of associations and images between it and his own work. This highlights the fact that although parallels may seem obvious between texts, it should not be implied that direct or conscious influence has occurred. This does not detract from the reader's response in equating the two. Such subjective reading is not a 'wrong' reading: if there are sufficient points of contact between the texts or evidence from other sources (such as interviews) that the original text was familiar to the writer. One must simply be careful not to presume authorial intention or exposure to the precursor.

Simon and Baudelaire

No direct references to poetry occur within the main body of Simon's novels. Simon actually admits his limited knowledge of and reliance on poetry: 'La poésie me touche assez peu, ou bien alors il faut qu'elle soit sublime: certaines choses de Rimbaud, de Mallarmé de Valéry...'(Knapp, 1969, p. 180). It is in one such statement that we find the only reference to a Baudelaire poem in Simon, to the second stanza of 'Correspondances':

> cette aventure [de l'écriture] dont je crois qu'il faut tout de suite indiquer que si elle se déroule sur deux niveaux (celui du pas à pas et celui du dessin général du trajet), ces deux niveaux, en réalité, fusionnent, comme on sait bien que dans un tableau le dessin d'un membre, d'une draperie, de la courbe d'une assiette est fonction de la composition d'ensemble où, selon l'admirable formulation de Baudelaire:
>
> Comme de longs échos qui de loin se confondent
> Dans une ténébreuse et profonde unité,
> Vaste comme la nuit et comme la clarté,
> Les parfums, les couleurs et les sons se répondent.
> (Ricardou, 1972, II, p. 84 [Simon's emphasis]).
>
> ...le caractère tout à fait artisanal et empirique de ce labeur qui consiste à assembler et organiser, dans cette *unité* dont parle Baudelaire et où elles doivent *se répondre en échos* toutes les composantes de ce vaste système de signes qu'est un roman (ibid., p. 96 [Simon's emphasis]).

This intertext is a literary crystallization of the concept Simon is trying to outline and define. He emphasizes the interplay of synaesthetic elements present in Baudelaire, but not on account of any search for hidden essences. It is only the metonymical relationships which are important. Robbe-Grillet, in discussion with Simon, clarifies this:

> '...dans tout ce que dit Baudelaire il y a quelque chose qui nous gêne terriblement, parce que son idée de symbole renvoie à une nature, à une essence divine qui serait par-derrière. Ce qui n'existe pas du tout dans votre travail, Simon, heureusement.' Simon replies 'Oui, je fais subir en quelque sorte à la Nature dont parle Baudelaire un déplacement de sens: je pense plutôt au langage dont les vivants piliers...' (ibid., p. 104).

By identifying with this compositional mechanism in Baudelaire, Simon establishes not only the importance of his own work in such a tradition, but also his divergence from its declared ideas. This is perhaps epitomized in Simon's quotation of the second stanza only of Baudelaire's poem, whereby the application of the whole is limited. Such practices are a cameo of the workings of quotation in general. One cannot rewrite the whole: only a part will be relevant to the new context, and its interpolation in the new frame will infer the original but will not demand the slant of the old context. Its rigour and density become a structural metaphor to describe the mechanisms of his own novel, *Triptyque,* which 'functions like a set of mirrors that reflect slightly modified images' (Simon, in DuVerlie, 1974, p. 7).

Simon's use of Baudelaire as poet is in fact secondary to that of Baudelaire as art critic:

> Baudelaire a écrit 'Tout l'univers visible n'est qu'un magasin d'images et de signes auxquels l'imagination donnera une place et une valeur rélative'— par exemple Monet peint le Hall de la Gare St-Lazare d'une certaine façon. Il a été séduit, frappé par certaines harmonies qu 'il a retenues, lui, sélectionnées rejetant d'autres composantes. Devant le même spectacle (référent) Manet ou Cézanne auraient peint un tout autre tableau (Grivel, 1979 pp. 96-7. Baudelaire's words come from 'Le Gouvernement de l'imagination', in *Curiosités Esthéthiques L'Art romantique et autres œuvres critiques* [Garnier, 1962], pp. 328-9).

Simon not only endorses Baudelaire's words, but also employs the method of comparing poets and artists as Baudelaire did before him. The exactness of the quotation and the relevance of its context suggest Simon's familiarity with the critical writings of Baudelaire and their shared knowledge and love of art. Simon's 'poetry' of language is inherited not so much of previous French poets, but of novelists highly conscious of style, like Dostoyevsky and Flaubert.

Simon and Dostoyevsky

Turning to the novel as the paradigm form of representation, Simon openly states the influence Dostoyevsky had in shaping his early work: 'Je dois dire que les littératures anglo-saxonnes et la littérature russe possède à mon avis de plus authentiques romanciers que la nôtre... Cela dit, le maître des maîtres à mes yeux c'est Dostoïevski' (Aubarède, 1957, p. 7). The elements which Simon particularly admires in Dostoyevsky's opus are ones which have something in common with his own literary techniques. First, there is a break with chronological time in preference to fictional time (*durée*). Simon compares the experience of reading one of Dostoyevsky's novels with that of his conception of *La Route des Flandres*: 'Tout le livre m'est apparu d'un seul coup, comme on dit... que les romans de Dostoïevski se déroulent en une seconde ou même en une fraction d'une seconde' (Chapsal, 1963, p. 166). Action is of minor importance. The spatiality of description takes over, and every detail counts in the completion of the overall picture. Thus, for Simon, Dostoyevsky's work epitomizes the representation of fictional time.

A second major lesson is learned from his forebear: description is intrinsic to characterization, but of a much more sophisticated kind, in Simon's opinion, than that practised by nineteenth-century French novelists like Stendhal (see Bourin, 1961, p. 7). The kernel of Dostoyevsky's writing in Simon's eyes is the ambiguity of character: there are no types, no two-dimensional figures embodying heroic virtues, no triumphing of good over evil. Hence the moralizing aspect is of secondary importance. Characters display both good and bad qualities, thus circumventing simple judgement of their actions (Paulhan, 1984, p. 44). Therefore, Dostoyevsky's novels represent, for Simon, the complexities and ambiguities of characterization evident in his early fragments, with particular regard to the sketching of character psychology. Direct references to Dostoyevsky produce an authentic mould into which Simon can pour his own character descriptions; the fragment *Babel* is an excellent illustration of this process. Simon uses the names of Russian writers to evoke an atmosphere of revolution, which indirectly mirrors the actual setting of *Babel,* the Spanish Civil War. In a tavern scene in *Babel,* the drunken conversation is reminiscent of Raskolnikov's meeting with Marmeladov. However, where the latter confessed his life history, Simon uses 'in vino veritas' to portray the inauthenticity of language as message-bearer. Later in the same fragment, the Dostoyevsky allusions become synonymous with the archetypal anguished Russian, which is set against its opposite archetype, the liberated American: 'Ivan et son âme, le Grand Inquisiteur Dostoïevski et la fameuse âme russe, les grands écrivains occidentaux, leurs glandes génitales et leurs âmes?' *(Babel,* p. 408). Simon is employing these literary references to make ironic comments on the political setting of his fragment. Economy and critical distance are achieved by the medium of these fictional stereotypes. However, the psychological nuances of characterization Simon so admires in Dostoyevsky are never inserted. Simon's Russian peasant remains a type to offset the virile bravado of the American freedom-fighter, à la Hemingway, and ridicules both. Interestingly, *L'Invitation* takes up precisely these elements and reworks them as a scathing attack on soviet attitudes towards the writer. However in this later work, Dostoyevsky is markedly absent.

It is only in Simon's early works that direct references to the nineteenth-century Russian novel again occur. The epigraph quotation of *La Corde raide* heads a set of impressions on art, war and society. Simon uses his precursor to emphasize the distinction between his private convictions and his public pronouncements as novelist. In *Le Sacre du Printemps,* Dostoyevsky's world is implied as being in direct antithesis to Bernard's, which is totally devoid of religious questioning: '...pourvu que tout ne soit pas comme dans Dostoïevski, comme dans la *Maison des Morts...* pas la palissade de pieux' (p. 260). More important are the Dostoyevskian overtones in *Le Vent,* for character psychology is still an important element in this text. Simon admits the influence of Dostoyevsky on *Le Vent*:

> Le dernier roman où comme Flaubert, je me suis cru obligé de raconter une histoire a été *Le Vent...* faute d'avoir quelque chose de particulier à dire. J'ai peut-être fabriqué, comme beaucoup de critiques l'ont dit, 'un remake' de *L'Idiot* (Paulhan, 1984, p. 44).

The essential parallel between the two novels is the similarly-expressed ambiguity of the central characters Montès and Myshkin (see de Magny, 1957, p. 784 and Sigaux, 1958, p. 79). Both are outsiders in their respective societies and refuse to conform. They are able to be brutally frank and to ask awkward questions, but can also communicate easily with other outcasts from society. They are totally devoid of class snobbery: both identify with children. Both portray moments of extreme perspicacity and utter imbecility: both are labelled as madmen, fools or saints, and their actions waver between these categories: both inherit a family fortune, and have dealings with lawyers to wind up their estates, losing vast amounts of money in the process due to their naive trust in humanity: both fall in love with unstable and loose women, Rose and Nastasya Filippovna respectively. Seen as a quasi-saint, Prince Myshkin is affected by and associated with Hans Holbein's painting of Christ taken down from the cross, his body already in a state of decay. The macabre elements of Dostoyevsky's novel—plots, visions, epileptic fits—find their baroque counterparts in Simon's novel. Montès is also equated with a saint, the retable representation in the church suggesting links with him. Yet, however close these parallels between character and theme appear, there are also vast differences between the Russian model and Simon's 'remake'. First, by turning Montès into a petit-bourgeois replacement of Prince Myshkin, the latter's authority is undermined and trivialized. Montès is an anti-hero and fades into the text, whereas Myshkin is a powerful central presence throughout. Religious enquiry is never far from the surface in the Russian novel, whereas it is firmly in the background in Simon. Moreover, the two settings and stories are poles apart: Russia in the late nineteenth-century is very different from France in the 1930s. The titles of the two novels also help to show the differences. *The Idiot* stresses the centrality of Myshkin: Montès is secondary to the forces of the wind, destroying and confusing the order of the world around him. The fictional coherence and control which are obvious in Dostoyevsky's text are questioned in Simon's novel, which is a '*Tentative* de Restitution d'un retable baroque', the stress being on the first word of the sub-title. At the end, Montès is the same indeterminate figure as at the beginning, despite the efforts of the lawyer and the narrator to construct his history.

It is evident that Simon has employed his nineteenth-century Russian precursor as a model for the ambiguities in his protagonist, but only in so far as Montès is an individual, suffering under the constraints of a society which desires to categorize him. The descriptions of the wind and the shift from introspective questioning amply demonstrate that Simon has developed away from his initial idea, to make a 'remake' of *The Idiot*. *Le Vent* is the point in his evolution where Simon turns his back on what he sees as the central representational concerns in Dostoyevsky as nadir of complex characterization, psychological introspection, moral questions and social portraiture. Simon's novels after *Le Vent* bear no such Russian trademarks because introspective analysis in characterization is inappropriate. It is from *L'Herbe* onwards that Simon begins openly to address questions of writing describing and representing its own processes. His own path as novelist becomes clear through his admiration for, and rejection of, Dostoyevsky. It is Simon's familiarity with and appraisal of the evolution of his own tradition, the French nineteenth-century novel, which touches and shapes the whole of his mature *œuvre*.

Simon and Stendhal

In his interviews, Simon openly states his lack of admiration for and distance from Stendhal: 'Je n'aime pas Balzac ni Stendhal, qui sont très loin de moi, mais cela aboutit à Flaubert et à l'impressionisme' (Senlis, 1960, p. 28). In keeping with the other *nouveaux romanciers,* Simon's reasons for this reaction are based on criteria of 'realism'. However, instead of criticizing the anachronistic aspects of Stendhal as novelist, Simon positively lambasts him. The best example of this is a parodic paraphrase, notably the only one of its kind in Simon, the 'reconstruction' of the early events of *La Chartreuse de Parme.* This is interrupted constantly by Simon's *sous-texte* (in brackets), which provides an ironic running commentary on the main text:

> Un personnage, X, est allé, pour passer le temps, surveiller un chantier (ici, *description* de la tranchée ouverte et *réflexions* de l'auteur sur l'état d'esprit des paysans dans les champs...). Soudain, d'un coup de fusil, X tue un oiseau qui va tomber sur une route traversant les champs et où, justement, roule une voiture où se trouve la maîtresse de X accompagnée... d'un souteneur. Voyant X armé d'un fusil, le souteneur lui prête des intentions hostiles (ici, un peu *d'analyse psychologique*) et tire sur lui un coup de pistolet qui rate son but. Il s'ensuit une bataille entre les deux hommes (*narration* la bataille) au cours de laquelle X échappe de justesse à tous les coups de son adversaire et le tue (truffant cette *narration*, encore un peu *d'analyse psychologique* pour expliquer au lecteur les sentiments qui agitent X pendant la bataille). Après quoi s'engage un *dialogue* entre X, sa maîtresse restée dans la voiture et la maquerelle qui l'accompagne (tandis que la jeune femme embrasse le héros avec passion, la maquerelle lui réclame de l'argent). Finalement X s'enfuit pour l'étranger, muni du passeport du souteneur qu'il vient de tuer. Arrivé au poste de police de la frontière... il présente son passeport au fonctionnaire de service qui, justement, se trouve être un ami du souteneur...
>
> ... j'avoue que j'ai beau réfléchir, je ne parviens pas à voir dans un tel récit (d'une consternante maladresse, y compris le style...) autre chose qu'une suite d'événements parfaitement fortuits, de hasards, de coïncidences qui confinent au miracle... Hormis cette 'continuité' à prétention réaliste... rien... ne permet de passer d'un élément à l'autre... Comme on l'a vu, je n'ai pas été prendre mon exemple dans *Les Trois Mousquetaires*... mais dans cette *Chartreuse de Parme*, que Balzac considérait comme 'le chef-d'œuvre de la littérature d'idées (Ricardou, 1972, II, pp. 74-6).

Not only does Simon's version show a total irreverence for the original, it also offers a gross distortion of it. The mock mystery ('personnage X'), suspense triggers ('soudain'), and the trowelling on of phrases concerning chance ('justement') are not so much satirical comments as grotesque, and even rather childish exaggerations. It is in fact Simon's *sous-texte* which is much more revealing, not about Stendhal's techniques or about *La Chartreuse de Parme,* but about his own criteria for appropriate fictional production. While seeking to decry chronology as an imposed textual logic, omniscient authorial interventions as a narrative stance and the biographical, didactic or psychological emphasis of characterisation, Simon only demonstrates his misunderstanding of Stendhal's own awareness of precisely these key pivots of the nineteenth-century French novel. Simon has thus failed to notice the *irony* of the original, precisely where the fortuitousness of the meeting of the hero and heroine is concerned, and in the 'logic' of the episode, that Fabrice murders someone personally known to the border guard, so that the borrowed passport gives him away. Stendhal also plays with the concept of 'omniscient' authorship. The character details he gives and the scenarios in which he places his characters all add to the *mockery* of simplistic authorial control, coupled with his even more sophisticated parody of the heroic tale, the fairy story convention, where chance plays a major role. It is the very mobility of the narrative and style (the author is both inside and outside his creations) which allows the ironies, parodies and humour to operate. At the end of Simon's somewhat facile comments on his parody of *La Chartreuse,* his explicit identification of the intertext only spoils any effect it may have had on the reader. Indeed, the fact that Simon feels the need to locate the original only underlines his fears as to the effectiveness of his reworking. His chief objection is to the domineering, engineering control of Stendhal: the irony is that he falls into this very trap himself, for by precluding readings contrary to his own biased one, he imposes his own authorial control over his readers.

In the same interview, Simon also attacks Stendhal through the mouthpiece of previous critics, first Balzac, then Martineau and Faguet, and at the same time criticizes their methodology; the yardstick of 'psychological realism' as a way of evaluating fiction:

> en lisant Martineau et Faguet, entraînés dans des considérations sociologiques ou psychologiques... et dont on se demande d'ailleurs en les lisant (car un romancier n'est ni un sociologue ni un psychologue) quelles sortes de rapports elles peuvent avoir avec l'étude d'un texte littéraire (Ricardou, 1972, II, p. 77).

Again, Simon's *prejudice* against, not his critical understanding of Stendhal, is made visible on two counts. The accuracy of the quotation from both these critics, demonstrates Simon's familiarity with his literary tradition, which, however, he uses to underline his own particular hobby-horses—ambiguity of character and synchrony of events. The frequency with which he refers to their debate when answering interview questions about his own views on the novel also signals their function as stalking-horse.

Despite his adverse comments on Stendhal, Simon does give due recognition to his precursor's contributions to the development of the French novel:

> Par exemple, la description de la bataille de Waterloo dans *La Chartreuse de Parme* peut être considérée comme la préfiguration de toute la littérature moderne: au contraire de ce qui se produit trop souvent chez Stendhal, les adjectifs de valeur en sont à peu près absents et, pour la première fois, un événement nous est présenté sous un angle subjectif, sans 'explications'. Fabrice, par les yeux duquel nous voyons la bataille se dérouler, n'en a qu'un aperçu extrêmement fragmentaire, il n'y comprend rien; c'est l'opposé de cet 'observateur privilégié' omniprésent et omniscient qu'est l'auteur du roman traditionnel... (Simon, 1978, p. 90).

Simon's appreciation of this episode is, of course, not original; Robbe-Grillet cited this very example in *Pour un nouveau roman* to illustrate the evolutionary qualities of Stendhal's writing (1963, p. 115). Much of Simon's reading of Balzac, Stendhal and Flaubert, it can be argued, stems directly from the ideas set out here by Robbe-Grillet. Simon responds to Stendhal positively in this instance only because the emphasis on limited (as opposed to omniscient) narrative viewpoint serves to underline his own priorities and narrative strategies. Once again, Simon's stress is clear: description rather than the event itself *becomes* the action:

> Et de citer un passage de *La Chartreuse* où il est uniquement question de *mouvements* de cavaliers et de chevaux, hors de la signification, hors de l'anecdote. Voilà l'écriture. Quelques lignes plus loin, Stendhal s'enfonce dans la chronique et cela ne vaut plus rien, c'est assommant (Chapsal, 1961, p. 33 [Simon's emphasis]).

Simon alludes to this particular passage, no doubt, because it mirrors the sensory descriptions in his own novels. In *La Corde raide*, the narrator alludes to Fabrice's experiences at the Battle of Waterloo, as a comic, yet apt, parallel for his own reflections on death:

> J'eus le temps de me voir, de penser que je devais être ridicule, de me comparer à une gravure de chasse anglaise où un monsieur en habit rouge tirait de la même façon sur un cheval, de me souvenir de Fabrice del Dongo, et de penser que c'était de cette manière ridicule que j'allais crever, participant à une grande bataille dont on parlerait plus tard (mensongèrement) dans les livres d'histoire... (p. 53).

The repetition of 'ridicule' underlines the unheroic stance of Fabrice, doubly mocked by his Simonian reincarnation. In *La Route des Flandres,* the passage portraying the rotting horse corpse, decomposing in the mud, is both thematically and stylistically similar to this segment of *La Chartreuse de Parme.* Georges's experience of battle is equally fragmentary and impressionistic: no historical reconstruction of events is possible—it is hard to ascertain which battle this is. So, Georges shares Fabrice's confusion; but Simon omits the mock-heroic stance of Stendhal's character. Georges is not pretending to be an 'archetypal' hero, so—whether serious or mocking—such inferences would be out of place in Simon's novel.

Simon also endorses Stendhal's descriptions which underline how facts when retold become distorted. He quotes frequently in interviews an episode from *Henri Brulard* as paradigmatic of this (and by extension of the autobiographical project). An engraving of the St. Bernard Pass replaces the historicity of the event in the narrator's mind. As with Fabrice's experiences at the Battle of Waterloo, temporal action is upstaged by spatial (atemporal) description, whereby past and present, real and imaginary become synonymous. 'Events' become mental frames within which analogies and associations interplay and become indistinguishable. Like Stendhal, Simon also employs the ambiguities of vision between painting and actuality in *La Route des Flandres.* Georges cannot tell whether a crack in the painting of his ancestor, de Reixach, is simply a flaw or the mark of a bullet wound, if and when the latter shot himself.

Simon also relies on literary and cultural generalizations culled from Stendhal as a familiar starting point from which he can proceed to portray his own divergent fictional production:

> on connaît la fameuse définition de Stendhal et que les romanciers traditionnels ont fait leur; un roman c'est un miroir promené le long d'un chemin. Pour moi, ce n'est pas ça du tout. C'est plutôt au contraire une très grande glace fixe où se reflète *en même temps* tout ce que l'on a à dire. Parce que si l'on essaie un peu de voir ce qui se passe en nous lorsque le passé nous revient à la mémoire, on s'aperçoit que ce sont un tas de choses, d'associations, qui resurgissent toutes mêlées en un

> instant (Knapp, 1969, p. 184. Reference is to the epigraph to I, 13, itself an *amorce* of the well-known digression in II, 19, of *Le Rouge*).

Simon's criticism (and misreading) of Stendhal's mirror is again caused by his antagonism to the supposed quest for 'realism' generated by such mirrorings. In Simon's view, the only valid option is that of the limited, and at the same time limitless, subjective perspective, be it the experiences of a single narrator or the knowledge available to the author. Consequently, the chronology and fictional logic of a Stendhal are ruled out because no firmly defined 'mirroring' structure is available to the writer to specify cause and effect, motive and reason. All that is at his disposal is a stream of *simultaneous* sensory perceptions which may be considered from various angles, but never definitively ordered. Therefore, Simon uses present-tense descriptions to *mirror* simultaneous mental responses, vision, memory and imagination. Again, Simon has failed to recognize the validity of Stendhal's metaphor for the novel as another means of actually subverting 'realistic' narrative through the self-conscious holding of a mirror by the Stendhalian narrator, who does not even adopt a single stance, but *moves* the mirror along.

For Simon, then, a remake of the nineteenth-century novel *à la* Stendhal would be an anachronism: 'On ne peut pas s'exprimer en 1960 avec la phrase de Stendhal, ce serait se promener en calèche' (Chapsal, 1963, p. 170). This sentiment is supported by the paucity of references to Stendhal in Simon's novels and their position in his early fiction. Here, Stendhal's world is considered to be anachronistic and serves as a butt of humour or exaggeration. In *Le Tricheur*, *Le Rouge et le Noir* features as an intertext, the novel which Ephraïm is reading. O'Kane has noted that it 'focusses on the alternatives of the Church and Army, open to Julien, as 'father-figure' models for Louis (in Duncan, 1985, p. 52). However, it seems more pertinent, from the context, to view the intertext as synonymous with *escapist* literature, because Ephraïm picks it up to divert his mind, or to pass the *time*—the irony being that he is a watch salesman (pp. 176, 182). Note that it is the *second* volume of the novel, when Julien is in Paris, which is emphasized. By interpolating Stendhal into his own fiction, Simon economically holds up two different, indeed opposite, fictional frames for the reader to compare and contrast; for both kinds of fiction are being read simultaneously: the reader is reading about Ephraïm reading about Julien Sorel. Times (the nineteenth and twentieth centuries) are also juxtaposed, but the latter effaces the former once Ephraïm ceases to read *Le Rouge et le Noir.*

In *Le Sacre du printemps* the anachronism of Stendhal's time but also milieu is highlighted:

> Je sais: un de ces mots dont le seul énoncé suffit à faire s'étrangler de rire nos jeunes admirateurs de Stendhal qui ont au moins en commun avec lui, en même temps que la prudence, ce goût pour les puissants, les salons, les comtesses, et la mauvaise peinture (p. 263).

This appropriation is particularly ironic, for Bernard's father, who has experienced the Spanish Civil War, is speaking against youthful idealisms and people living in a falsely 'unrealistic' Stendhalian fictional world. In *Les Géorgiques,* Simon also uses Stendhal and his court scenes as a foil for LSM, who spends little time at court:

> Il regarde d'un œil froid le brillant parterre, les épaules nues des éblouissantes comtesses italiennes qui fascinent le jeune Stendhal arrivé avec l'Intendance, évaluant en termes de marchés d'aciers, de contrats de forges et de fournitures avariées les diadèmes et les colliers payés par leurs vieux maris aux interminables titres de noblesse, occupés de minuscules intrigues politiques et mercantiles (pp. 222-3).

The glitter and unreality of Stendhal's courts are made brutally mundane by LSM's observation of everything in terms of material value. The reference here is, however, barbed and ironic, for there is ample evidence in the novel of LSM's *own* petty family intrigues, together with his preoccupation with the buying of goods for his estates. But more important, perhaps, is the misreading in both these instances. Simon takes Stendhal's alleged fascination with court life and its depiction *at face value*: he appears not even to have noticed the satire of the aristocracy in both *Le Rouge* and *La Chartreuse.* This comment is relevant to Simon's uses of Stendhal in general. He is acknowledged *en passant*, but distance from him is quickly established. Throughout, Simon equates Stendhal far too simplistically with 'realism' and thus apparently rejects this model for his own fictional practice. One may also speculate on the crassness of this rejection, which may cover over unacknowledged admiration, or jealousy, of a Stendhalian wit in which he is deficient.

Simon and Balzac

Simon responds to those of Balzac's fictional practices which mirror Stendhal's in equally pejorative ways, and for the same reasons: the lack of 'realism' in characterisation as biography or mouthpiece for a 'message' or the causal chronology imposed by the omniscient narrator. 'Je ne pense pas que le rôle... du romancier soit contrairement à ce que voulait Balzac, de délivrer un enseignement quelconque' (Haroche, 1981, p. 15). This criticism of didacticism Simon levels at both character descriptions in Balzac and his portrayal of society in general, especially the moral implications.

> Le roman français se veut avant tout didactique, utile. Ainsi dans la préface/dédicace à *César Birotteau*, Balzac écrit qu'il espère que l'on verra, dans la publication simultanée de ce roman et *La Maison Nuncingen*, 'tout un enseignement social' (Paulhan, 1984, p. 44. Simon quotes Balzac's words to Zulma Carraud).

For Simon, social criticism is an outdated concern for the novelist because sociology and psychology are now much better equipped to describe these phenomena. In these areas, Simon sees himself as diverging radically from his nineteenth-century precursor. To attempt to construct from Simon's novels a story *à la* Balzac is also an utterly wrong approach, as Simon notes: 'The reader is free to interpret a work, but some readings will be wrong, for example a reader insisting on reconstructing a Balzac or Zola-type story from one of my novels' (DuVerlie, 1974, p. 17).

In Simon's early novels, which might tempt the reader to reconstruct a story, allusions to Balzac occur sporadically. Critics have for example equated the 'Georges' cycle with the recurring characters of *La Comédie humaine,* but again without developing this statement (Fletcher 1975, p. 59). As was the case with Stendhal references, the Balzacian borrowings are all used ironically, to mock the precursor and distinguish between his writing and Simon's. Thus by reiterating stereotyped literary connotations of Balzac, these allusions herald their own extinction in Simon's novels through their becoming generalities. These connotations rely on reader familiarity with the money-oriented, social-climbing world, where characters are larger than life. In *Le Sacre du printemps,* Simon describes the society surrounding Bernard 'comme si elle faisait elle-même partie intégrante du quartier au même titre que les plaques émaillées et racoleuses avec leurs mains aux index pointés, leurs raisons sociales vraies ou fausses et leur nostalgique et littéraire pouvoir d'évocation d'une société aux infrastructures balzaciennes, besogneuses et avides (p. 95). This reference surfaces at a key point in the text, for the literary world of Balzac's money-lenders ironically interplays with

Bernard's own experiences. He is on the brink of initiation into the arena of underhand dealings and exchanges of goods as he tries to pawn a ring. Even though the fictional situations are parallel, and each takes place in the sphere of a literary world, the exactness of the situation is an anachronism. Bernard may be in a romantic world at this juncture—hence the relevance of the comparison—but it is also clear that he must re-evaluate accepted social labels; and indeed this is what happens as the novel progresses. *L'Herbe* also uses the phrase 'héros balzaciens' (p. 142) as a shorthand reference to another, bygone, and inappropriate world, triggered by the description of Marie's meticulously logged account books.

In *Le Vent,* Balzac's characters are used as a ready-made metaphor:

> dans les poussiéreuses et hymalayennes montagnes de contrats et d'actes rédigés sous la dictée d'innombrables *Pères Goriot* par l'obscure et victorieuse armée d'innombrables notaires semblables à celui, et au prédécesseur de celui, et au prédécesseur du prédécesseur de celui, et au prédécesseur du prédécesseur du prédécesseur de celui en face de qui j'étais assis dans ce même fauteuil où Montès revenait lui aussi de temps en temps (p. 110).

The excessive repetition of lineage directly following the plural 'Pères Goriot' traces a complete, logical and chronological ancestry which can only belong to fiction, and moreover to Balzac's brand of fiction, not to reality. The line of lawyers having as their genesis a fictional figure also undermines their reality: in addition, they lose their individuality by being lumped together in the 'Goriot' category. Simon's own ignorance also strikes the reader: Goriot was a pasta king, not a lawyer! Simon's presentation of Balzac through these adjectival allusions is therefore clearly partial and derogatory. They are to evoke an 'unreal', money-oriented, clear-cut and ridiculous social world.

Simon's antipathy to Balzac is, however, not all-encompassing, for, as we have seen, he admits that the development of techniques instigated in part by Balzac 'aboutit à Flaubert et à l'impressionisme'. Simon appreciates and lauds elements in Balzac such as his portrayal of a certain society, a portrayal which Simon sees as having a historical importance, and the literary-historical role he played in the shaping of the French novel. We might describe this as his 'bakhtinian' understanding of the dialogic principles at work because of Balzac's contributions to the French novel as genre:

> Bien sûr, dans les romans que j'appellerais non pas traditionnels... mais plutôt conventionnels (et non pas 'balzaciens', comme le font abusivement certains critiques en oubliant que les formes romanesques de Balzac étaient: *a.* absolument neuves et propres à Balzac et *b.* étroitement liées à un moment très précis de l'histoire dont nous sommes loin)... dans ces sortes de romans, donc, l'écriture prétend 'narrer' ou 'raconter' les aventures d'un ou plusieurs personnages (*Entretiens*, p. 18).

Whilst, then, particular vestiges or aspects of Balzac's work are being attacked by Simon, the whole is certainly not discounted by the label 'balzacien'. Balzac's chief contribution—indeed chief merit—is, for Simon, his innovatory development of description for itself. It was not simply the 'petit détail qui fait vrai', nor Balzac's methods of conveying 'realistic', Gidean *tranche de vie* settings to illuminate character or highlight the plot.

> Et je ne suis pas, comme vous, aussi méprisant pour les descriptions de Balzac, même si ce sont des inventaires. Cela peut être passionnant, un inventaire, même sans commentaires, parce que l'inventaire nous met aussi la chose décrite en rapport avec un tas d'autres concepts (Simon, 1978, p. 91).

Objects were seen to be as interesting as the protagonist of the story, providing 'action' in their own right and paving the way for the 'set-piece' descriptions in Flaubert.

> Tout à coup, comme si le romancier prenait soudain conscience de la faiblesse démonstrative de sa fiction/fable, voilà qu'avec Balzac (et c'est peut-être là que réside son génie) comme pour donner plus de crédibilité, de véracité, de 'réalité' à la fable, on se met à l'étoffer de descriptions de plus en plus abondantes et détaillées, qui vont peu à peu avoir avec Flaubert la même importance que l'action (Paulhan, 1984, p. 44).

We have seen how Simon himself employs just this strategy of description of objects in the section 'Inventaire' in *Le Palace*. Various objects from different centuries are juxtaposed within a common locus, the building of the title, Palace/Bank. This storehouse of objects is what generates a fictional 'plot'. However, crucial distinctions must be drawn between Simon's descriptions and Balzac's. This same inventory in *Le Palace* opens and closes the novel, thus destabilizing the implication and fixity of each object as signifier of an historical period. A corollary is that, unlike Balzac's descriptions of objects, Simon's are bereft of emotional implications, because they just *are*. In this sense, Balzac's 'tranche de vie' descriptions, which suggest moral and social dimensions, are not, for Simon, 'realistic'. Simon does not, however, equate the name 'Balzac' totally with 'realism'. On the contrary, because no description may ever exhaustively describe an object, he qualifies the term to allow his precursor due regard:

> Balzac non plus n'est pas 'réaliste' en ce sens que le réalisme ça n'existe pas. Même quelqu'un qui veut copier platement un cheval ne 'reproduit' pas un cheval: il produit toujours l'image déformée d'un cheval (Grivel, 1979, p. 90).

In the light of more subtle readings of Balzac evident in his interview statements the intertexts in his novels should perhaps be viewed through the screen of Bakhtin's dialogism. Their main interest is then not so much the comparison (or lack of it) between Balzac's world and characters and Simon's, but the *place* where they occur: at the pivot between Simon's imaginary narratives and the more autobiographical novels commencing with *L'Herbe*. Here, the more 'traditional' elements of plot and character are left behind. However, it must also be said that Simon seems to ignore the fact that Balzac's descriptions are often profoundly ambiguous, especially where the moral standpoints and motivations of his characters are concerned. Moreover, it appears that Simon's rather simplistic (mis)reading of Balzac has led him, and indeed other *nouveaux romanciers,* to reject this precursor on somewhat erroneous grounds.

Simon and Flaubert

As already mentioned, Flaubert is, for Simon, pivotal in the development of the French novel—a point for new departures, leaving behind what Simon calls the 'roman à thèse':

> à partir de Flaubert, le roman s'est divisé en deux courants assez divergeants; d'un côté le naturalisme avec Zola et ceux qui ont poursuivi cette voie; et de l'autre côté, Flaubert et les pères du roman moderne: Joyce, Proust et Kafka (Le Clec'h, 1971, p. 6).

Simon sees his own novels belonging firmly in the latter category. There are no uses of Zola, for example, in his works, because 'naturalism' and the wide portrayal of social classes are not what concern him. Surprisingly, there are also no direct references or indisputably Flaubertian allusions in Simon's novels either. Evans has explored the intertext of *Madame Bovary* in *Leçon de choses* (Evans, 1980, pp. 33-44) by picking up such traces as the names 'Saint Charles' and 'Sainte Emma' (*LC,* p. 108) and suggesting similarities between Rodolphe and the anonymous lover in Simon's text, together with the details of the cows in the field and the frogs croaking as the characters make love. All these may be parallels, or hints to the reader, but there is no substantial evidence in the novel to suggest that *Madame Bovary* is the stimulus to these traces. The list of saints also includes such names as Alexis (which might equally well suggest *Anna Karenina*), and although the name 'Charles' appears several times (pp. 81, 94, 108, 168), it could equally well connote Proust's Swann, given that the names 'Gilberte' and 'Odette' occur together on page 172 or the character from Simon's own earlier novels. Furthermore, the cows and frogs are not unique to this novel. Both appear in the same context in *Triptyque* without the name 'Charles' (pp. 98-9 & 208 respectively) thus only further undermining Evans's certainty as to the particular intertextual reworkings of *Madame Bovary* in *Leçon de choses*.

There is a direct reference to *Madame Bovary*, however, in one of Simon's textual fragments: 'Et elle, Bovary paisible et sanctifiée, s'éventant avec mollesse' (*Correspondance,* 1964, p. 31). The whole fragment reappears in *Histoire*, but its details are reworked, and interestingly, this specific reference is omitted. So, like Flaubert himself, Simon makes studied changes between versions of his text. As fragment, Simon's *Correspondance* explores its title, communication being in the form of postcards and the Baudelairean sense of interassociating ideas. The inferences of the allusion to Emma Bovary are that the receiver of letters is looking for some romantic attachment from an updated Rodolphe, and that she is a sensually langorous creature. These associations both undergo change in their reformulation in *Histoire* (p. 399). What Simon has done, by omitting the Bovary allusion, is to erase all keys to psychological response or characterization in his protagonist. No direct authorial insights into character moods are left. It is Simon's use of Flaubert's *style indirect libre* which alone maintains the authorial position of a writer behind the text.

Flaubert's importance for Simon is marked, however, by the proportionately greater emphasis and space given to him in interviews; Proust tops the rating only marginally because praise for him is unreserved, as we shall see in the next chapter. With Flaubert, Simon still has reservations, particularly where traces of the 'traditional' nineteenth-century French novel still surface. So while Simon lauds the relative decline of the chronological / logical plot, with what he sees as its accompanying moral or didactic implications in *Madame Bovary* (Simon, 1963, p. 26), he rankles against traits of the novel which do not allow it to break free from its tradition, such as the 'Mœurs de Province' and the particularized historical milieu (Poirson, 1977, p. 38). Similarly, Flaubert's characterization, in Simon's eyes, fails to realize its full potential. Although moving away from creation of heroes *à la* Balzac or Stendhal, Flaubert's Emma and Charles Bovary still have the inevitability of their destinies written into their characters. Once again, for Simon, features of 'realism'—the social and local colour—still imprison Flaubert's writing.

Yet the issue of realism is the focus whereby Flaubert is seen by Simon to be in an altogether different class to Balzac or Stendhal and to be one of his own 'poncifs':

> Il est caractéristique de l'époque que Flaubert qui... vomissait le réalisme ('j'exècre ce qu'il est convenu d'appeler le *réalisme* bien qu'on m'en fasse un des poncifs') se soit cru obligé de se soumettre à cette sorte de totalisation rationnelle fondée sur des critères psychosociologiques et rejetant au second plan les impératifs proprement littéraires (Poirson, 1982, p. 36. Simon quotes from Flaubert's letter of 6 fév. 1876 to George Sand, *Correspondance,* VII, p. 285.).

His aim is to define where Flaubert's literary investigations part company with his own. Simon may poke fun at the 'fantastic' story of Emma and Charles, but he excuses the content of Flaubert's novel because of *how* Flaubert wrote (Nuridsany, 1981, p. 16). It is in the operation of literary creation that Flaubert's influence on Simon is most evident. Our investigation of the one direct Flaubert reference above provides the clue. To entitle his fragment *Correspondance*, Simon pays tribute to, and fully acknowledges his study of Flaubert's *Correspondance*, which furnishes, for Simon, various cameo statements in his interviews to describe his own efforts:

> Pour en revenir à Flaubert, il me semble qu'au delà de ses roman, au delà des fulgurants 'scénarios'... son importance tient justement au fait qu'il a mis en question le dogme du 'réalisme'. Dans une lettre à Louise Colet, je crois, ou à George Sand, il a, pour la première fois, posé les bases d'une littérature où le sens se dégagerait d'un travail de la langue:

> non plus *l'expression* d'un sens mais la *production* de sens pluriels (Simon, 1978, pp. 90-1 [Simon's emphasis]).

First and foremost, then, Flaubert is the archetypal artisan, working, reworking and modelling his text, aware of the importance of finding the right word or sequence of words, because that combination will make certain requirements in the ensuing narrative. The rhythms, cadences, assonance, dissonance and ambiguities in Flaubert come from work on the language itself, beyond the exigencies of plot progression. This allows the potential musicality and poetic associativeness of language to come into their own. Simon prides himself on this aspect of his own prose style, quoting Flaubert as an illustrious precursor:

> Je dirais qu'il est impossible d'écrire si on n'est pas dans un certain tempo... [le problème] hantait Flaubert. Vous savez qu'il a écrit dans une lettre à George Sand: 'Pourquoi y a-t-il un rapport nécessaire entre le mot juste et le mot musicale? Pourquoi arrive-t-on toujours à faire des vers quand on resserre trop sa pensée? La loi des nombres gouverne donc les sentiments et les images... et ce qui paraît être extérieur est tout bonnement dedans'. Il y a une chose très troublante: c'est de constater que l'on est souvent amené *uniquement par les nécessités (je dirais même; les exigences) musicales de la phrase* à rejeter un mot que l'on croyait juste ou, au contraire à rajouter un mot qui alors, s'avère *juste*!... Une phrase qui n'est pas 'bien balancée'... est *ipso facto sur le plan du sens*, vide, creuse. (Poirson, 1977, p. 39 & *Correspondance,* VII, p. 345 [Simon's emphasis].

Despite the similarities between the two writers, there is a distinction of emphasis to be made. The context of Flaubert's letter shows how he is striving to achieve Beauty and capture essences: Simon on the other hand is more interested in the sense of abundance and self-perpetuation that the surface collisions of verbal play bring into being. Both writers, however, contend that form and content are one because of their view of language, which is not a vehicle of meaning, but part of meaning itself. To illustrate this very aspect, Simon again quotes Flaubert: 'le style... est une manière absolue de voir les choses' (Simon, 1978, p. 88, and letter to Louise Colet, 16 janv. 1852, *Correspondance,* II, p. 345). One may note that such attention to style implies strict authorial control. Simon seems unaware of the contradiction inherent in his praise of Flaubert here and his comments on its working out in *Madame Bovary*, 'la terrible mise en forme'. Simon is himself a controller of fictional elements in the same manner as his literary forebear, *Triptyque* offering a paradigm of these processes.

Because Simon balks at the stylistically strict control to be sensed in *Madame Bovary*, this is a major reason why he prefers the earlier, more descriptive versions of the novel:

> Connaissez-vous cette édition intégrale de *Madame Bovary* que publiait... l'éditeur Corti? C'est le premier état du roman avec toutes les notes de travail de Flaubert, les brouillons où il relevait le détail de la pensée de ses personnages, saisie 'à l'état brut'..Il faut bien convenir que cette première version à l'état sauvage était infiniment plus riche... que le chef-d'œuvre qui en est sorti après la terrible mise en forme que nous savons (Aubarède, 1957, p. 7).

Simon is mistaken in thinking that this version is the 'Ur-Bovary'. It is in fact a reconstruction by the editors from the notes and scenarios for *Madame Bovary*, but it is *their* reconstruction, not Flaubert's original draft. This aside, however, Simon is obviously familiar with the *Nouvelle Version,* which he quotes exactly and extensively to illustrate his admiration for the impressionistic description in Flaubert's style. The most revealing part of Simon's reusage of the *Nouvelle Version* is his dogmatism concerning style. As description provides the key to textual dynamism for Simon, the absence of it in *Madame Bovary* (final version) denotes for him a regression, a thinning of textual richness. By over-accentuating simultaneity of description, Simon misses the refinements in *Madame Bovary* itself: the greater weight of each word means that descriptive details are not excrescences, but in fact contribute to textual purity:

> Il y a à ce sujet dans *Madame Bovary* une toute petite phrase d'une importance capitale, et qui a présidé à tout un aspect de l'évolution du roman contemporain. C'est celle-ci: 'Tout ce qu'il y avait en elle de réminiscences, d'images, de combinaisons, s'échappait *à la fois, d'un seul coup* (comme les mille pièces d'un feu d'artifices). Elle aperçut nettement et par *tableaux détachés*, son père, Léon, le cabinet de L'Heureux; leur chambre là-bas, un autre paysage des figures inconnues'. Comme vous voyez, il introduit là pour la première fois dans le roman les notions de simultanéiïté et de discontinuïté (Knapp, 1969, p. 185 [Simon's emphasis] Flaubert's words are found in the *Nouvelle Version* p. 597. The final version is *Madame Bovary*, p. 369).

In fact, greater simultaneity is achieved when the 'tableaux détachés' are removed. No signposts are given to indicate the shift of viewpoint; Flaubert depends on the alertness of his reader, so that he is drawn directly into Emma's flood of impressions, instead of being kept on the outside by 'separated scenes'. Although Simon does not recognize it, it is actually the final version of *Madame Bovary* which is closer to his own use of unmarked perspective shifts (for example 'je' becoming 'il'), rather than the *Nouvelle Version.*

Simon reiterates his views on style and his own prejudices by quoting the *Nouvelle Version* in a closely-studied commentary which is unique in Simon's interviews.

> Visite à son hôtel, confidences—ressouvenirs menant à la baisade, Vous rappelez-vous. Ah! Je vous ai bien aimée... très calme sans pose—rendez-vous pris d'avance pour tirer un coup.
>
> impatience des rendez-vous du jeudi—descente de la côte de Boisguillaume. Rouen dans la brume—cailloux qui craquent sous les roues—entrée à Rouen—odeur d'absinthe qui sort des cafés, manière féroce dont elle se déshabille.
>
> après les f...ries va se faire recoiffer—odeur des fers chauds—s'endort sous le peignoir—quelque chose de courtisanesque chez le coiffeur—intérieur de la gondole, en s'en retournant, un peu ivre, etc. cul de jatte dans la côte.
>
> Sur le port. Chaleur. Tentes de coutils—coup sain [...] différence avec Rodolphe/Léon (plus) ému qu'elle. Elle rentre à Yonville dans un bon état de f...rie normale. C'est l'epoque des confitures—fumiers roses—colère cramoisie d'Homais—arsenic. Faublas'.
>
> Que subsiste-t-il dans la version définitive de *Madame Bovary* de ces fulgurances (fumiers *roses*—colère *cramoisie* d'Homais) qui éclataient l'une après l'autre comme autant de fusées dans les petits scénarios, où tout à sa vorace sensualité, Flaubert faisait se bousculer et se répondre par fragments, images, odeurs, paroles et actions? Quelques-unes surnagent ici et là, prises dans un tissu conjonctif qui voudrait reconstruire une totalité et où abondent les commentaires explicatifs (*d'ailleurs il se révoltait contre l'absorption toujours plus grande de la personnalité*) quand ce ne sont pas les fadaises (*Cela lui descendait jusqu'au fond de l'âme comme un tourbillon dans un abîme et l'emportait parmi les espaces d'une mélancholie sans bornes*) Scenario XLVIII in Simon, 1982, p. 74 [his emphasis].

Simon actually makes several mistakes in this transcription. The paragraph commencing 'sur le port' should follow 'pour tirer un coup'. Simon then omits two paragraphs of the original, before accurately following the text, 'impatience des rendez-vous', and then omits 'Charles et son enfant' which should follow after 'cul de jatte dans la côte'. The second inaccuracy is the plural forms of 'confidences' and 'ressouvenirs' which are singular in Flaubert's notes. By comparing the scenario version and the relevant sentences in Part Three of *Madame Bovary*, Simon shows his preference for the sensuality of the former, the collusion of sense impressions, colour and language. This immediacy of visual description is subjugated in Flaubert's final version to refine out the overt sensuality. The particular instances Simon picks out illustrate this distinction perfectly. The 'fumiers roses' become 'Au coin des rues, il y avait de *petit tas rose qui fumaient* à l'air, car c'était le moment des confitures, et, tout le monde à Yonville confectionnait sa provision le même jour' (p. 292). Homais's 'colère cramoisie' becomes his heated words to Justin, in a 'realistic' build-up of anger, where *what is said* is given more weight than the quality of the anger itself (p. 294). Again, there is failure on Simon's part to see in the final version the increased ambiguities and colours of sensuous experience, shaded in by the avoidance of the noun/colour adjective formulation.

From this commentary, it is clear that Simon also reacts strongly against the author's manipulation of reader reaction, and the rigour of the narrative progression. The first sentence Simon chooses comes from Part Three, chapter 6, p. 334. It is a pity that Simon changed the order of events in his repetition of the scenario, for this quotation comes from Léon's thoughts after the section developing 'manière féroce dont elle se déshabille', becoming, in *Madame Bovary*: 'Elle se déshabillait brutalement, arrachant le lacet mince de son corset' (p. 333). The main focus is now on Léon, whose disgust is intrinsic to the further relationship of the lovers. Flaubert presumably changed Emma's importance (in the scenario) in the definitive text, because the structure of the novel and its conclusion demanded it. Similarly, the second quotation Simon gives, taken from *Madame Bovary,* Part Three, chapter 5, gives insights into Emma's psychology—character and action taking precedence over sensual (and peripheral) descriptions. The quotation comes in the section concerning Emma's trip to Rouen, the 'impatience des rendez-vous du jeudi' in the scenario. The pebbles rattling beneath the carriage wheels, here, become 'la terre résonnait sous les roues': and 'Rouen dans la brume' becomes 'Descendant tout en amphithéâtre et noyée dans le brouillard... On entendait le ronflement des fonderies avec le carillon clair des églises qui se dressaient dans la brume' (p. 311). The café smells are mentioned (p. 313), and after their lovemaking ('f...ries'), Emma goes to the hairdresser: 'L'odeur des fers, avec ces mains grasses qui lui maniaient la tête, ne tardait pas à l'étourdir, et elle s'endormait un peu sous son peignoir. Souvent le garçon, en la coiffant, lui proposait des billets pour le bal masqué' (p. 315). The heat of the curling tongs is omitted in the novel, because it is again, apparently, a detail which detracts from the main subject, Emma Bovary. Simon reacts to Flaubert's amendments negatively, simply because of his preference for the associative and sensual nature of description. His praise for the scenarios is a subjective response, and fails to allow for the change in Flaubert's intentions from these notes to the novel. Each 'devaluation' of the descriptions comes from Flaubert's awareness that they were a distraction from the mainspring of the text. A reading of *Madame Bovary* shows, however, that sensuality, colour and description have not in fact been expunged by the corrections. Indeed, the use of suppressed and ambiguous impressions and the complication of interpretation caused by *style indirect libre* demonstrate clearly Flaubert's masterful *improvements*, together with his move away from 'realism', a move so much at the heart of Simon's own narrative objectives.

Thus, Simon's reworkings move in the *reverse* direction to Flaubert's, but from similar motivation—the refinement of the prose to serve its new purpose. In Flaubert's case, it is a shift from hamperingly sensuous description to increased psychological nuance of response in his characters; with Simon, it is an ironing out of all psychological investigation to smooth the way for the equal prominence of all surface descriptions. *Both* move away from 'realism' in what they describe and how they describe it, but Simon does not do full justice to his precursor by recognizing this aspect of his writing.

*****

It is clear, then, from Simon's interviews and papers, that he has many prejudices against his nineteenth-century precursors, especially in the realm of 'realism' and its representation. Simon might see these precursors as his literary 'relations', their writing then acting as a catalyst in the development of his own prose style away from 'traditional' ingredients such as psychological realism, chronology, and the omniscient narrator. In this, he participates fully in the dialogical principle of evolution of a genre as Bakhtin outlines. However, his often simplistic reactions and blatant misunderstandings of examples taken from the highly ambiguous narratives of Stendhal, Balzac and Flaubert serve only to show his deficiencies as a critic. It was by mixing these ingredients afresh that Simon's forebears were, in fact, subverting 'realistic' narrative, to form the 'Nouveaux Romans' of their own generation. It is to this tradition that Simon belongs. It might even be argued that in view of his requirements of achronology, shifting and limited viewpoint and the flow of impressions that Simon's novels are just as 'unrealistic' as say those of Balzac.

Therefore, while the few references to nineteenth-century works in Simon's fiction are in the main defamatory, and highlight his move away from this literature, comparisons to these precursors actually define Simon's debt to many aspects of the nineteenth-century literary tradition, both Russian and French, and establish him firmly in a line of prose writers whose art and artifice is to describe and represent realities. Simon's reactions are therefore anti(pa)thetical and synthetic in the dialectic of the evolution of the novel in Bakhtinian terms. Simon's particular place as artisan of intertexts and reshaper of the novel out of his literary tradition *à la* Flaubert has also emerged strongly from this chapter. We shall be looking more closely in the final chapter to the corollary of these processes; how evolution of his own writing is enhanced by revisions and enhancements from *intra*textual fragments and other novels within his *œuvre*.

Chapter Five

Simon and Proust

The present chapter connects with and builds on the investigations of the previous one, where focus centred on the more general relationship of Simon to the tradition of the nineteenth-century novel as exemplified by the interest certain specific precursors showed towards description. Simon's prejudice and preference were all too apparent. The corollary of dialogism as a literary stance is that by relating to a generic evolution, one necessarily opts for one trait among many and hence participates in a highly critical manner towards one's tradition. Thus Simon can speak of the novel in such broad terms as 'Je dois dire que les littératures anglo-saxonnes et la littérature russe possèdent à mon vis, de plus authentiques romanciers que la nôtre... Balzac et Proust mis à part, bien entendu' (Aubarède, 1957, p. 7). This chapter scrutinizes what this 'authenticity' might entail, by studying the influence of a single novelist-progenitor, Proust, on Simon. The specific and pervasive inheritance from this literary 'father', as revealed in his interviews and novels, can be usefully viewed in the light of Bloom's theory of intertextuality, the 'anxiety of influence'. By this is meant the 'son's' recognition not merely of his literary inheritance, but his endebtedness to one particular writer, his literary 'father'. This filial bond is then coupled with an awareness of the necessity of breaking free of such parental dominance in order to create independently. This occurs when the 'son' deliberately misreads the 'father':

> *Poetic Influence—when it involves two strong poets—always proceeds by a misreading of the prior poet, an act of creative correction that is actually and necessarily a misinterpretation. The history of fruitful poetic influence... is a history of anxiety and self-saving caricature, of distortion, of perverse, wilful revisionism* (Bloom, 1973, p. 30).

Bloom discusses the literary father / son relationship and conflict in specifically Freudian and psychoanalytical terms, which I choose not to adopt fully. I prefer instead, to keep the sense of 'father' and 'son' separate from any particular psychocritical approach which would involve a project larger than this book can incorporate. Useful criticism has already been started by Britton (1987) and Duncan (forthcoming). Neither shall I adopt Bloom's six categories (clinamen, tessera, kenosis, daemonization, askesis and apophrades), which he uses to define the various stages in the divergence of 'father' and 'son'. These are too technical to be of practical value. Instead, the overall concept, the 'anxiety of influence' itself, will be the theoretical polemic of the chapter.

Literary 'sonship' requires kinship to, and recognition of the dominance of, the 'father', before the birthright and independence can be claimed. This chapter will thus establish and examine Simon's recognition of Proust's influence upon him. Description is again the subject in question. The extent to which this is 'Proustian' will then be illustrated first by the frequent and reverent allusions to Proust's writing practices in Simon's interviews and papers. The fragments chosen from Proust as exemplar often recur in some guise in Simon's novels. It is the form of the disguise these take which gauges the 'anxiety of influence' proper and the need to break with this father's dominance. Hence, a chronological investigation of Simon's novels, will be the method adopted to establish where and how Proust's influence is apparent throughout Simon's *œuvre*. Furthermore, the novel-by-novel investigation which is peculiar to this chapter enables the success of Simon's development away from this literary father to be more clearly assessed. As Bloom indicates above, the marks of this to be borne in mind are 'misinterpretation', 'self-saving caricature', 'distortion', and even 'perverse, wilful revisionism'. Such quintessentially intertextual operations will then themselves be evaluated with regard to the particular dexterity or sophistication Simon's usage presents.

References to Proust in Simon's interviews

Proust's dominance may be established first through the very frequency of Simon's allusions to him in interviews. Early in his literary career, Simon subordinated Proust to Dostoyevsky (Aubarède, 1957, p. 7), but rapidly the roles were reversed in all following interviews, whether as direct forebear, favourite author (for example Bourdet, 1961, p. 141), or as a primary influence on contemporary writing in general in the propelling of the nineteenth-century novel towards a poetics of pure description (Senlis, 1960, p. 27).

Contrary to his interview judgements of his precursors in the previous chapter, Simon does not evaluate Proust according to models of psychological or biographical realism. Thus, he is not concerned with issues such as whether or not Proust was a homosexual, or how closely his descriptions of the faubourg Saint-Germain mirror the morality and values of that world (Poirson, 1982, p. 37). Where character sketches as given blocks of description, delineating and fixing a personality in the 'realist' novel, were lambasted by Simon, he lauds Proust's 'impressionistic', highly evocative figures, such as Odette de Crécy 'la dame en rose qui mangeait des mandarines', characters 'réduits à quelques-unes seulement de leur composantes (ainsi nous ne savons rien d'autre de Proust que: dame, rose, manger et mandarines...)' (Simon, 1978, pp. 81-2). Simon highlights here the incompleteness of descriptions refined to such a limited choice of components, yet this incompleteness is essential if textual ambiguity and development are to occur as the novel unfolds. This passage also exemplifies for Simon the fragmentary collation of sense impressions: the accumulation of descriptive fragments in the text acts as a mirror for the workings of the consciousness—perception, memory and imagination (Eribon, 1981, p. 21). Simon also notes the specific and universal when it comes to Proust's use of names. Thus Simon guards against equating Marcel Proust, the author, with the fictional Marcel, just as for Proust himself, Elstir is not Monet, nor Albertine Proust's chauffeur (Ricardou, 1975, p. 415). Even place names cease to operate as atlas referents. The name 'Quimperlé', which takes on heightened evocations in the boy's mind functions as personalized and private signifiers as well as stimulating verbal play in the wider text (Grivel, 1979, p. 93). Proper names, like any noun, act more as synecdoches and are public signifiers of a category of objects. This is why names are often interchanged in the course of a Simon novel: their particularity—however imaginary—does not count. Indeed, it is their structuring dimension which for Simon reveals harmonies and reverberations between seemingly disparate occasions and objects: they accumulate and condense significance. Such operations are at the core of Simon's works, and he recognizes his legacy from Proust by citing Albertine, both her name and the harmonies between her and the other 'jeunes filles' (ibid. p. 92). In *Les Corps conducteurs,* description by association of common qualities, not by temporal contingency, is intrinsic to the workings of Simon's prose. He illustrates these by referring to the famous 'madeleine' episode (Knapp, 1969, p. 186) where sensory, linguistic and associative functions of language generate densely poetic prose. To the same end, Simon also in the same interview cites the episode of the 'pavés inégaux'. However, he does not comment on how the latter encompasses the 'madeleine' section, nor how both fit into the overall architectural structure of Proust's novel.

Proust's 'madeleine' also encapsulates the workings of memory, perception and language, a cameo illustration of his 'mémoire involontaire'. Simon, by locating it within the context of his precursor's work, can also use it as a shorthand for equivalent operations in the production of his *Triptyque* (DuVerlie, 1974, p. 6). The difference between the memory associations here and in Proust, however, lies with the person doing the remembering. In Proust, it is the narrator recalling Combray as he eats the madeleine. In Simon, it is the *reader* who must piece together the associations between the three strands of the novel by the process of his own memory: the memories or emotions of any internal protagonist are not at all involved.

Expressly vague description also allows for excursions into the realm of the poetic and Simon gives as example the 'haie des aubépines' to illustrate language as epiphany (Haroche, 1981, p. 15). He also cites the set of generators or structural motifs in *Le Temps retrouvé* (a cloud, a triangle, a steeple, a flower, a pebble) to illustrate how selection of catalysts heightens their every appearance, thus throwing into relief the writer's concentration on capturing the relevant properties of ordinary objects, or, as with the 'clochers de Martinville' to show condensation of images (Joguet, 1976, p. 14). The latter are paradigmatic of the principle of association between instances of a given motif: the belfreys signify periods in the narrator's life, each new instance of the motif indicating another stage in his experience and contributing to the structural pattern of the whole text. Another important feature for Simon of the 'clochers de Martinville' passage is the link between a particular stimulus (the 'clochers') and the act of writing. Simon breaks off the verbatim quotation *just before* the boy asks the doctor for paper to compose his very first piece of writing. For Simon, the materiality of the act of writing cannot be separated from the material of the writing itself. A figure writing within the space of the novel is not a necessity.

Elsewhere, choosing a single sentence from Proust as paradigm, Simon illustrates his own writing priorities:

> Pour ma part, afin de garder, pour pouvoir aimer Balbec, l'idée que j'étais sur la pointe extrême de la terre, je m'éfforçais de regarder plus loin, de ne voir que la mer, d'y chercher des effets décrits par Baudelaire et de ne laisser tomber mes regards sur notre table que les jours où y était servi quelque vaste poisson, monstre marin qui, au contraire des couteaux et des fourchettes, était contemporain des époques primitives où la vie commençait à affluer dans l'Océan, au temps des Cimmériens, et duquel le corps aux innombrables vetèbres, aux nerfs bleus et roses, avait été construit par la nature, mais selon un plan architectural, comme une polychrome cathédrale de la mer (Simon, 1978, p. 83).

This description of the fish on the plate in the restaurant in Balbec is indeed quoted frequently by Simon as epitome of dense writing. Simon focusses on the power of Proust's language to 'susciter soudain dans cette salle à manger... tout un ensemble de majestueuses résonances ou harmoniques mettant en jeu les concepts de préhistoire, de biologie et de structure' (ibid.). He underscores the unreality of the description, its non-photographic reproduction, and hence emphasizes the poetry and suggestiveness of the words chosen. Thus, identification of a particular kind of fish is not the issue; its universal qualities are the main concern. These act as metaphors or synecdoches for the structuring devices of the total composition, of which this segment is a part: 'cet objet n'est pas un accident isolé mais un élément de cette immense et rigoureuse organisation dans l'espace et le temps' (ibid.). Simon indicates several important components of this sentence which have wider implications, such as the theme of the sea, the linking with Albertine of the words 'passion'/'poisson', and the cathedral structure mirroring that of the whole novel (ibid., p. 86). It is rather unfortunate that Simon digresses from a close textual analysis of Proust to speak on the more theoretical ideas of 'accumulated' and 'static' description based on his understanding of Tynianov. Description is action in its own right, not just a support for events. What Simon seems to overlook is the fact that Proust, as well as developing description for itself, employs much so-called traditional descriptive technique to portray salon society at the turn of the century.

Although Simon pinpoints the devices of composition of this sentence as a cameo for the whole work, he does not analyse the applications of time and space in this sentence to the whole of Proust's novel. This passage is an ideal focal point for both. The present, the narrator's past, the time of Baudelaire, the 'époques primitives où la vie commençait', and the 'temps des Cimmériens' are all condensed vertically within a ten line fictional space, which encompasses Balbec, 'la pointe extrême de la terre', 'plus loin', 'la Nature', and the space of the imagination and metaphor, 'cathédrale de la mer'. Simon does not comment either on the immense superimposed network of cited writers in Proust: nor does he make any overt connection between Proust's use of Baudelaire in this segment of *A la recherche* and his own reference to Baudelaire's 'Correspondances' later in his exposé. A deeper penetration of Proust's text on Simon's part would have revealed more clearly to what extent Simon understands Proust and therefore how much he has absorbed from his precursor, not least lessons on the use of intertexts.

Simon's continuing and deep admiration for Proust, together with his close knowledge of *A la recherche* or three volumes of it: *Du côté de chez Swann, A l'ombre des jeunes filles en fleurs* and *Le Temps retrouvé* make this precursor unquestionably Simon's paternal paradigm, especially where descriptive techniques are concerned. Thus by referring to and analysing large numbers of passages from this novel, Simon uncovers the practice of his *own* writing to show where it is akin to Proust's in intention. 'Ce que j'ai tenté donc c'est de pousser encore le processus amorcé par Proust et de faire de la description... le moteur... le générateur de l'action' (Poirson, 1977, p. 35). Particularly innovative in *A la recherche* as a whole for Simon is also its description of writing describing its own processes; and he cites the reception of Vinteuil's sonata as a cameo to illustrate this (Biro-Thierbach, 1970, p. 33). Again traditional and innovatory writings are contrasted, and, by quoting this passage, Simon can justify the newness of his own writing against charges of 'difficulty' (DuVerlie, 1974, p. 19). However, the interviews also show a potential limitation of such direct and close literary kinship: they have a propensity to comment, catalogue or collate, with little critical discussion, perhaps because admiration is uppermost. The dominance of Proust remains central to Simon's interpretations of the elements chosen, for these are never distorted, caricatured or wilfully revised. Respect, not mockery of Proust, then, establishes the literary kinship of Simon and Proust and is the nexus of Bloom's 'anxiety of influence' out of which disrespect must stem. It is in Simon's novels that this second stage, the break with this 'strong' father, comes about. How his move away from his 'progenitor' establishes his own independent voice will become apparent in the ensuing novel-by-novel survey.

References to Proust in Simon's novels

The very earliest Simon novels offer no sustained borrowings but only cultural references of the kind mentioned already in chapter two. In *Le Tricheur,* the names 'oncle Charles' and 'la petite Odette' appear in the text, but without intertextual development (pp. 27 and 84 respectively). In *La Corde raide,* Proustian reverberations such as its incipit and structure are reminiscent of *A la recherche* but in an abridged form. Compare 'Longtemps, je me suis couché de bonne heure' with 'Autrefois je restais tard au lit et j'étais bien'. As in Proust, the narrator lies in bed and this position is the common locus of places and experiences, different times in his life, and a means of superimposing ideas and events from different spatial and temporal locations: Perpignan, Paris, Berlin, Avignon, and Italy all exist synchronically in the space of memory. Similarly, in *La Corde raide,* one 'dôme' recalls another, a direct allusion to Proust, where steeples and churches are major stimuli and structural symbols of the workings of the text. The narrator in *La Corde raide* 'travels' by means of different rooms, as does Marcel, but his journeys are more literal, less inner explorations. The limited content and scope of Simon's essay compared with the vast canvas of his precursor, matches the weight of each. The two works rapidly part company after the opening because the remainder of Simon's essay discusses less complex ideas. The borrowing of Proust's technique is effective, however, for it lends authority and credibility to Simon's early writing, without, at the same time, deflating the 'father'. *La Corde raide* may be seen as a struggle less with the precursor, Proust, than with conventional, more representative writing.

With *L'Herbe,* there is increasing confrontation between the precursor and Simon. References to Proust are integrated more widely throughout the novel and operate as a means of comparison, both positive and negative. Thus distortions of the precursor begin to appear. The chief example is Tante Marie, ironically called a 'jeune fille de fleur' (pp. 12-13). She is an old dying woman, the direct antithesis of Proust's 'jeunes filles en fleurs' at Balbec, young and unafraid to explore their sexuality. Simon uses this allusion ironically, to build up an impression of Marie by negative simile. Comparison is further established by Marie's name, Marie-Artémis-*Léonie* Thomas. Simon, then, borrows a character and section from his literary parent, Proust, to expand them into his own novel, guarding some elements while simultaneously veering away from the original. Both Marie and Léonie are powerful central presences in their respective contexts, signalled by their particular smell (*Herbe* p. 10 and *ALR,* I, pp. 49-50). Both are the focus of family life by their immobility, this concentration being their autocracy. Simon also borrows Léonie's incessant monologue, another marker of her presence apart from the perfume, but has transformed it into the wordless and unconscious death-rattle, which is no less omnipresent (pp. 19, 135 and *ALR,* I, pp. 50-1). This reworking of Proust shows Simon moving beyond his precursor, for Marie is a *textual* mouthpiece; her very wordlessness is a powerful means of communication. She never speaks herself: it is her life which speaks, both the records of the past as found in her account books, and her relentless breathing and presence.

Time is another central concern for both women. Léonie measures time by her medications and the church bells. Marie's life is marked by the diurnal shadow changes. Simon's stress of the word 'Temps' links *L'Herbe* indirectly to *A la recherche du TEMPS perdu*. The past is retold in both novels, but in Simon is not found again for it is fictional time alone which presides. Moreover, where Léonie fills up time, Marie *is* time—she is as unaware of it as she is of her breathing. By simply being in the present, with no conscious recourse either to her past or her future, she overcomes the anxiety of time and boredom that are Léonie's experience. In tandem with these characters' interaction with time is their interaction with space. Léonie imposes her space on others—she needs to know everything going on around her, seen within the frame of her window and the area of her room and mind. Marie is utterly passive and unconcerned with others' space: yet by the paradox of her inert omnipresence throughout the whole text she inhabits its space totally.

The physical appearance of the two women is also similar (p. 142 and *ALR,* I, p. 52). They are both a heap of bones, but where Léonie attracts attention to her thinness and uses it as a subject of conversation and means of power (by getting Eulalie to visit her), Marie just *is* thin, a living corpse, yet the focus of undemanded attention. Facial details also compare: for example Léonie's baldness is echoed in Marie (pp. 60, 79 and *ALR,* I, p. 52). Léonie, however, attempts to retain her femininity, whereas Marie is so near the point of death that she is sexless, a skeleton with a bald skull.

The second borrowing from Proust, which underwrites the links between Marie and Léonie, is the presence in *L'Herbe* of a manservant, Julien (pp. 31-2 and *ALR,* I, p. 53). He is kept in the background in his servant's place in both texts, and Simon seems to use him as a way of authenticating the other Proustian borrowings rather than for any particular purpose in his novel. Later in the text Gilberte, another unmistakeably Proustian name, appears, this time ironically, to expose character traits in Sabine and Pierre. The latter is arguing with his wife, who believes he is having affairs with other women. This reference introduces the theme of jealousy, but in this case Gilberte is just one of Sabine's girlfriends, with whom Pierre danced at their wedding, a minor character divested of Proustian significance in Simon's text (p. 198). Because Simon has appropriated and reworked rather minor characters from Proust in *L'Herbe,* but remains largely faithful to his forebear, it may be said that at this stage of his fictional development the precursor's dominance is being questioned, but has yet to be overthrown.

The same can be said of both *La Route des Flandres* and *Le Palace*. The former contains somewhat disguised allusions to Proust, which invert the implications of the original. One example of deflation of the precursor in this way occurs in the description of the women at the races, which hints at the scene of the girls appearing at Balbec. Comparison with Proust is provoked by the singularity of this passage in Simon, for numbers of women do not appear frequently in his writing (p. 19 and *ALR,* I, p. 829). A closer parallel is Simon's reworking of the meeting of Marcel and Gilberte at the hawthorn hedge in the reported encounter between Iglésia and Corinne (pp. 48-9 and *ALR,* I, pp. 139-41). It is the light Simon's interviews shed on such traces which helps define his familiarity with this extremely famous exerpt from Proust and which seals it as a deliberate intertext. One obvious parallel is the reciprocal voyeurism of the figures glimpsing each other on either side of the hedge, which prevents a good view. As in Proust, the hedge also divides the sexes and the protagonists from each other. In both passages, colour (pink) links taste imagery: the similes and metaphors of eating and desire are evoked by highly sensual painting of interrelating sensations. Another parallel is narrative viewpoint: Georges and the narrator of *A la recherche* both act as commentators on the couple in question, and neither can determine the full meaning of the encounter, for the particular actions and exchanges are intensely ambiguous.

Shifts and deflations in Simon, however, are also evident. Corinne, like Gilberte, comes from a wealthy family, and both share the same hair colour, Gilberte being a 'blond roux' and Corinne a russet. However, Gilberte is still a girl, whereas Corinne is already a woman and fully sexually aware, this fact almost emblazoned in her transparent red dress. Furthermore, Simon takes over Proust's image of the pink hawthorn blossom looking like 'une jeune fille en robe de fête au milieu de personnes de négligé... souriant dans sa fraîche toilette rose l'arbuste catholique et délicieux' and concretizes it in Corinne. Her 'robe en voile' is her new 'party' dress specially for the occasion, but its net-like transparency also makes it like the girls in Proust's image 'en négligé'—a cover for nakedness which makes their state of *déshabillé* more obvious. The shift occurs in that Simon transfers the undress of Proust to the dress worn in public by Corinne, where it becomes like undress. In Proust, eating and delectation are closely interrelated: the pink hawthorn blossom is associated with 'fromage frais' mixed with strawberries, and leads by suggestion, as the passage unfolds, to desire for Gilberte. In Simon, it is Corinne, again, who is lent edibility associations; in her dress, she looks like a boiled red sweet 'enveloppée[s] de papier cellophane'. The comic implications lie in the fact that the cellophane is indeed wrapping, but indecorous, as it is total transparency. The sense of value and luxury associated with pink food is also removed, and perhaps devalued in Simon in that the sweets are 'acides'.

Towards the end of both passages, the narrators try to interpret the ambiguous meanings of what they have witnessed. In Proust, the narrator and lover are the same person. There is no obvious difficulty, then, in reconstructing the events of the meeting, only in interpreting the particular meaning of Gilberte's gestures. In Simon, the situation is more complicated, because the narrator (Georges) and lover (Iglésia) are two separate people. Iglésia is not comparable whatsoever to Marcel as he is the burlesque embodiment of virility, a kind of *commedia dell'arte* figure, who postures masculinity, but is comically seen in garments which are almost feminine in evocation ('voluptueux travestissement'). This may point obliquely to the sexual inversions in Proust, where the surface belies the actuality beneath, or where protagonists enjoy a dual sexuality. In total, the 'aubépine' scene in *La Route des Flandres* is utterly mundane, whereas for Proust it is a moment of fictional intensity opening up the diegetic progression in the text. The 'anxiety of influence' is mounting, however, for Simon has chosen to deflate, in *La Route des Flandres,* Marcel and Gilberte, characters of much greater significance in *A la recherche* than Tante Léonie, and a well-known moment of Proustian epiphany.

Le Palace, rather than offering distortions of Proust's characters, presents a new intertextual glance at the precursor, encroachment into his *stylistic* territory: Proust's structuring principle of his 'vases communiquants' which opens the third paragraph of Simon's novel. He is making this allusion a metaphor for the whole of his novel, and the way in which its parts are intercalated and superimposed. This compositional principle in *Le Palace* may be seen to uncover a deep level of influence between the two writers, which goes beyond a mere purloining of tropes or themes. So, while the 'early' middle novels of Simon's *œuvre* demonstrate that his own style and language are largely supplanting Proust's topoi and characters, the actual creative processes are still recognizably those of the precursor. Confrontation with Proust as influence must occur if Simon is to challenge his dominance. For this to happen, larger adumbrations from Proust's prose must be seen within Simon's works for these, in turn, to reject them. Confidence of the 'son' is the corollary: to permit the 'father' to exist in the same textual space attests the knowledge that the 'son' can create independently.

It is in the late 'middle' novels that evidence of this very process emerges so markedly and with increasing intensity, until the 'anxiety of influence' has been surmounted. This progression towards independence can be seen to begin in *Femmes,* gather momentum in *Histoire* and finally culminate in *La Bataille de Pharsale.*

Femmes is a reworking of the scene where the girls appear on the beach at Balbec. However, to my mind, this is *not* a pastiche or parody of Proust's writing so much as an alignment: only a limited number of pages are selected from the antecedent as the raw material to be paralleled with Simon's text (*ALR,* I, pp. 787-830). Within these pages, only very specific thematic and general structural elements are chosen. The Simonian variation lies precisely in the lack in *Femmes* of narratorial comment, general statements about art, life, love, personal reactions, questions concerning the psychology and motivation of other characters and the deeper significance of names or acts. A further distinguishing feature is the omission of Proust's wider plot, determined again by the taking of only a fragment of the textual tapestry which is Proust's novel. The intertext Simon borrows comes immediately before Elstir is introduced in Proust as a model of innovation in art. Simon parallels and goes beyond Proust by including reproductions of twenty-three Mirós as loose leaves in his text.

What is endowed by Proust and guarded from him is, not surprisingly, description: the poetry formed from association, selection, imagery, colour, sensation, light, and linguistic devices. Instead of generalizing away the particular, essentially Proustian details (as seen above in the reworking of the hawthorn epiphany in *RF*), the particular—as I shall show—is emphasized, concentrated and intensified. This draws attention to the model as model, but also to the new context and how it has changed the implications of that model.

What, then, are the common motifs? First, the group of women in both texts is differentiated from everything and everyone else on the beach (p. 9 and *ALR,* I, pp. 788, 793, 796-7). However, where Proust begins with the group which splits into individuals, the movement in Simon is the reverse: the individual introduces the collective. In both cases, it is the particularity of the group which separates it from the rest of the beach scene. This is marked by two major principles of perception: movement and colour. For the former, presence can be mapped by whether the group is moving or static. At various points on the journey, a 'maintenant' indicates whether movement or stasis is in operation, not only as promenade, but as textual progression (p. 10 and *ALR,* I, p. 792). Colour is the second mode of differentiation used by Proust and Simon. Greyness (non-colour, for the purposes of both texts) acts as the foil against which daubs of colour stand out and catch the observer's and reader's eye. The same vibrant colours, black, green and pink, are associated with the group of women. In Simon, Albertine's 'polo noir' becomes the head description of the woman who generates the text, 'lourde tout entière vêtue de noir la tête couverte d'un fichu noir' (p. 7) and the two other women have green or pink dresses to distinguish them from each other (p. 11). Simon takes Proust's facial colourings and transforms them into blocks of colour representing the whole figure. The borrowing is more a transcription because of the unusual tone: 'géranium ou plutôt rose cyclamen' (p. 11) mirroring 'le rose avait cette teinte cuivrée qui évoque l'idée de géranium' (*ALR,* I, p. 790). Throughout *Femmes,* the colour/figure disappears and reappears, again marking the progression of both women and text (p. 17). *Femmes* concludes 'celle en noir disparue les deux corsages géranium et vert même plus visibles maintenant' (p. 17). Compare this with the ending of the section in Proust: 'Mais c'est peut-être encore celle au teint de géranium aux yeux verts que j'avais le plus désiré connaître' (*ALR,* I, p. 830).

Another common locus of motifs centres on the cosmic, made even more apparent in the reprint of *Femmes* as *La Chevelure de Bérénice*. Proust compares the band of girls to the luminous path of a comet (la chevelure), visible because of the darkness of space around it (*ALR*, I, p. 791). This comet image becomes the 'chevelure' of Simon's *La Chevelure de Bérénice* and constellation: the girls wade in the sea in which the stars are reflected, joining the micro- and macro-cosmic worlds (p. 12). The same interpenetration occurs in Proust's text, the sparkle in the girls' eyes joined by metaphor to the sparkle of constellations (*ALR*, I, p. 823).

Where colour and movement structure the progression of both episodes, similar uses of sensation and language portray the musicality and poetry in the prose of both writers, illustrated as bird imagery and birdsong. In Proust, the girls are described as 'une bande de mouettes' and possess 'un esprit d'oiseau' (*ALR*, I, p. 788). This is reproduced in *Femmes* by the appended Mirós, their titles linking women and birds. The most striking comparison is the description in Proust of servants, transposed by Simon into whores (p. 15 and *ALR*, I, p. 812). The exotic, brightly coloured birds brought to Proust's 'jardins zoologiques' appear also in Simon's text, but they are not *alive* in a zoo; they are preserved under a taxidermist's glass dome or decorate a musical box. Thus, despite the differences in *what* is described, the closeness of literary techniques (association) can only confirm the still entrenched influence of Proust on Simon.

Histoire is even more pervaded, indeed invaded, by allusions to Proust than *Femmes*. The change, though, is that instead of association affinity and alignment operating in tandem, the Proust references suffer mockery, caricature and distortion in *Histoire*. It is these very criteria which alert us to the 'anxiety of influence'. Mockery of the precursor is evident on two levels: Proustian protagonists are parodied, while at the same time Proustian narrative strategies are caricatured. It is the latter incursion into the deeper prose structures of the forebear which distinguishes Simon's use of Proust in *Histoire* from that in *Femmes*, and suggests Simon's grappling with the characteristic, unique and influential in Proust.

In *Histoire*, the uniqueness of Proust's protagonists is emptied out so that they become rather banal figures. However, they are not so generalized that their origins are not recognizable. The most consistent re-embodiment from Proust is 'l'oncle Charles'. For the narrator in Simon, as for Marcel, this is a model of love and literary pursuits. Like Charles Swann, Charles has had an unfortunate love-affair, but the difference is that in the 'remake' it is this single feature which remains, making this new Swann a 'Charlot', the butt of pity or mockery (p. 68). The breadth of Swann's character, his literary tastes, his marriage to Odette and his fatherhood are absent. Uncle Charles has been unable to form a relationship with any woman, and ends up as a stuffy pedant (p. 114) the 'story' of his failures never revealed. Uncle Charles may also have an overlay of the Baron de Charlus, although his relationships are not specifically homosexual, the hint of this coming through a reference to 'Morel', this being Charlus's partner (*Hist*, p. 142). The theme of homosexuality is thus brought into Simon's text, but the context stresses the friendships between the contemporaries of the boy-narrator at his seminary school, not *adult* relationships as in Proust.

Other names from Proustian characters punctuate *Histoire*; 'Marcel' appears twice, but this name is a false clue (pp. 118 and 379). 'Marcel' is doubled with the Latin, historical figure Marcellus as Marcell... T... Cillia, thereby linking once more the historical and the fictional and compressing them into one name in the same set of letters. The direct consequence is that the individuality and singularity of both Proust's Marcel and the hero of antiquity are emptied out. It is deeply ironic that Simon's boy-narrator translates and reads the Latin concerning Marcellus, and at the same time, as boy-narrator, pastiches the activities of Proust's main character.

Similar ironic and parodic treatment of Proust occurs in the visit of Lambert (Simon's reworking of Bloch) to the narrator's home (pp. 215-23 and *ALR*, I, pp. 90-3). By superimposing on Proust a figure from Joyce, Simon condenses name-parody. The result is an over-riding mockery, not just of social (middle-class) values, but of previous literature as well, for the parallels with Proust's episode are striking, and the criticism found in these previous texts is thus pushed to new extremes. First, there is the admiration of the narrator for the older friend Bloch / Lambert, for his experience, taste and 'knowledge'. In both cases, outspoken eccentric language and sarcasm mark the friends' speech, a means whereby 'nice' words and values in the host families are undercut. In both texts, there are personality and generation clashes between guest and host family. Again, social rules and etiquette are under attack; the modern comments on the establishment. However, shifts of emphasis prevent Simon's text from being a mere repetition of the antecedent. There is mockery of the family as 'religious' group, with unimpeachable rules (repeated in the authority of the religious school the boy attends), which mirrors and transposes the strict background of Proust's Marcel. Second, Marcel's father is replaced by oncle Charles. This weakens the Proustian emphasis on family hierarchy, yet the element of the leisured head of the family is retained and mocked. As dilettante writer by occupation, Simon's Charles is seen to be indicative of his class and generation, and as unproductive and non-innovative writer, he epitomizes an anti-Bergotte. In both texts, the visitor also displeases and upsets the women present, both incidentally 'souffrantes' in differing ways, another hint at decadence, as opposed to the rude health of the guest. Bloch and Lambert commit social *faux pas* as far as eating arrangements are concerned, although the details are again different. Both are outspoken outsiders but to different degrees; Simon's transcription presents a new, cruder level of behaviour, language, and frankness, which is overtly Joycean in irreverence but Proustian in inspiration, whilst offering to some extent a parody of Proust.

This parody is more overt as regards the particular fabric of *A la recherche*. For example, there are common activities and scenes: the 'soirées de musique de chambre' remind one of faubourg Saint-Germain social gatherings (p. 60). In both texts, architecture is equated with cakes and food: the 'clocher en pâtisseries roses' is a metaphor reminiscent of Proust's church at Combray, with its evocations of pink biscuits (p. 188 and *ALR,* I, p. 139). Similarly, there is a description of a sunset over 'la cathédrale en pain d'épice du château médiéval en pain d'épice des maisons en pain d'épice' (*Hist,* p. 263) and later, an aquatint, 'd'où sortent çà et là des cheminées d'usines, les pointes rigides et gothiques des clochers et des coupoles surchargées de pâtisseries... une sorte de pâte molle boursouflée tartinée sur une planche' (pp. 362-3). Both these images point back to Proust, but by repetition ('pain d'épice') and exaggeration ('surchargées') the idealizing and gently ironic tone of the original is destroyed. Simon's church spires are not, as in Proust, epiphanies or points of association which link moments of importance for Marcel. Instead, they are grotesque excrescences in a conglomerate landscape which is almost baroque in flavour. It is this revision of Proustian techniques of association which is central to *Histoire* and which spawns its digressions and structure.

The opening of the novel sets the intertextual scene, for it is highly reminiscent of Combray. The tree outside the narrator's window in *Histoire* is scrutinized for hidden meanings (which are never divulged) and 'becomes', by association, a grotesque genealogical tree whose members are depicted as birds with human heads. This mirrors and then parodiesMarcel's preoccupations with family names and meanings behind them, such as the name 'Guermantes'. Simon's version is triggered by these human birds which conjure up the word 'jais' in its multiple senses:

> leurs sombres et luisantes toques de plumes... les serres des aigles héraldiques, et jusqu'à ces ténébreux bijoux aux ténébreux éclats dont le nom (jais) évoquait phonétiquement celui d'un oiseau, ces rubans, ces colliers de chien dissimulant leurs cous ridés, ces rigides titres de noblesse, qui, dans mon esprit d'enfant, semblaient inséparables des vieilles chairs jaunies, des voix dolentes, de même que leurs noms de places fortes, de fleurs, de vieilles murailles, barbares, dérisoires, comme si quelque divinité facétieuse et macabre avait condamné les lointains conquérants wisigoths aux lourdes épées, aux armures de fer, à se survivre sans fin sous les espèces d'ombres séniles et outragées appuyées sur des cannes (p. 11).

What Simon does here is deflate and invert the time-resistant and magical qualities found in Proust, while at the same time using and disintegrating the association to form his own text. Exactly the same process occurs on the next page of *Histoire,* where the word 'toque' is picked up, used in a mock-Proustian way, and then distorted by associations which play with the original model of Marcel's grandmother:

> le mot toque lui-même amenant à mon esprit... le qualificatif de toquée qui paradoxalement la nimbait pour moi... parce que si dire toquée d'une femme encore jeune, comme je l'avais parfois entendu faire par oncle Charles, impliquait mépris ou apitoiement, son accouplement avec le mot vieille lui conférait au contraire dans mon esprit une sorte de majesté et de mystère l'englobant dans cette aura d'obscure puissance qui les entourait toutes: vaguement fantastiques, vaguement incrédibles retirées dans leur royale solitude, cette roide majesté qui contrastait avec leur fragilité... puisqu'on disait d'elles qu'elles allaient bientôt mourir (pp. 12-13).

This clustering of Proust's stylistic features at the beginning of *Histoire* is not sustained throughout the novel, but concentration on them, and on their subsequent distortions as new prose digression (transgressions?), is important to uncovering the 'anxiety of influence'. Simon is using association to structure his work as Proust before him. The difference, however, is that in mocking Proustian 'depths', and the overall impossibility of reconstructing events from memories in *Histoire,* Simon eschews layers of meaning, replacing this form of association by a linguistic juxtaposition to link seemingly unrelated objects. The colour 'rose', for example, appears frequently in *Histoire*. It not only joins things spatially and pictorially, but also emerges in the related guises of 'arroser', 'rosette', 'Rosa' and 'roseaux'. This punning, of course, harks back to Proust and thus caricatures the precursor at the same time.

While *Histoire* boasts much intertextual borrowing and distortion of Proust, actual quotation from the precursor is absent. The reverse is true in *La Bataille de Pharsale,* which contains the largest number of direct and verbatim quotations from Proust in Simon's novels, thus defining even more clearly the precursor's *stylistic* presence. Distortions of Proust are visible in this novel not only in terms of the treatment of prominent Proustian motifs: overt undermining and debasement of Proustian language and structure also occur. The frequency of the intertexts signals the intensity of the conflict. Permitting the 'father' to speak directly, to dialogue with the 'son' on the level of style, suggests that this is the nexus of the 'anxiety': their duel and confrontation will determine who will win 'la bataille de la phrase', to borrow Ricardou's anagrammatical rendering of the text. Recently, Lefere has argued that 'On a l'impression que Simon rivalise avec Proust dans l'enrichissement de la phrase, que tous deux s'efforcent de la distendre' (1990, p. 98). To my mind, the 'anxiety of influence' moved beyond rivalry to the more aggressive antagonism of writings. The very interpolation of Proust's words into Simon's text shows the two proses locked in combat, in a battle of writings.

Despite two more recent studies by Lefere (1990) and Peyroux (1987) re-examining the role of Proust in *La Bataille de Pharsale*, the most comprehensive appraisals of Proustian intertextuality in *La Bataille de Pharsale* remain those by Van Rossum-Guyon (1971, pp. 71-92) and Birn (1977, pp. 168-86). The former pinpoints and identifies the quotations; the latter studies their significance for the development of Simon as writer. Later in this chapter, I shall discuss my own contribution, which is connected with the description of the fish on the plate at Balbec. Van Rossum-Guyon concentrates mainly on the Proustian structures from Part One of *La Bataille de Pharsale* relegating to a footnote other quotations, names, and allusions also present in the text (which Birn picks up and expands). Van Rossum-Guyon investigates four quotations in detail: the 'raidillon aux aubépines' for its thematic denaturation from the Proustian context and re-usage as intensifier of sexual themes centring round 'raidi' and 'pine'; 'coiffées de hauts turbans cylindriques' as a generator of multiplying associations in Simon of 'casque' and 'coiffé'; 'je souffrais comme', which becomes synonymous with the way imagination, love and jealousy deform reality—this critic considers Simon's use of this phrase to signal emotions of despair, and the confrontation of love (sex), time and death in the repeated action of love-making; and fourth, 'altérés en leur matière même', as a trace of psychological change in Proust, but one which Simon translates into non-progressive, achronological repetition of action, thus rejecting psychological characterization and the focus on the single 'cellule', and recognizing the equivalence of all fragments. Peyroux, without acknowledging Van Rossum-Guyon's study, lumps these together as Simon's engagement with Proust to extract his own metaphor which 'renvoie à ses obsessions: l'érotisme' (1987, p. 30). She then castigates Simon for his impoverishment of the suggestive and understated in Proust by his 'débauche' to conclude that 'Déclarer que Claude Simon et Proust sont proches parents pour leur type d'écriture semble donc une affirmation hâtive... Il faut faire table rase de prétendues analogies, de légendes fragiles, fruits de l'ignorance et de la flatterie calculée' (ibid.). Van Rossum-Guyon's analyses of the Proustian borrowings within Simon's new context demolish these counter claims while also showing where Simon departs from Proust. His chronology of events, and the subjective time of memory reorganizing the past, are replaced by a non-unified, fictional time which is a refusal of unified reconstitution. The equivalence and reversibility of elements become, in Simon, the substitute for the hierarchy of signs in Proust. Van Rossum-Guyon sees in the fragments Simon has chosen to rework in *La Bataille de Pharsale* an alternative structure for his own novel which she summarises as a 'une nouvelle lecture de Proust' (1971, p. 91). *La Bataille de Pharsale* through Proust gains universal dimensions as 'l'apprentissage qui n'a rien de scolaire puisqu'il est celui de la vie même et de la mort' (ibid., p. 73).

Birn expands study of these four quotations in her article, adding other traces she has noticed: the woman wearing the kimono is like Odette or Albertine, the old machine is like La Berma as abandoned prima donna and the end of the second part of Simon's novel strikes chords with Marcel's watching of the sunset from the train. Birn concentrates her attention on interpretation of Simon's uses of Proust to conclude that the final outcome is Simon's rejection of *A la recherche* as model of the quest novel (1977, pp. 170-1). She focusses on two areas: the sense of filial guilt in the text, the jealousy and mental anguish in the desire to know; and the failure of erotic fulfilment which cannot be worked out through art. She claims that suffering and questing are useless, and therefore a search for form, not deeper knowledge through art, is the only way forward for art itself. In addition, she believes that psychological probing is not a fruitful path for the modern novel and that novelists of this type are relegated to the past (ibid. p. 181).

While these two critics' insights are invaluable, both have over-emphasised the psychological/erotic connotations of the Proust quotations and concentrated too much attention to the first two parts of *La Bataille de Pharsale*. For me, both critics miss the point by largely neglecting part three: what the Proustian quotations show is the 'apprentissage' of the writer on other writings. Writing, and composition itself, are the deep structure they reveal. My reading does not contradict the (correct) interpretations of Van Rossum-Guyon concerning the broken combine-harvester as a cameo of the fragmentation of Proust's text, or Birn's insight that the graffito 'Marcel' on the toilet wall represents the smear of Proust's influence, whose eradication is the only way in which Simon's personal development will take place. Both of these perceptions fit neatly into my reading of *La Bataille de Pharsale* as metaphor of writing in composition and decomposition, the movement of practising ('apprentissage') on Proust becoming practice ('tissage') in the new text. Therefore, my study of the Proustian quotations will attempt to avoid reading *into* the themes signified (as Simon's interview comments on Proust would endorse), and instead study the *place* of the quotations within the new composition which *replaces* them.

Counter to Van Rossum-Guyon's refusal to classify the quotations in their context in Proust, considering this order to be 'très sécondaire, sinon absolument sans importance puisqu'il s'agit d'une composition spatiale et non temporelle' (p. 78), my argument is that they map the composition of Simon's novel as battleground of texts. Their place or repetition in Simon's text is vitally important, and warning is given directly to the reader from the outset that the *process* of writing is the action of the text signalled overtly by the first instance of non-roman script: 'mais peut-être as-tu raison après tout tout savoir ne débouche jamais que sur un autre savoir et *les mots sur d'autres mots*' (p. 18). Although the direct context is 'discussion' between oncle Charles and the narrator-reader of the dead Latin texts, this comment is relevant to a reading of all the intertexts and particularly Proust. Thus heralded, the first Proustian quotations are introduced by the focus on their *place* in the text:

> Disant que la jalousie est comme... comme...
>
> Me rappelant l'endroit: environ dans le premier tiers en haut d'une page de droite. Pouvais ainsi réciter des tartines de vers pourvu que je réussisse à me figurer la page et où dans la page (p. 19).

Furthermore, and contrary to Van Rossum-Guyon's interpretation, these 'tartines de vers' which follow, the fragments from Proust, *have nothing to do with jealousy*:

> coiffées de hauts turbans cylindriques chaussaient des lanières rappelant les cothurnes selon Talma ou de hautes guêtres
>
> avant que l'Allemagne ait été réduite au même morcellement qu'au Moyen Age la déchéance de la maison de Hohenzollern prononcée et
>
> une certaine migraine certains asthmes nerveux qui perdent leur force quand on vieillit. Et l'effroi de s'ennuyer sans doute
>
> sur d'impalpables ténèbres comme une projection purement lumineuse comme une apparition sans consistance et la femme qu'en levant les yeux bien haut on distinguait dans cette pénombre dorée
>
> pas seulement les coiffures surmontant les visages de leurs étranges cylindres
>
> arrêter un instant ses yeux devant les vitrines illuminées je souffrais comme (p. 20 and *ALR*, III, pp. 723, 728, 730, 737, 725, 735).

What they do display, however, is the chronological *skim-reading* of *Le Temps retrouvé* by the narrator, who is recalling Proust in order to borrow a definition *for his own use.* He can vizualize the *place*: the 'reprise' in his search (at fragment five) indicates this.

The irony of the whole venture is that the word 'jealousy' does occur in the top third of a right-hand page, but *before* these detailed fragments (*ALR*, III, p. 705). Does this underline the abortiveness of any attempt to couch personal experience in the exact words of another writer and the reason why the 'comme... comme' is left open? At the very least, it underscores the inappropriateness of delving (as Birn 1977, pp. 174-5 and Van Rossum-Guyon 1971, pp. 85-90) into the theme of jealousy in Simon's narrator. Both critics digress into speculations on jealousy and anguish because they take this leitmotif purely as a thematic and psychological signpost. In my reading, however, this phrase must be treated as a fragment of the same status as the others: it is integrated with the other quotations, not singled out for special 'psychological' significance. It actually comments indirectly on such readings, for the simile (like that of the search for a definition of jealousy) is never completed. Simon is not rejecting outright the theme of jealousy in *La Bataille de Pharsale,* but redefining it *in his own terms*: the trigger word 'jalousie' stands for the whole Proustian intertextual enterprise in the novel, what I see as the 'anxiety of influence'. There are also scenes portraying a jealous lover, and in Part Two of the novel occurs a veiled reference to Françoise's deciphering of Albertine's gold and ruby ring for the jealous Marcel (p. 123 and *ALR,* III, pp. 165, 463-5). However, it would seem appropriate in the context clearly signalled above not to read jealous motives into the narrator within the novel but into the jealousy of the writer, Simon, regarding the status of his 'father', Proust. This jealousy and its extent are necessarily indefinable overtly: it is the text itself which brings them to light.

Elsewhere, other potentially psychological phrases taken from Proust are divested of their old implications. Simon's reusage of 'je souffrais comme', for example, is made non-psychological again through its new context: the phrase follows a description of clouds (p. 40). Later, the suffering is connected to *war* experience (p. 73). Printed in italics, Proust's phrase is further rejected by its emergence in the *negative*: 'Je ne souffrais pas'. Thus the Simonian voice challenges Proust's by parodically varying the precursor's words. Again, the suffering perhaps has more to do with the 'anxiety of influence' for the struggle with Proust is not quite over: '...*ne souffrais pas*' (p. 75). Without a subject, grammatically or thematically, the independent writer is not fully present or secure. The context indicates that it is the Simonian 'je' who is speaking, but is not yet separate from Proust, whose voice re-emerges at the end of the same paragraph, the two writers then visibly locked in textual combat over the same sentence. However, with the increased space given by Simon to the *war* context, the 'je ne souffrais pas' recurs, with the 'je' now fully voiced (p. 104), to become completely independent (p. 117). By the end of Part Two, in the middle of a *bedroom* scene, the victory is complete: the 'je ne souffrais pas' is voiced, not in its earlier war context, but connected to love-making (p. 177), the original Proustian context, now defeated. Not surprisingly, then, there are *no* references to suffering in Part Three of the novel. Although Simon holds his writing open again to Proust references, no suffering of overriding influence is present, for

Simon is now using Proust for his own purposes, overwriting his forebear.

This *skim-reading* is further endorsed by the details chosen. Their singularity and adherence to the then fashion and times assert their uniqueness to Proust, but also their insignificance, both for Simon's narrator and within the massive thematic canvas of *A la recherche*. These fragments mark the specific point reached in Proust as remembered (recited) text. When re-sited together in this way by Simon, they show that his narrator is not attracted or engulfed by the storyline of the original.

Building on the last quotation, a further block appears, to fix the new point in the skim-reading (the fragments now grouped together, rather than being separate entities):

> *tissue seulement avec des pétales des poiriers en fleurs Et sur les places les divinités des fontaines publiques tenant en main un jet de glace... édicules Rambuteau s'appelaient des pistières Sans doute dans son enfance n'avait-il pas entendu l'o et cela lui était resté Il prononçait donc ce mot incorrectement mais* (p. 22 and *ALR*, III, pp. 736, 750).

The space between these quotations 'suppresses' Proust; the longer interval between them in their original context may also be seen to signify distance from the precursor. Simon's text is now literalizing the fragments in their ability merely to decorate ('tissue seulement'), or fix language ('jet de *glace*').

Use of Proust is therefore *indirect commentary* on what Simon is doing to *A la recherche* as intertext, indeed an intentional *travesty* of the original. Pronunciation ('Hohenzollern *prononcé*', above) becomes mispronunciation, as indicated by the absent 'o' in 'pistières'. The original is further debased in this block, for the focus is on urination, and parallels the graffito 'Marcel' on the toilet wall. Later, open vulgarization of Proust occurs to mock and deflate the measured language of the Proust: 'Sodome et Gonhorrée Page combien', after which comes a mangled version of the love between Swann and Odette which occurs in *Du côté du chez Swann* not *Le Temps retrouvé* where the main block of quotations occurred (pp. 178-9 and *ALR*, I, p. 276). Simon *chooses* to return to the earlier sections of Proust because his writing is in control.

The textual autonomy of Proust is further broken, as return to the initial marker, the first quotation, is now *fully integrated* typographically into Simon's writing, and changed slightly as *paraphrase* (p. 38). Mispronunciation of a given structure becomes pronunciation of a new structure. The context of the block from Proust again signals what is happening at an *intertextual* level: 'choses en *décomposition* comme un cadavre' (p. 38 [my emphasis]). Is Proust this 'cadavre'? This decomposition is imitated directly in the truncation of the reference to the 'pistières', which is used to introduce the next fragment from Proust:

> que nous appelions le raidillon aux aubépines et où vous prétendez que vous êtes tombé dans votre enfance amoureux de moi alors que je vous assure (p. 38 and *ALR*, III, p. 756).

The love declaration between Marcel and Gilberte, here, suffers the same gross deflation as the 'édicules Rambuteau', the continuation of the 'toilet' humour via the particles 'raidi' and 'pine'. Note also the implication of *fixing* old language in the former. The context in Proust for this quotation is 'la bataille de Méséglise'. Are we then to infer that the battle of writers is reaching crisis-point?

Near the end of the first part of *La Bataille de Pharsale*, familiar patterns are repeated, but differences thereby become more visible. There is no recall of the page, or trigger of 'jalousie', however, only 'puis de nouveau *le* livre' (p. 84 [my emphasis]). Now only one major book absorbs the narrator-reader, Proust. Interest is focussed on the image of the *broken* combine-harvester, which is 'sur les bricoles', and introduces material from Proust as resource of 'bricolage' for Simon's text. The 'raidillon' reference is requoted to pick up the thread before new material is added, but this time it is interspersed by Simon's text, which thus distances segments of Proust from each other:

> *avec Albertine n'avaient été que des querelles particulières n'intéressant que la vie de cette petite cellule particulière qu'est un être Mais qu'il est des corps animaux* (p. 85 and *ALR* III, p. 771 ['cellule *spirituelle*' in the original]).

The particular love quarrels of Proust's characters are past, unrelated to the emotions of the present narrator. However, the quarrel between Proust as the 'cellule particulière' and Simon's writing continues. The narrator breaks off the precursor's words before their enormity overwhelms him: these 'corps d'animaux' are 'assemblages de cellules dont chacun par rapport à une seule est grand comme le mont Blanc'. A break with this threat is required, embodied in his gaze which moves from Proust's novel to contemplate the woman opposite him in the carriage, also reading, but a different novel. This further *particularizes* and reduces Proust, for his text is only one among many. Difference from Proust is then asserted through 'pas une moissonneuse dans le raidillon', the negative again inferring *not Proust* (p. 85). The 'raidillon' is associated not with love, but with conflict.

Part One of the novel ends with a block of Proustian references, which repeat the pattern established, but with variations. Jealousy, as word not emotion, is displaced ('où donc'), then the page in Proust noted as usual. 'Tissue seulement' introduces two new quotations; the word 'divorce' is singled out:

> entendu dire me demanda-t-il en me quittant que ma tante Oriane divorcerait Personnellement je
>
> une gradation verticale de bleus glaciers Et les tours du Trocadéro qui semblaient si proches des degrès turquoise (p. 90 and *ALR,* III, pp. 738, 762).

Oriane's divorce as event is not the issue; the divorce from Proust as forebear is, to *Orion,* fixed in Simon's own writing and new context several pages later, the Proustian 'jet de glace' and 'bleus glaciers' transformed: 'cet Orion titubait en aveugle sur les monumentales assises de ses pieds rougis par le *froid glacial du ciment'* (p. 140). Oriane (Proust) turns into Simon's Orion through the intervening passage of an exerpt from Apuleus's *Golden Ass.* Petrification of Proust's language and influence over Simon's narrator is also visible in the new material they are presented and updated in, cement. Thus, it seems that while the themes and characters in Proust, even his language, have no power over him, Proust's associative style and use of detail continue to hold his attention, without stultifying him.

In Part Two of *La Bataille de Pharsale,* the rereading of *A la recherche* unfolds, but the pre-text is transformed by Simon's reusage: 'car chez les duchesses c'est pour les roturiers un peu poètes *le nom qui diffère* mais elles s'expriment selon la catégorie d'esprit à laquelle elles appartiennent' (p. 158 and *ALR,* III, p. 733 [my emphasis]). Simon now rewrites and overwrites the application of Proust's original words. Another example is Simon's re-shaping of Proust's 'étranges cylindres': 'allant en s'évasant, c'est-à-dire cylindre *au départ,* autour du front, puis coniques' (p. 104 and *ALR,* III, p. 723 [my emphasis]). Here, the physical shape of Proust's image is first introduced before being distorted by its remodelling, then paraphrased: 'les coiffures aux *formes* extravagantes' (p. 154

[my emphasis]) until, finally, being ridiculed by verbal rearrangement (p. 155). The *Proustian* trope is thus locked in its historical singularity through its new, devisive and derisory Simonian context. By tampering with the linguistic components through parody, Simon shows increased distance from the influence of his forebear. This is further underscored by the repeated search to define jealousy: it too is over, '*pas* page de droite' (p. 168). The Proust quotation which follows is the passage previously mangled, concerning Swann's jealousy of Odette (*ALR*, I, p. 276). The termination and obliteration of personal involvement with the sentiments of Proust (Marcel's jealousy over Albertine) are restated at the end of Part Two (p. 169 and *ALR*, III, p. 518), but in a passage *outside* the main intertextual area used previously in *La Bataille de Pharsale*. Intertextual plundering from the precursor is now free of the 'anxiety of influence' for the control and purpose is utterly Simon's and not Proust's. This is further underlined by the truncated 'raidillon aux aubépines où vous prétendez que' (p. 181). Proust has no *claim* on Simon's language now: the narrator is totally distanced from the words and the feelings they imply: 'ça doit être vite fait *On* ne doit pas souffrir longtemps' (p. 181 [my emphasis]). Through the different perspective ('On'), the suffering of the 'anxiety of influence' has been overcome.

In Part Three, O writes a card and a letter to Odette Pa (pp. 191-2) and, possibly due to the overlap of the name Odette with Proust's text, he is unable to send either. The fate of these writings is complete destruction. The first is torn up and put down the lavatory in the train (note the ironic connections here with the graffito 'Marcel'). In the second instance, the card is torn up and put in the ashtray. This action mirrors the tearing up of *A la recherche* within *La Bataille de Pharsale*.

Van Rossum-Guyon asserts that Proust has been expunged from O's writing by Part Three, but this is an erroneous reading. Several large chunks appear, triggered by

> O feuillette un livre *à la recherche* d'une phrase dont il croit se rappeler qu'elle se trouvait dans le haut d'une page, à droite. Il lit quelque lignes. Ce ne sont pas celles qu'il cherche. Il est parfois entraîné par sa lecture plus qu'il n'est nécessaire. Mais il l'interrompt, tourne la page et lit de nouveau (pp. 203-4 [my emphasis]).

The fragments in this section are descriptions from *Le Temps retrouvé* ('le ciel... vertige', p. 762; 'grands hôtels... perles qui', p.

759; 'une gradation... turquoise', p. 762; and 'n'avait été... animaux', p. 771) and represent the reading of the mature writer who is able to break off and remain separate from Proust at will and turn over a new page. He is aware that he is still at a precarious point, in danger of being sucked in by the power of the forebear, but is strong enough himself to pursue a rereading of the text. The repetition of reading the same section as the reader-narrator of Part One disengages O from him. The familiar 'une certaine migraine' marks the starting point for a new chronological sequence of fragments, but the quotations O picks out from Proust centre on events of the First World War: the sinking of the Lusitania, Belgian neutrality, Lenin, conscription, aeroplanes and room 43 in billets (pp. 204-5 and *ALR*, III, 'reprit son... besoin de', pp. 772-3; 'toujours... chez eux', p. 776; 'ce régent... l'est de', p. 779; 'parents qui... hommes qu'ils', p. 780; and 'encre... telles que', p. 790). The battle with Proust is over—fragments from *A la recherche* end on p. 206 (*ALR*, III, 'tous les... répétait que', p. 794; 'plus obscure... consolant pour', p. 800; 'projecteurs... aéroplanes', p. 801; 'tandis qu'il... probablement', p. 808; and 'Le 43... fumée ici', p. 812)—and can be used as specific cultural references to wars on a par with the other Latin intertexts on the theme of war. These are manipulated to fit into O's structure, this interweaving then diminishing the importance of 'le livre' within the overall collage of related intertexts, because Proust is being cited for elements which are *peripheral* to the intent of the original text. O now fills the blank page before him with the first line of the novel we have just been reading, a tongue-in-cheek glance at Proust, but the product is very different from *A la recheche*. The intertext is reduced, as before, to a physical non-literary object on his desk: the card portraying a trumpeter (herald of Simon?) whose forehead is described as being cut off by 'une haute coiffure... d'une forme bizarre et d'une hauteur démesurée, commençant d'abord en cylindre et s'évasant ensuite en tronc de cône renversé' (p. 269). Caricature of his forebear could hardly be better matched, for Simon has reduced the weight of influence of Proust to a thin, two-dimensional clown figure. The axe he holds is also ironically of the same blue ('bleu glacier') associated with the Proustian quotations, the intertextual 'souffleur' and prompter of writing silenced once and for all.

The termination of Proust, chronologically, is the epigraph quotation to Part Two, the pivotal point of the novel. Both Birn and Van Rossum-Guyon note the central location of this, but fail to comment further in their articles (1977, p. 175 and 1971, p. 83, respectively). References from Proust in Part Three all come *before* it, so it represents the culmination point of Proust for Simon, marking the breakpoint with the precursor and the springboard for his individual writing:

> Je fixais avec attention devant mon esprit quelque image qui m'avait forcé à la regarder, un nuage, un triangle, un clocher, une fleur, un caillou, en sentant qu'il y avait peut-être sous ces signes quelque chose de tout autre que je devais tâcher de découvrir, une pensée qu'ils traduisaient à la façon de ces caractères hiéroglyphiques qu'on croirait représenter seulement des objets matériels (p. 99 and *ALR*, III, p. 878).

The privileged status of the epigraph and its place have already been displayed in Simon's interviews, the words being used to exemplify Proust's stylistic genius. Its reusage in this novel, concerned essentially with the emergence of new writing, is doubly significant. Separated, intact and acknowledged as epigraph, Simon treats it again as a paradigm, and likens his own efforts to what it signifies (the privileged position of detail in description, and its function as structuring principle). However, if our reading of all the Proustian quotations as commentary on Simon's emerging writing is to be consistent, then this epigraph must also yield comment from within itself, and suffer distortion as a result of being re-employed in a totally 'un-Proustian' way. Appearing in the middle and not introducing the last section of the novel, it has a dual function: not only does it act as a kind of epilogue to all the Proustian references in the text, summing up the apotheosis of *Le Temps retrouvé* for Simon, it also dissolves as intertextual force upon him. Metaphorically speaking, Simon has had to reach the end of Proust's novel before being able to start out on his own. This is perhaps why the preponderance of references from Proust in *La Bataille de Pharsale* are from *Le Temps retrouvé*, an intertext not found in any other Simon novel.

The Proustian 'je fixais' is in fact itself fixed into a block of text, an object, without any *thematic* influence. Consequently, it is from this object, broken up, that creation can occur. Detail and the importance of individual objects are now to take precedence in the ensuing text. The message to the reader of *La Bataille de Pharsale* is that we are to focus attention on the individual words of the epigraph itself—'nuage', 'triangle', 'clocher', 'fleur' and 'caillou'—within their Simonian context, broken free of the bounds of Proust as a storehouse of new signification.

We have seen how fragmentation of Proust occurred as re-sited sentence. Through a fixing and reformulation of nouns from Proust's lexicon in Part Three of *La Bataille de Pharsale* (as Ricardou's close study of the words of the Valéry epigraph as generators in this novel illustrated the linguistic reverberations and the necessity to read details closely (1970, pp. 118-58)), fragmentation and distortion are also visible at the level of the individual word. The first section focusses on 'nuage'; this description not only re-writes Proust within Simon's context, but also joins his epigraph to the epigraph of the whole novel, the stanza from Valéry, 'Achille immobile à grands pas'. Here, Zeno's paradox of Achilles and the tortoise (movement leads to a constant, unchanged state) is reformulated in the formations of these clouds. The superimposition of Proust and Valéry is masterful, and demonstrates the density of Simon's emerging writing and its capacity to manipulate and combine the writing of others. Simon's clouds become first a simile and then a metaphor to emphasize their potential to engender description (pp. 104 and 110 respectively).

The second section, 'César', is a parodic exploration of 'clocher' by the mockery of religious imagery. The narrator is with his grandmother in Lourdes (a little like Marcel arriving in Balbec with his grandmother). The hieroglyphic function of an object is also parodied, as Simon secularizes highly charged religious and material symbols in the grandmother's necklace, which combines hieroglyphs from several registers, thus preventing 'depths' of significance being attached to any: 'quelques médailles, une croix d'or et ce cœur... en or et serti de rubis' (p. 123). This leads to speculation on and rejection of depths of significance (p. 125) in a manner not unlike that of Marcel, who eventually rejects the cryptic potential of objects, but not, as does Simon's narrator, a heightened, 'religious' significance to experience.

Section three, 'Conversation', sets out 'triangle' first as a frame of vision, and then as a formal composition, the legs of the artist's easel (pp. 128 and 131 respectively). By extension, the idea of threes emerges set within the context of a trite conversation between the artist's model and the narrator, the artist himself being absent. The abstract concept, triangle, also shapes *La Bataille de Pharsale,* which is tripartite in form.

'Guerrier', the fourth section, explores 'caillou', and plays with the idea of matter, not abstract geometric shapes. Materiality is not just limited to stone, but remodelled comically as concrete as well:

the fighter 'adhérant au ciment comme des ventouses' (p. 135) and his eyes are 'durs et fixes comme des morceaux de verre' (p. 137). This links back to the epigraph, 'je fixais' itself and forward to the Orion reference already quoted (p. 140).

The next section, 'Machine', takes up the image 'fleur', parodically as it is not living, but made of metal. The description of the combine harvester transposes Proustian imagery, its '*tiges* et barres de fer s'entrecroisent' (p. 148) into the mechanical through verbal intertwinings, the driving seat being

> un siège métallique en forme de feuille de nénuphar... De l'autre côté de la machine... une tige horizontale projette très à l'extérieure de l'ensemble un autre trident... faisant penser à l'une de ces fleurs appelées ombelles et dont il ne resterait plus que la tige affaissée et quelques-uns des pédonculés de la couronne, sans fleurs, et cassées (p. 149).

The section 'Voyage' is the last confrontation of Simon's narrator-writer with Proust (and indeed with the other intertexts summarized here) before he becomes the independent writer, O. Proust is almost doubly important, for a description of his photographic image is included (fixed) alongside his prose (p. 158). The 'message' of this section, however, is that intertexts are all of equal status in the conglomeration of materials they represent as potential components in new writing. 'O', the last section of Part Two, is a zero point, the start for the independent writer. Influence and its anxiety have been left behind by the metaphorical journey of development. O is now in charge of his own fictional space-time, not dominated by those of the past. *A la recherche* has been plundered as intertext and as word-field to generate Simon's text. Details are lent new Simonian associations and are combined in new relationships.

However removed Simon now is from Proust's language, one major question of influence remains, the use of association itself as a textual generator. Has Simon broken with this also? The epigraph to the third part of the novel serves partly as an answer. Heidegger's words provide a key to the new 'Chronologie des Événements' which is the textual and fictional time of O's writing, beyond former historical times and events in the previous intertexts. This epigraph sums up the activity of O upon the Proustian text, as broken machine to be plundered for its parts, but unable to operate in its former state (*A la recherche* is suggested to be redundant). However, the *words* of this epigraph mirror those of Proust's; but the variations display the differences of each as separate entities. I have juxtaposed both, to demonstrate the central mechanism of the generative power of the word (Proust's voice is in square brackets):

> Un outil apparaît endommagé, des matériaux apparaissent inadéquats... C'est dans ce découvrement de l'inutilisable que soudain l'outil s'impose à l'attention [Je fixais avec attention]... Le système de renvois où s'insèrent les outils ne s'éclaire pas comme un quelque chose qui n'aurait jamais été vu, mais comme un tout qui, d'avance et toujours, s'offrait au regard [m'avait forcé à la regarder... quelque chose de tout autre que je devais tâcher de découvrir]. Or, avec ce tout, c'est le monde qui s'annonce [une pensée qu'ils traduisent à la façon de ces caractères hiéroglyphiques qu'on croirait représenter seulement des objets matériels].

Perhaps Simon's 'monde qui s'annonce' is generated by means of association and juxtaposition rather than by Proust's use of layers of association which imply significance and depths of meaning. The principle of construction and association, however, remains. Its differing emphases mark the rejection of direct Proustian influence, but admit a fundamental mode of fictional creation which Simon shares with Proust.

I now return to the allusions to the fish which I identified at the beginning of this chapter. It recurs, transformed but no less significant, appearing in all three parts of *La Bataille de Pharsale* (pp. 57, 161-2, 177, 269). The attentive reader will have become aware that all the major excerpts from Proust studied so far in Simon's novels are matched by those allusions Simon chose as paradigms in his articles, except the Balbec fish. I suggest its relevance here; for like the broken harvester this image, by analogy, stands for *A la recherche* as intertext broken free of its parent, but still usable in *La Bataille de Pharsale* in a different form.

Invitation to compare the fish and Proust comes when the narrator hurts his hand in rage against a closed door:

> poing qui avait frappé quelque chose de cassé peut-être petits os métacarpe squelette de poisson ou de ces nageoires de mammifères marins (p. 57).

In Part Two of the novel, the reference highlights the 'Cimmérien' qualities of the Balbec fish and the levels of time it represents, especially here as it has 'arêtes de *basalte*' (p. 161). The fish motif is reiterated in the same context as in Part One (the jealous lover): not only has the Proustian whole been broken, but the influence and emotional attachments have also been rejected. The final appearance of the trope is at the end of the novel, where the word 'cimier', the crest on the helmet of the postcard trumpeter, is likened to the fin of a fish (p. 269). This word 'cimier' again links with 'Cimmérien', Proust and all the intertextual implications of the trumpeter already discussed. Although direct influence of Proustian description has passed (seen in the form of the card), indebtedness to Proust is perhaps being obliquely recognised through the rewriting of it into Simon's text. This is further reinforced by the pun on 'cimier' and 'cimetière'. I do not wish to over-read, but, just as O begins to write at the end of the novel the first line of the text that we have been reading, so the 'mammifère marin', this fish from Proust, can also be linked back to the epigraph at the beginning of *La Bataille de Pharsale*, the stanza from Valéry's *Cimetière MARIN,* 'Achille immobile à grands pas', which signifies revolution round a fixed point and, by extension, the circularity of the text. The message is that developing writing through intertexts in the hands of a skilful writer yields multiple reverberations for the reader who fixes his attention on the details of the text.

*****

The reworking of Proust's lexicon in Part Two of *La Bataille de Pharsale* released Simon from the influence of his precursor's language and much of his structuring technique, except certain kinds of association which may include intertextual references of the kind found in Part Three, the First World War quotations from Proust. Independence of style and form are clearly apparent demonstrating the indisputable overcoming of former 'anxiety of influence'. Yet the positive family resemblance remains through such independence: association purged of the specifically Proustian is the endowment which Simon inherits and develops. Indeed, it is this associativeness of language which is the hallmark of Simon's 'third cycle', which includes *Orion aveugle, Les Corps conducteurs, Triptyque,* and *Leçon de choses*. Here, although *no* references to Proust appear, the Proustian lexical density of association is clearly visible. With *Les Géorgiques,* Simon opens his work again to the themes and considerations of *La Bataille de Pharsale* (that is, to a more 'Proustian' kind of novel in its length and sustained association building); and thus avoids a potentially sterile solitude in the formalistic interplay and *mises en abyme* of language and self-referential representation of the third cycle. The boy narrator of *La*

Bataille de Pharsale re-emerges to translate Latin for uncle Charles, and goes to the opera with his grandmother (a glance at Marcel and his experience of hearing La Berma), but it is obvious that Simon's strength is such that Proust has no hold over the shape of the novel: these traces sit alongside other intertexts and hark back as much to *La Bataille de Pharsale* as to Proust.

The extent of Proustian influence and dominance, then, can be endorsed as paradigmatic in Simon's interviews and articles which, in turn, shed light on Proustian intertexts in his novels. These, on the contrary, illustrate Simon's questioning of, and break with, his literary 'father', visible through increasing caricature, distortion and parody. The theory and hallmarks of Bloom's 'anxiety of influence'—manipulation, extension and pastiching of his progenitor's themes, characters, and adumbrations of language and structures—shed light on what constitutes Simon's individual style and ways of combining language associatively after the battle of writings is over. Simon's direct, French, lineage from Proust and the Proustian novel is also beyond doubt. Furthermore, I argue that it is through detailed study of Simon's intertextual relationship with Proust that his development as a writer can be plotted. Many critics have remarked on the very different (inferior) nature of the 'third cycle', commencing with *Orion aveugle,* and then the seeming return to old patterns with *Les Géorgiques* (see Britton, 1987, p. 15). Instead of seeing these as two separate and unrelated stages in Simon's development, a 'continuum' reading is also feasible, association then being the thread which links together the two phases. With *Les Géorgiques* and *L'Acacia,* it is Simon's own, post-Proustian, use of association, intertextual and intratextual reverberation which separates him irrevocably from his literary 'father'. The patterns to be emulated, as the boy-translator's copies from uncle Charles, are discarded when literary adulthood is reached. It is in the mature writings from *La Bataille de Pharsale* onwards that Simon's style can thus be said to be authentic, sufficiently individual and autonomous to be copied in its own turn.

Chapter Six

Twentieth-Century Literature

The intensive and single focus which was the hereditary relationship between Proust and Simon is unique in his work, but not singular in terms of his reliance on important novelist precursors. The area of particular concern in this chapter is Simon's varied and extensive employment of twentieth-century intertexts although many of the *issues* that will emerge find reverberations in previous discussion. A second circuit round familiar yet divergent territories opens out proper investigation of the intertextual scope of Simon's *œuvre*. Crucial though layers of influence and revision of French tradition is to the poetic development of his work, the literary edifice he builds depends also on the dynamic of the other, the not-French. To this end, Genette's concept of the intertext as participant in an 'architexte' provides a theoretical frame for the chapter:

> L'objet de la poétique... n'est pas le texte, considéré dans sa singularité..., mais l'*architexte*, ou si l'on préfère l'architextualité du texte..., c'est-à-dire l'ensemble des catégories générales, ou transcendantes—types de discours, modes d'énonciation, genres littéraires etc.—dont relève chaque texte singulier (Genette, 1982, p. 7).

In its totalising capacity, the 'architexte' thus encompasses all languages, cultures, discourses, and structures of rhetoric outside a national identity, and is also larger than any of the three main genres (lyric, epic or dramatic). Such circumscription pertains to Kristeva's definition of 'Texte'. The difference of emphasis here is that the paraliterary dimensions discussed in the third chapter will be displaced by the interliterary. Laurent Jenny formulates this central, international, aspect of intertextual activity in terms of 'archétypes':

> on ne saisit le sens et la structure d'une œuvre littéraire que dans son rapport des archétypes, eux-mêmes abstraits de longues séries de textes dont ils sont en quelque sorte l'invariant... Vis-à-vis des modèles archétypiques, l'œuvre littéraire entre toujours dans un rapport de réalisation, de transformation ou de transgression (1976, p. 257).

In the closing stages of his article, Jenny emphasizes the ideological implications of these now familiar modes of intertextual interaction by stressing their literary universalities 'comme détournement culturel', 'comme réactivation du sens', 'comme miroir des sujets'. Such considerations underscore the *contextuality* of the new writing and its intertext as foreign and signalling itself as such. Simon's tribute to writers of international repute and to the distinctly literary innovations they represent are the overarching heritage within which he also works. Any reading of his interviews yields a host of foreign writing to which he ascribes innovatory power—Borges, Beckett, Hemingway, Conrad, to name but a few. The concept of the 'architexte' I wish to pursue, then, in this chapter is avant-garde writing. The chapter will ultimately raise the question where Simon stands in relation to this umbrella category. *En route,* the chapter will assess the 'archétype' of revolutionary literature as thematic genre. The first part of this chapter will therefore focus on twentieth-century foreign revolutions *of* the novel, and in particular the formal contributions of Faulkner and Joyce, to shed light on the changes these provoked in Simon's practice. Simon, in fact, sees revolution of both form and content as essential to the process of writing. The epigraph he chose for *Le Palace*: 'Révolution: Mouvement d'un mobile qui, parcourant une courbe fermée, repasse successivement par les mêmes points' epitomises the importance ascribed to this subject. Simon also quotes Maïakovski to make his point as theory of the novel: 'il n'y a pas d'art révolutionnaire sans forme révolutionnaire' (Simon, 1963, p. 26). Thus the second part of the chapter will consider revolutions *in* the novel. Simon writes overtly political novels and his use of intertexts concerning war and revolution—from Reed and Orwell—is an important means, for him, of 'universalizing' experience and social 'message'. 'Message', here, by being denationalised, ceases to be a *particular* message or 'propagandist' statement, to both of which Simon shows much antipathy. Simon's use of such intertexts also presents the formal problems of recording 'action' and 'activism' in literature. They reflect revolutionary writings and reflect upon them. This chapter, then, raises questions for specifically intertextual innovation and repetition and will ask how Simon's usage makes him a revolutionary of writing practice.

Revolutionaries of the novel

Simon and Faulkner

Of all the twentieth-century writers who have been compared to Simon, critics cite William Faulkner most frequently as a major influence, or inspiration for stylistic or linguistic devices, the non-French equivalent of Proust as it were (See Amette, 1971, p. 101). Other critics have pinpointed various 'Faulknerian' themes in Simon such as memory (Chapsal, 1957, p. 29) or the 'Faulknerian' confusion of time and chronology (Nadeau, 1957, pp. 17-18). Simon himself is no less averse to quoting Faulkner as one of his major precursors (for example Knapp, 1969, p. 180). While Simon's reading of Faulkner opened his eyes to a different kind of writing, and although, unlike his immediate attraction to Proust, his learning to like Faulkner was a more gradual process (Bourin, 1960, p. 4), yet Faulkner's writing appealed to Simon for exactly the same reasons as did Proust's: the highly sensorial qualities of the prose, 'tout ce qui me donne beaucoup à voir, à toucher, à sentir, à entendre' (Chapsal, 1963, p. 169). Simon's admiration for Faulkner is not, however, uncritical. The general appeal of this American writer is contrasted with those Faulknerian 'quirks' which run contrary to Simon's views on writing and will now be familiar after our study of nineteenth-century French novelists. Simon objects to the parabolic element in Faulkner's fiction, his use of 'grands mots' ('la justice', 'le devoir', 'le courage', 'l'amour') and the pursuit of 'message' or 'moral' behind the fiction (Simon, mars 1967, p. V) as well as grandiloquent titles (Moncelet, 1972, p. 207). Descriptions are however worthy of imitation and are thus quoted like the Balbec fish *ad infinitum.* A passage from *The Sound and the Fury* to demonstrate the associative play of the English used as well as the economy and verbal density of Faulkner's prose becomes Simon's *pièce de résistance:*

> a man in a dirty apron came to the door and emptied a pan of dishwater with a broad gesture, the sunlight glinting on the metal belly of the pan, then entered the car again (Simon, 1978, pp. 87-8. See *The Sound and the Fury* (Penguin, 1970) p. 273. .

The language, as Proust's, thus seeks to enmesh the transitory, the sensory, the irrational. This mastery of allusive description, word-coinage and name reverberation (as the personal significance Benjy attaches to the name 'Caddy' in Simon, New York, 1982, p. 20) epitomize, for Simon, Faulkner's 'génie d'écrivain', which is contrasted again with his 'sottises d'écrivant (pour employer la terminologie de Barthes) les messages "ésotériques"... puritains et moralisateurs' (Poirson, 1982, p. 37).

The late forties and early fifties were a period of excited reception of Faulkner in France, and Simon was caught up in this enthusiasm. It is therefore not surprising that admiration will be transcribed into attributable 'Faulknerisms' in his early novels. In *Le Tricheur,* Duncan has noted the exploration of archetypal woman (exemplified by Caddy) in Simon's Belle (1973, p. 236). In *Gulliver,* Sykes sees in Herzog the epitomization of Faulkner's polar antithesis between men and women, in both their physical and mental make-ups. Herzog is a kind of Joe Christmas, initiated into the nature of women (*Light in August*) but an *old* man, and therefore the antithesis of Joe's youth. Such links posit only traces of influence, however, and are too isolated to prove it.

Le Sacre du printemps is more overtly Faulknerian, as many critics at the time of its publication and subsequently have stated. Blanzat even goes so far as to speak of Simon being overshadowed by Faulkner, both in the composition of the narrative (the two levels in the text) and in the style: 'abondant, insistant, pressé, chargé d'effets répétés, d'adjectifs triples, quadruplés' (Blanzat, 1954, p. 9). What Blanzat sees as a worse crime of plagiarism on Simon's part is the very substance of the novel, 'la façon de voir et de sentir'. Emulation and influence tip over into imitation of a non-creative kind. Edith has 'toute psychologie faulknérienne'; Josie, 'c'est la sauvage morale puritaine et aussi sa mythologie'. However, I would suggest that these moral, religious and psychological investigations are quite foreign to the mainspring of Simon's practice and therefore, when so blatantly present in this novel, are seen to point only to their Faulknerian origins. Although Blanzat does not classify this novel as an actual copy of Faulkner, Kanters does:

> Le malheur c'est que de l'ensemble Claude Simon a fait un pastiche ingénu de Faulkner. C'est plus clair, plus cartésien que *le Bruit et la Fureur* ou que *Absalon! Absalon!* soit: mais cet effort de vulgarisation était-il bien nécessaire? Symétries chronologiques, constante veulerie du langage intérieur, ellipses de la mémoire ou de l'association des idées, tous les poncifs du faulknérisme se retrouvent. Mais il y a chez Faulkner le plus souvent, un puissant effort de création, une poussée de sève... Cela est beaucoup moins sensible dans ce *Sacre*-ci: et les procédés du maître américain sont tellement particuliers qu'on finit par avoir

> l'impression pénible d'une histoire jetée dans un moule d'emprunt (1954, p. 121).

Again, I argue that while *Le Sacre* seems only a repetition of Faulknerian techniques, it is also a novel about adolescence, and not least the adolescence of the writer dependent on, but growing away from Faulkner, because his style and language are inimitable.

Fleeting parallels have also been drawn between Faulkner's writing and *Le Vent* (see, for example, Duffy, 1985, p. 8). Beyond these similarities, Sykes, in the second chapter of his thesis, likens Montès more overtly to Benjy, as a successor in the line of simple innocents. Duncan also likens Montès to Faulkner's character and sees him as a foil for the hierarchical and closed provincial society in which he lives, noting that the elemental dimension of his nature—man pitted against time, fate and Nature—gives Montès an archetypal role like that of the wind in the title of the novel. However, I refer the reader to Simon's comments on the subject in chapter five: Montès is in the mould of Dostoyevsky's *Idiot,* much more than remade in the form of Benjy, who, despite being disowned from his land, is not an active participant in society in the mould of Prince Myshkin and Montès.

More importantly, however, Duncan links *Le Vent* to Faulkner not just in terms of character and theme but also stylistically: the particular technique of reconstructing events from the past in a series of fragmented narratives. Simon comes closest to Faulkner in *Le Vent,* according to Duncan, adopting the latter's obsessive style of writing: 'The tortured syntax, the idiosyncrasies of style, the extravagant use of words conjure up in both cases worlds larger and more vivid than life. No single detail of these is unrealistic: Faulkner and Simon rarely portray anything but credible human experience in a recognizably real world: but they describe their worlds in such obsessively elaborate, such supernaturally vivid detail that their novels stand ultimately quite outside the realm of realistic writing' (1973, p. 250). While *Le Vent* is closest to Faulkner in the pitching of an anti-hero against the forces of society and the elements of nature, Simon in this novel is exorcising the 'psychological' hero and the narrative composed of multifarious viewpoints, and instead plants narrative firmly in the present. Therefore I see *Le Vent* as a pivot novel, balanced between pastiche of Faulkner and rejection of his stylistic techniques (such as several narratives and mouthpieces). Evidence of this is the extent and variety of non-Faulknerian material in the novel, for example references to Spanish drama we discussed in chapter two. There is also the question of the adoption of Faulkner's language, especially his word-coinage, which is hardly copied by Simon for obvious linguistic reasons. Proustian density of association and imagery, using already-existing words is always Simon's preferred option. Furthermore, Richard Howard, Simon's American translator, states categorically that through his work on Simon's language he can find no inherent Faulknerisms (1972, p. 163). This is one reason to explain why Simon eventually escapes the influence of Faulkner as a major precursor: he is free from the deep language patterns of his forebear. This level of influence is also a gauge to judge the extent of influence of Faulkner as opposed to Proust. The former's is much less entrenched, and thus Faulkner may be seen as a major, but not *the* major influence on Simon.

Simon is *not,* however, totally free from Faulkner until much later. In fact, he may be *more* indebted to him in *L'Herbe* and *La Route des Flandres* than in *Le Vent. L'Herbe* is to my mind the most Faulknerian of Simon's novels, both in its themes and technique. This novel has also yielded the greatest diversity of comparison with one or another of Faulkner's novels. Duncan likens it to *Absalom! Absalom!*, drawing parallels between the human fortitude of Rosie Coldfield and that of Simon's Marie (1973, p. 241). Hinkle's thesis (1971) analyses *L'Herbe* and *The Sound and the Fury*. He argues that the thematic structures in Faulkner dealing with modes of perception, the nature of time, values, and different means of controlling reality are also present in Simon. Faulkner's Dilsey embodies the convergence of these themes, as does Marie: both are selfless, timeless, impassive in theface of experience and willing to sacrifice themselves. Hinkle concludes, however, that the mystery of Simon's Marie is 'awesome in significance' and that all hierarchies of values in Simon's novel are levelled. 'Thus *L'Herbe* might be called the absurd novelist's answer to *The Sound and the Fury*'. In a curious piece of critical (intertextual!) plagiarism, Leonard, in an article called 'Simon's *L'Herbe*: Beyond Sound and Fury', repeats Hinkle's evaluations and even the conclusion just quoted (1976, p. 30). His only additions are remarks about the thematic overlappings of degeneration of a family, and about usage of the stream-of-consciousness narrative technique.

The novel which cries out for comparison with *L'Herbe* is, of course, *As I Lay Dying*. This parallel has been mentioned by Chapsal (1958, p. 25) indirectly: the title of her article is 'Tandis qu'*elle* agonise' [my emphasis]. As early as 1961, Isaacs saw the likeness of the two novels. Outlining the plot of *L'Herbe,* he states, '*The Grass* might well be called *As I Lay Dying*'. He then enumerates the similarities of technique—time shifts, interior monologue, association of ideas, dialogue in dialogue and dual or treble points of view. However, Isaacs stresses that in Simon

> there is neither the depth of perception nor the breadth of vision. The points of reference, which in Faulkner render everything manifoldly meaningful, are missing. Faulkner's people may be drab and dreary at times: but there is always the relationship to the author, almost always to the reader, invariably to Yoknapatawpha county, sometimes to the South, frequently to Man, and more often than realized, to God (1961, p. 432).

Isaacs considers that Simon and the other Nouveaux Romanciers read Faulkner too well, adopting the American novelist's techniques' and carrying them to extremes he never intended'.

Simon, in my opinion, 'remakes' *As I Lay Dying* to condense elements in Faulkner's prose which lie at the heart of his own practice, while at the same time *rejecting* the grandiose, the universal and the authorial commentary, those very elements which Isaacs sees as properly Faulkner's. My earlier comments on Simon's rejection and dislike of the grandiose in Faulkner in his interviews endorses this view. Simon chooses not to work his characters into a grand scheme, but to leave their relationships ambiguous and particular to each novel in which they (re)appear. I contend that, by making Marie a reworked Addie Bundren, Simon wants to stress neither shifting time nor narrative perspectives but the expression of *absence*. Neither Marie nor Addie can speak, but both are the overriding presence and voice in their respective novels (*As I Lay Dying* pp. 134-40). Even though Addie is dead, she still speaks through the unfolding of the narrative. In fact, the women speak more powerfully by their silence than the other characters who use words. The noise of the sawing as Addie's coffin is being made is a descriptive voice, which plots the progress of Addie's illness and demise and the passing of time more effectively (and affectively) than any explicit remark on the part of a character or the narrator. The same is true of the noise of the rotting pears dropping outside Marie's window and the wheeze of her death-rattle in *L'Herbe*. It is precisely the voice of comment and description from the non-person for which Simon is most indebted to Faulkner. Marie's rattle, her status as moribund, are comparable to Benjy's moanings as a simpleton in *The Sound and the Fury*. Paradoxically, these speakers, Benjy, Addie and Marie, all demand attention, not just from those characters around them but from the reader as well. So it is the *implicit* vocalization of time, decay, death and change through description which I consider Simon 'purloins' and guards from Faulkner as essential to his own purposes, and which he admires so much in Faulkner's descriptions: the capture of the indefinable in words—flashes of light, sensations, fleeting impressions, all that is elusive and present. It is therefore not so much the themes, characterization or stylistic tics which interest Simon: it is Faulkner's penetration of the inexpressible.

This is further exemplified in the speculation on death in *L'Herbe* and *As I Lay Dying*. Simon condenses Addie's death-throes into Marie's static death-rattle, but magnifies their significance by extending them throughout the whole of his novel. Thus, such major changes signal a break with Faulkner. It is from *L'Herbe* onwards that Simon's own style of narrative emerges. Simon needed Faulkner in his early novels to enable him to learn new fictional and descriptive techniques, but, these mastered and interiorized, Faulkner's influence is either stemmed or moulded in a completely different and recognizably Simonian way.

La Route des Flandres has also been classed as Faulknerian in style and compared to various Faulkner novels, the most common parallel being with *Absalom! Absalom!* Studies of the similarities between these novels have come to very different conclusions as to the importance of Faulkner's influence on Simon. Aarseth focusses on the structural and mythical similarities of the two novels and champions their universal dimension, that of painting a coherent, mythical landscape superimposed on a recognizably historical one: 'Instead of the myth of the South, represented in the Sutpen story, Simon is exploring the mythical shadows of the de Reixach family with its roots in the ancien régime. As in Faulkner's novel, the emphasis is not on the story itself, but on its genesis as myth, the meaning of the past subjected to the act of narration' (1982, p. 345). Weinstein, on the other hand, sees *La Route des Flandres* as Simon's last truly anthropocentric novel because the style is still in the service of its characters, and there is obvious Faulknerian rhetoric (treatment of the imagination, and use of the present participle). However, Weinstein stresses that in Simon disintegration is the principal theme, as against the inherent reordering which characterizes Faulkner's work: 'Simon's novel is the reverse image of *Absalom! Absalom!* ... it registers a failure of the imagination, an inability to believe in depth, penetration... The imaginative effort of Georges and Blum to create a story out of portraits is a brilliant—but pitiful—parody of the ritual of story-telling enacted by Quentin and Shreve' (1974, p. 242). Simon maps the failure of the mind to make sense of experience or one's past, whereas *Absalom! Absalom!* testifies to a belief that feeling is a means of knowing, a way to penetrate the past. Developing Weinstein's main arguments, Labriolle studies in detail the parallels between *Absalom! Absalom!* and *La Route des Flandres,* in order to plot Simon's emerging individualism (1979, pp. 358-81). The similarities he notes are: the obsessive reconstruction by Sutpen/Reixach of 'histoire'; the overlaying of private drama on a national one; the grouping of personal memories (Quentin/Georges) with secondary 'récits'; and the demystification of war and heroism and their compensating antithesis in the myth of the eternal feminine—Caddy and Corinne are seen by Labriolle as Lilith figures. This critic also pinpoints formal analogies—monologues, time jumps, style indirect libre, use of the present participle, association, animal imagery, dry humour, wordplay, parenthesis and corrective descriptions. Retrospection and the muddling of anecdote are essential structuring devices in both novels. Labriolle however compares in order to distinguish Simon's approach from his precursor's; the former 'donne *à voir* une identification que Faulkner se contentait à analyser'. Simon also, in this critic's opinion, focusses more on language for itself rather than as a means of description. Labriolle, however, uses this shift as an evaluation of Simon, suggesting that the post-*Route* cycle is therefore inferior to the Faulknerian period, where 'la recherche formelle... se trouve équilibrée par le choix de thèmes cruciaux (la mort et la solitude, fût-ce dans l'amour) et par un souci de mimétisme envers une conscience traumatisée par la guerre' (ibid., p. 378). Thus, for Labriolle, Simon's work stands or falls by the yardstick of Faulkner the more important precursor novelist, for whom theme and style weigh equally in the production of 'good' novels. Simon's statements on Faulkner would lend a different emphasis to this point of divide. Sykes also compares *Absalom! Absalom!* with *La Route des Flandres,* enumerating the similarities of style and theme, but this time to demonstrate the potential of Simon working beyond Faulkner: 'In the chemistry of memory, perception and imagination... Claude Simon adds his concern with the generative potential of language itself' (1979, p. 349). Sykes neatly sums up the differences by stressing the strong thematic and experiential nature of Faulkner's prose, set against a backdrop of historical / emotional defeat, while in Simon the principal events narrated are only surface manifestations of the defeat of language itself as a reconstructive tool. The main theme, then, is the impossibility of narrative itself. It is for this reason, not on the grounds of mystification of the stories or puzzlement of the reader, that temporal layers are interwoven and exchanged.

It seems clear that it is after *La Route des Flandres,* with the increasing decline in the importance of the anecdote and psychological investigation, that Simon parts company with Faulkner. There are certainly many thematic and stylistic parallels between Simon and Faulkner, which serve to reiterate the former's openly stated admiration for his precursor. However, my contention is that *La Route des Flandres* is the break-point with Faulkner by its clever integration of 'Faulknerian' style, coupled with Simon's own material and style. The result of this integration and coupling is to envelop and seal into a new form Faulkner's use of language which is thus re-evaluated in and through Simon's. It is Faulkner's descriptive techniques and uses of language which are *the* central issue, their richness (and also limitations) for Simon promoting innovation, a working on and beyond the precursor. Faulknerian hallmarks (such as time prolepses) are not lasting influences on Simon because his usage of such devices (learnt, admittedly, from Faulkner) bears his own stamp due to the particular needs of *La Route des Flandres.* Because the overall novelistic aims of Simon and Faulkner are, in fact, very different, the points of common interest (themes and style) diverge. The same tools of narration are used to very different effect. 'Faulknerisms' have been spotted in Simon's later novels and the episode of the boys fishing in *Triptyque* (p. 15) can be seen as reminiscent of episodes in *The Sound and the Fury.* However, I maintain that the pervading Faulknerian influences cease with *La Route des Flandres.* Recourse to them in *Les Géorgiques* as noted by Duncan and Duffy can be explained in the light of the fact that Simon reuses his own fiction to regenerate his later novels. *Les Géorgiques,* in fact, contains many elements from *La Route des Flandres,* so the Faulknerian components such as long involved sentences will automatically be carried over (but to a lesser degree) and reworked at the level of a sub-text in a novel which is essentially Simonian throughout, despite the numerous intertexts blended into it. As with the influence of Dostoyevsky, Faulkner's influence on Simon can be seen as important, but only at a particular time in Simon's stylistic development. The degree of this, however, may be gauged by the fact that lessons learnt from the former are visible only in Simon's early work. Faulkner's place is much more essential in shaping Simon's awareness of language as a persona in its own right, and as a means of describing the indescribable and immediate. This comes at the point in Simon's *œuvre* where he establishes his own particular prose style, the point where, with *L'Herbe* and *la Route des Flandres,* he turns his back on psychological ambiguities and opts instead for associative prose (in so far as these can be separated). Simon's appreciation of, and work on, Faulkner can then be seen as the springboard for the properly 'Simonian' novel of the 'middle' period.

Simon and Joyce

Alongside Proust and Faulkner, Simon classes Joyce as one of his three major precursors and 'un des maîtres du roman contemporain' (Aubarède, 1957, p. 7). As paradigm craftsman of intertexts and references, in the vein of Rabelais, Simon sees Joyce as an innovator and revolutionary of the novel within the tradition of the self-reflexive novel (Simon, 1982, p. 17).

While unhappy with the 'esoteric' depths of metaphor and linguistic allusion in Joyce, Simon praises the Joycean novel which undertakes 'to construct... texts, in which, as a matter of priority, considerations of quality will govern the linking [and] the confrontation of elements' (ibid., p. 20). Simon, however, rejects the extremes of punning and self-engendering verbal play in novels, where

> vous tombez dans le non-communicable, le bégaiement, l'informe, l'inflation verbale du Joyce de *Finnegan's Wake* (qui est, disons-le franchement, proprement illisible ou encore la limite dans le lettrisme)... Le lettrisme ne m'a jamais semblé une solution littéraire (Grivel, 1979, p. 102). .

As Simon has an insufficient reading knowledge of English to read Joyce in the original, one wonders how much translation has prejudiced his views of Joyce's skill at linguistic acrobatics. Suffice it to say that *Ulysses,* at any rate, is for Simon a cameo of sensuous prosody (see *Disc,* p. 22). Non-causal association is the vehicle of such writing: Joyce is set in the tradition which Flaubert began. Simon illustrates this by quoting from Molly Bloom's erotic reverie at the end of *Ulysses* in French translation and uses this as a passage for critical analysis (ibid.). Much of the earthiness of Joyce's language in this passage is lost in the French, and it is noteworthy that Simon does not comment on Joyce's words, indeed leaves this aspect untouched, his remarks centring only on the stream-of-consciousness technique and the suppression of punctuation. As with Faulkner, the language usage itself is inimitable.

Joyce's influence reaches beyond comments in interviews: traces visible in Simon's novels have generated critical attention. Morrissette has commented on the Joycean sentence length in Simon (1962, p. 12), while Thiébaut has equated their use of interior monologue (1960, p. 159). More specifically, critics have hastened to equate *Ulysses* and *Histoire*, but without developing their reasons for the comparison (for example Pugh, 1982, p. 178). For Albérès, both novels, though in different styles, are concerned with a day in the life of the protagonist (1967, p. 7). Levitt examines the Joycean elements in *Histoire* in greater detail (1969, pp. 129-31). He sees Henri as a quasi-Ulysses and the narrator, his son, as a quasi-Telemachus, but concludes that, in Simon, the narrator never expects to find his father, or thereby his own identity, even though he hunts through the postcards and family stories for clues, like Bloom, who sifts through the memorabilia of the past.

Histoire undoubtedly comes closest to *Ulysses,* it being Simon's most epic novel, with many classical references embedded in it, but not according to any elaborate scheme like that to be detected in *Ulysses*. Despite the similar banality of narrating the events of a single day, the underlying mythic element of Joyce is suppressed. It seems to me that Simon is doing more than simply borrowing the *Ulysses* structure of a twenty-four hour period or making his narrator a Leopold Bloom. Possibly his commentator-figure Blum, in *La Route des Flandres* is nominally closer to Joyce's character, but expunged of the precursor's heroic qualities. Where Joyce's intention was to overlay the banal with the mythic to create a new kind of universal dimension to his figures, Simon is to my mind rejecting the mythic nature of his precursor. By inverting references to classical mythology through almost crass deflation, they are rendered utterly banal. This emerges in *Histoire* first through the frequent usage of Greek myth, with its depths of symbolic or universal implications removed. The Stymphalian birds are remembered, not for their harpy qualities, but for their lacustrine habitat (*Hist,* p. 39). This in turn jogs the narrator's memory and reminds him of his trip to Greece. Apollo and Pegasus are however demythologized by their new opera setting (p. 55) and 'Nausicaa' is simply a Latin word in a list of others beginning with 'N' (p. 109). In fact, Simon may be pushing this anti-mythic use of language to the point of gently mocking Joyce's practice of presenting Bloom as a contemporary Ulysses. One hint of this is the exaggerated recreation of a Theseus figure, not in the labyrinth killing Minotaurs, but in a boiler-room, to show the incongruity of such mythical comparisons (p. 71). Again, whereas Joyce's Molly Bloom is a conemporary Helen of Troy figure, Hélène, Charles's wife in *Histoire,* is utterly without personal or national importance. The ironic suggestion is that she may have committed suicide, an act of deleting personhood, or, on the fictional plane, of preventing mythic structures from emerging.

Not only is the mythic interwoven into the structure and language of *Ulysses*; Joyce also incorporates into it religious language and form. *Histoire* again has the largest number of references to Christianity in Simon. These, I suggest, are used to explore and create language associations, but in order to bypass the *mystical* elements of such vocabulary. Borrowing from Joyce is again the key, particularly his character Lambert, who in *Histoire* perverts the words of the Kyrie to produce pornographic statements. In Joyce, Ned Lambert introduces pastiches of literary style, especially bombastic pretentious language (*Ulysses,* p. 125). Simon's Lambert provokes pastiche, but of a more sacrilegious kind, compressing much of the tone of religious criticism in *Ulysses* within the confines of the single character, who echoes Joycean punning and the deflations of mystical language as well.

> Arsenal de calembours et de contrepèteries censé d'affranchir par la magie du verbe des croyances maternelles et des leçons du catéchisme. Donc je suppose quelque chose comme Introïbo in lavabo (p. 43).

This post-Joycean, non-mystical language in Simon is best demonstrated by his deployment of Joycean vocabulary and style, but inflated to incongruously exaggerated proportions. Lambert's Kyrie in *Histoire* vulgarizes as it demythologises language: 'Lambert chantant tue-tête Qui riez et les frissons ou j'ai z eu ta bite si gloire il y a au lieu de Kyrie Eleisson ou de Jésu tibi sit gloria' (p. 336).

Similarly, there is play on the letters 'INRI', both novels punning on the assonances between the letters and the names Henry/Henri respectively. In Joyce, the letters are made to stand for something other than the irreligious meaning:

> Letters on his back INRI? No, IHS. Molly told me one time I asked her. I have sinned: or no: I have suffered, it is. And the other one? Iron nails ran in *(Ulysses,* p. 82).

In Simon, the letters lead the boy to consider the incongruity of the religious atmosphere and the priest himself, the sign not matching the signified:

> la soutane et plus bas les gros souliers noirs cirés... ce qu'il y avait écrit au centre de la croix par devant trois ou quatre lettres en caractères épineux eux aussi griffus gothiques et entrelacés INRI sans doute ou ce P et ce X entrecroisés XPISTOS et quel mot grec encore dieu symbolisé par un poisson (p. 16).

The demystification of every religious scene in *Histoire* is the linguistic intention of Simon's novel: it presents the banal, even ridiculous nature of ritual and ritualistic language, which breaks into meaninglessness when repeated as, for example, the word 'Miséricorde' (p. 27). This is the antithesis of repetition as incantation, the inverse of any heightening of language to capture its mystical intensity. Intertextually speaking, the borrowing of Joycean proclivities to punning and mocking repetitions, permits the exploration of multifarious language registers in *Histoire,* not least Joyce's multifacetted language as well. By encompassing Joyce, however, Simon fails to supersede him. This is partly due to a vocabulary consisting of mythical and mystical components, but constructed so as to demythologize and demysticize them in a new banal context. In part also, it is the erotic associativeness of Joyce which holds sway in *Histoire* at the expense of other elements form *Ulysses.* The biggest hurdle to further Joycean intertextual activity on Simon is the erudite density of the English which is quite beyond Simon in ways which Proust's is not. Thus the lessons Simon appears to have learnt from Joyce centre on verbal association and wordplay as structuring and puncturing devices. Latin, Lambert, and vulgarising language in Joyce conjoin intertextually with Apuleius and Proust's Bloch so that Simon can universalise the particular 'histoire' of the boy-narrator in *Histoire.* The epic project of *Histoire* permits 'one-off' collision with Joycean avant-garde writing, but on a reduced scale to *Ulysses*. For Simon, it is being a revolutionary in a different thematic way to Joyce which then expurgates Joycean tendencies of language usage in *Histoire* and indeed from his subsequent novels.

Revolutions in the novel

As we have seen throughout our study, and particularly in the third chapter, Simon's novels operate by the intermingling of various time strands which, although not specific enough to be limited by exact dates, nonetheless evoke particular historical events. The 'times' Simon chooses are notable for, to show their differences, they are unique moments, charged with political and historical import. In addition, the choice of periods of historical and political turmoil matches the upheavals of 'meaning' and produces a breakdown of established political and linguistic structures. Revolution and war thus become privileged and intense moments in Simon's writing. This writing, however, contains no moral or call to commitment to particular ideologies, nor incitement to the reader to act. Simon thus rejects 'committed literature' in the manner of Camus and Sartre, for in his view, these writers use plot as an apology for, or a vehicle of, ideas (Simon, 1978, p. 80). Because Camus and Sartre focus on 'signification', *littérature engagée* is for Simon a sub-category of the *roman à thèse* (Chapsal, 1961, p. 32). Perhaps this is why Simon lampoons the Existentialist's emphasis on commitment in the Writers' Conference episodes in *Orion aveugle* and *Les Corps conducteurs*. Simon's view of the author is more modest: not a superior being with a mission to reorientate the blind, but a presenter of a chaos of impressions. The evocation of unrest and turmoil, confusion and change is uppermost in Simon's descriptions of these intermingling revolutions and wars. The reader is then left free to make his or her own connections, interpretations and evaluations. It is precisely in such depictions of social change that Simon's novels are intensely political and revolutionary. While it is the Spanish Civil War which has provoked most comment from critics, this political event will be considered along with Simon's use of other writings which document political revolutions. *Les Géorgiques* will thus be discussed in this context and through the intertextual references to Orwell's *Homage to Catalonia* which dovetail with the Virgil intertext already examined in Chapter One.

While it is the most 'architextuel' of Simon's works because it contains most intertexts from writing on revolution, it can only do so because of what Simon learns in *Histoire*. I shall therefore explore first how this text holds in tension and contains large sections from Reed's *Ten Days that shook the World.* By showing the range of revolutionary literatures in Simon, this chapter will then consider how these, when they are incorporated into Simon's writing, and coupled with his own personal experiences of war, enhance the political and revolutionary nature of his prose. The personal revolution itself we will consider in the final chapter when the revolution of *Histoire* comes full circle in *L'Acacia.*

Simon and Reed

In Chapter Four, I showed how Dostoyevsky's influence as Russian novelist on Simon's early novels proved an essential training ground for his own development as writer. Few critics have, however, remarked on Simon's use of Reed as a Russian 'novel' with a difference: the eye-witness report of the events of the Russian Revolution in *Ten Days that shook the World.* Brewer sees in Reed 'the mode of intertextuality in *Histoire* [which] operates to displace the historical *récit*. It intertextualizes it in a fiction whose auto-reflexive practice of writing and reading emerges as *its particular fiction*' (1982, p. 495 [Brewer's emphasis]).

Ten Days and *Histoire* share obvious themes—the convergence of history and revolution—and while the thematic reverberations of Reed universalize the narrator's experience in *Histoire*, it is not this which I feel is particularly 'revolutionary' in Simon's reusage. The actual quotations taken from *Ten Days* in fact form no *thematic* entity in their new setting, for segments from different chapters of Reed are juxtaposed, so that only a semblance of continuous cited discourse occurs. This is most clearly visible in a list of the quotations from Reed. They are given here according to their order of appearance in *Histoire*, their source references being to the relevant chapter in Reed (*TD*), put in brackets .

1. *Hist*, 108: *TD*, 129 (5)
2. *Hist*, 111: *TD*, 94 (4)
3. *Hist*, 118 'apotheosis... end': *TD*, 201 (9)
4. *Hist*, 118 'de là... routes': *TD*, 209 (9)
5. *Hist*, 119 'les vagues... mitraille': *TD*, 183 (8)

6. *Hist,* 119 'des milliers... du mur': *TD,* 183 (8)
7. *Hist,* 119 'matelots... sol': *TD,* 184 (8)
8. *Hist,* 119 'prises... mal': *TD,* 184 (8)
9. *Hist,* 120 'ils essayaient... rue': *TD,* 184 (8)
10. *Hist,* 121 'à quelque... disparu': *TD,* 209 (9)
11. *Hist,* 121 'apotheosis... end': *TD,* 201 (9)
12. *Hist,* 121 'des voix... armes': *TD,* 107-8 (4)
13. *Hist,* 121-2 'Grâce... édifice': *TD,* 108 (4)
14. *Hist,* 122 'dans le lointain... isolés': *TD,* 186 (8)
15. *Hist,* 127 'l'intérieur... édifice': *TD,* 154 (6)
16. *Hist,* 127-8 'Jamais... guerriers': *TD,* 155 (6)
17. *Hist,* 128 'Le commissaire... arrière': *TD,* 156 (6)
18. *Hist,* 128 'Trapu... uniform': *TD,* 156 (6)
19. *Hist,* 128 'Comrades... paix': *TD,* 156 (6)
20. *Hist,* 328: *TD,* 129 (5)
21. *Hist,* 352: *TD,* 129 (5)

While the identification of these sources seems rather basic, no one to date has collated them, and such 'groundwork' is essential to subsequent intertextual analysis and interpretation. Several observations instantly emerge, which may be clues as to Simon's purposes in re-using Reed here. When one compares the quotations from Reed and Simon's transcriptions of them, they are all seen to be direct, the word order remaining unchanged, even though the original is translated into French. This 'non-tampering' with the actual words contrasts strikingly with Simon's later tinkering with Proust's language parodied and vulgarized in *La Bataille de Pharsale.* This rather unique purity of transcription in *Histoire* is matched by a consistent typographical representation. All the quotations from Reed are in italic script, which acts as a constant signal to the reader that the writing is an intrusion, different, foreign to the main body of *Histoire.* It is worth noting that this fixity of typographical convention is again unique to *Histoire,* a simplification of intertextual signposting which Simon eschews in later works by mixing typographies and thus burying the intertext more deeply within his own.

Not only are the Reed quotations direct, they are also concentrated into one section of *Histoire,* the fourth 'chapter' of the novel: the only exceptions are two traces taken from the Reed quotations given and repeated in the penultimate 'chapter'. Through this textual condensation, Simon apparently focusses attention on *Ten Days* as intertext, compressing its span into a small part of his own. Thus, its comprehensiveness is, as it were, spotlighted. Indeed, within Simon's *œuvre* as a whole, this idea of comprehensive condensation has wider implications. *Histoire* is the first Simon novel to display such large-scale quotation, as opposed to incidental reference, paraphrase or allusion. In addition, the quotations in *Histoire* are all from the one intertext, this purity of source never again repeated in Simon's works. The one exception, a quotation from Caesar, does not however detract from the main intertext for it is actually framed by it, Reed then being seen to stand overall as the active intertextual force of *Histoire*. Thus the weight of the intertext as an example of both other and *particular* writing is increased. It paves the way for the use of *A la recherche,* for example, as one intertext among many in *La Bataille de Pharsale* and Virgil's *Georgics* in *Les Géorgiques.*

Thus far, my comments on the large-scale thematic overlappings, the accuracy of transcription, the signalled integration by means of typographical conformity and the confinement of the intertext to part of the host, sum up the basic ingredients for the simple reusage of any intertext within a new work in general. These bases, I would suggest, are however deliberately simple, to *show* intertextuality in action and to experiment with it. *Histoire* is therefore not just an exploration of the facets of (hi)story, fact and fiction as discussed in chapter three. It is also a 'workshop' novel for text and intertext as fictional generators. Past writing is then set against present writing in its simplest form: a one-to-one relationship. Experimentation in *Histoire* thus opens up the way for even richer intertextual activity and crafting, such as the inclusion of multiple intertexts in later works such as *Les Géorgiques* and *L'Acacia.*

Given this general reason for Simon's choice of just one intertext, why is Reed's *Ten Days* singled out for attention, especially as the source itself is deliberately suppressed? One major clue emerges from the frame for the Reed quotations in *Histoire*. 'Chapter Four' begins 'Disant Tout y est Mon notaire a vérifié' (p. 99) and the Reed intertext is closed off by the Latin and its translation:

> commemoravit: il rappela
> testibus se militibus uti posse: qu'il pouvait prendre témoin ses soldats (p. 128).

This context establishes that a textual memory is at stake. More specifically, the eye-witness as central figure of narration, and the 'place' of truthful verification of reports on an event is underlined. The Reed intertexts mirror Caesar and expand and contemporise the context. Like Caesar, Reed was the eye-witness recorder of major international upheavals, *Ten Days* being his written record of the events of the Russian Revolution. His position of detached observer, unlike Orwell in *Homage to Catalonia* as we will see, is crucial to Simon's project here. It is the experience of the writing, not the writer which is uppermost. Reed does not justify his position: he documents what he sees, emphasis on historical accuracy, then, the objective reason for the choice of *Ten Days* as intertext in *Histoire*. Moreover, as exemplum of the genre of documentary itself, *Ten Days* adds further layers to the strata of 'H/histoires' already examined in chapter three.

Simple juxtaposition of Reed as the paradigm of the genre of historico-political reportage and *Histoire* as collection of 'H/histoires' implies a parity and autonomy for both texts, such as to allow thematic and narrative comparisons to be drawn. Simon's reusage of Reed, however, completely overturns any such notions of parity. A.J.P. Taylor's introduction to Reed draws attention to its unrivalled universal, particular and generic excellence: 'Reed's book is not only the best account of the Bolshevik revolution, it comes near to being the best account of any revolution'. Simon certainly seems to recognise such qualities in the singling out of this intertext for special consideration. However it is the nature of his experimentation in cutting and pasting this work into his own which, in fact, deflates the genre of reportage. The alleged historical veracity of Reed is distorted, and both the chronology and rigour of Reed's eye-witness report disintegrate. It is not just, as Britton has noted, 'the drama and seriousness of the Reed passage [which] is corroded by the context which frames it' (1987, p. 107): it is, I suggest, through the individual instances of each quotation that Simon punctures every paradigmatic universalising and individualizing quality of Reed. Let us now return to these quotations and examine them in more detail.

Reed's text, as reportage, offers clear, precise narration of reality as he sees it. It is the *imprecise* and the unrealistic which Simon stresses by prefacing his first borrowing from Reed by the description of a black and white photograph of an orator:

> qui leur confér[aient] quelque chose d'à la fois mystérieux, anachronologique et barbare en accord avec les caractères Cyrilliques et incompréhensibles (en quelque sorte les contraires des caractères connus, leur réplique inversée) (p. 107).

As a *Russian* speaker the orator is only identifiable through indirect clues given by the editor such as the colours 'en réalité de rouge' (referring to the flags in the picture), and the Cyrillic script. It is the Russian alphabet, writing at its most basic level as individual letters, which signals and introduces the Russian Revolution quotations from Reed. The slide from this frame to the Reed quotation about an orator is unmediated except for a change of typography. Through the overlap of the familiar and the unfamiliar, comparison occurs—the two speakers are identical, both unnamed orators. So while the Reed text thus seems to authenticate a fictional report (Simon's text) by a 'real' piece of reported speech, the very authenticity of the words of the intertext are actually questioned: it is the new frame which casts doubt.

It also seems that Simon is questioning the validity of oratory itself, together with the power of propagandist speeches. This is suggested by the repetition of the first Reed intertext in 'Chapter' Four of *Histoire,* which appears in fragments near the end of the novel:

> *se tenant sur le rebord de la tribune, il promena sur l'assistance ses petits yeux clignotants, en apparence insensible à l'immense ovation qui se prolongea pendant plusieurs minutes Quand elle eut pris fin il dit simplement Nous passons maintenant à l'édification de l'ordre socialiste De nouveau ce fut dans la salle un formidable déchaînement humain... immense ovation qui se prolongea pendant quelques minutes* Quand elle se répète pour la deuxième fois plus rien qu'une farce (pp. 108 and 352)

The opinion that history repeats itself but as farce, echoed in an ironically negative version here by Simon, is from Marx (on the Eighteenth Brumaire). Of course, one reason for repeating the Reed intertext is to frame the language of *Ten Days* in order, as it were, to seal off its influence. More important, however, is that 'speechifying' in *Histoire* of an incoherent and disjointed kind is set against Reed's reported oratory, and its effects on the crowd. While their reaction in Reed only enhances the power of the message, Simon's repetition of this same noise of applause and general hubbub is used to blot out the intertext, so that it fades away completely. Furthermore, the rhetoric of the speech is punctured on two accounts. What is actually said smacks of oversimplification and is disproportionate to the response it elicits; and the crowd reacts before the orator can finish, which suggests an audience responding more to the delivery of the words than to what such construction of a new order would entail. Second, the rhetorical principle of repetition to enhance a point and intensify its significance is mocked by the recurrence of the quotation with the additional comment on such repetitions: 'plus rien qu'une farce'. Such political rhetoric and oratory have no power to hold back the new prose, which, even within the oratory of the Reed frame, constantly interrupts and therefore undermines the forcefulness and coherence of any such speech-making.

The final Reed intrusions in 'Chapter' Four, to return to the bulk of the borrowings, record a second speech and its reaction:

> *Jamais je n'avais vu des hommes s'appliquer avec une telle intensité à comprendre et à décider Ils ne bougeaient pas dirigeant sur l'orateur un regard d'une fixité presque effrayante les sourcils froncés par l'effort de la pensée la sueur perlant à leurs fronts géants aux yeux innocents et clairs d'enfants et aux visages de guerriers... Trapu court de jambes et tête nue il ne portait aucun insigne sur son uniforme Camarades soldats je n'ai pas besoin de vous dire que je suis un soldat Je n'ai pas besoin de vous dire que je veux la paix* (pp. 127-8)

Once more, the rhetorical repetitions banalize the words, and the speaker's words are emptied out through the discrepancy between what is said and the exaggerated response. By cutting off the Reed intertext at the crucial moment, anticlimax, not a rhetorical peak, is achieved. Simon has not changed the words in any way. He has simply chosen a breakpoint which ridicules the original. Again, as with the first speech, textual comment and repetition are intrinsic to the deflation of the oratory. In this instance, a doubling and repetition of the last words from the Reed intertext come through mirroring: a Latin text and the boy-narrator's *halting* translation of it: 'pacem petisset: il avait demandé la paix' (p. 128).

Further irony emerges when we turn to these original speeches in Reed. Simon takes great care to omit the orators' names, thereby reducing their historical importance, and thus reducing the weight of their words as well. The first speaker is none other than Lenin, and the second Krylenko, another major leader in the Revolution. For the same reasons perhaps as the suppression of Reed's authorship of the intertexts themselves, this removal of the speech-makers' identities forces us to examine what is said and how it is said, separated from any historical import or particular charisma in the speaker (which is obvious given the audience reactions). By extension, the quotations are separated from reverence for a particularly exemplary writer, as Reed clearly is. Therefore, by disembodying the original words of the speakers and the intertext, Simon highlights the dubious veracity of any reported speech or verbatim quotation, because, once speech is repeated by a new author, it is given a new persona. What *Histoire* suggests is that speech itself cannot be used as a tool to persuade, or to activate (political) response. The propaganda potential lies in the speaker (so, at least, Simon implies). Because Simon's narrators in *Histoire* constantly produce fragmented, even confused utterances, rhetoric and polished speech as exemplified by Reed is nullified, to leave room for Simon's more favoured kind of language—protean, open, with the power of suggestion and ambiguity.

It is not only the precise language of oratory and reportage which Simon deflates by using the Reed intertext: the documentation of events is also questioned. Documentation entails a chronological ordering of eye-witness accounts to present as full a picture as possible of the incidents. By setting up parallels between the action and descriptions of the Russian revolution in Reed and his own accounts of war, Simon would again appear to be authenticating and universalizing the experiences of revolution and war in general. However, while this element certainly plays a part, Reed and the authenticity of any historical documentation are severely questioned.

As before, visual representation is the trigger: a photograph introduces Reed's description of events, the photograph stressing confusion and depicting 'd'autres petites formes noires s'enfuyant, se dispersant, comme une poignée de billes lancées vers la droite entre les hautes façades'. Without interruption, again like the preface to the orator's speech, the Reed intertext takes over:

> *A ce moment une fusillade éclata à peu de distance Sur la place les gens s'enfuirent... les soldats courant en tous sens et empoignant à la hâte fusil et cartouchières en criant Les voilà! Les voilà! Quelques minutes plus tard le calme était revenu Les izvoztchiks reprirent leurs places* (p. 111)

Immediately striking is the contrast between the dispersal and disorder in Simon's description and the renewal of calm and order in Reed's. Here, everything returns to 'normal', helped by the measured nature of Reed's prose.

Disarray as action within each text is matched on a bigger scale by Simon's complete dispersal and confusion of Reed's original order of narration. This is coupled with a complete inversion of the chronology and historical developments in Reed's account. By glancing again at the list of quotations from Reed and the chapters they came from originally, we can see that for descriptions of the happenings of the Revolution (quotation three onwards), Simon starts near the end of *Ten Days* and then moves towards the beginning. There can be no greater deflation of historical records than this achronological reusage. Thus we begin with 'apotheosis and millenium without end' before the turmoil and bloodshed. This quotation is an intertext to a double degree, the only one Simon retains in English. Reed quotes these words from Carlyle to define Victory, a thematically ironic chapter-heading in *Ten Days,* but doubly so in Simon's context. Utter decimation is his new setting: 'massacre quel moutonnement de mourants entremêlés exsangues grisâtres dans le grisâtre crépuscule' (p. 118). Such satirical re-implantation of Carlyle's words can only emphasize Simon's implied message: the cost of such victory and the veneer of lasting peace after any political upheaval.

On a textual level, this is underlined heavily by the repetition of Carlyle's words, a frame as before, giving a mock order, but showing only the more clearly its contents within it: several fragments from 'Counter-revolution' which comes earlier in Reed's text. The borrowed details of violence, fear and anguish in revolution are put in a different sequence by Simon to form a new 'story' of revolution: the horror and confusion, not the ideals. Such chaos cannot be contained within the mock-stability of the reiteration of Reed's words, let alone Carlyle's. To underpin the point further, Simon then chooses fragments from the earliest section of Reed in *Histoire,* 'Fall of the Provisional Government' (quotations 12-13), which report the optimistic advance of the soldiers. This retrospection of course completely undermines the tenor of the words quoted. Especially ironic is the 'cri de triomphe': this victory we know to be illusory because we have already been exposed to the later events in 'Counter-revolution'. Indeed, Simon then turns again to this section to underline this:

> *dans le lointain résonnaient encore quelques coups de feu isolés* tué par un tireur isolé embusqué derrière une haie peu après être ressorti de cette ville bombardée Très fière parce qu'il avait raconté qu'un de ses ancêtres un Reixach s'était fait (p. 122)

Reixach's experiences of war are knitted to Reed's linguistically: the bursts of gunfire during the Russian Revolution are linked with Simon's 'un tireur isolé'. The pride of the narrator as he recounts the death of his ancestor, Reixach, is somewhat akin to pride in revolutionary ideals, such as being a martyr to the cause: this fails to convince, for the ugly side of war cannot be smothered. The isolated quotations from Reed, then, set in their new pattern, are indirect but no less powerful commentators on the horrors of revolution. It is this side which has always come second in importance to the overall developments, successes and politics presented in traditional historical documentation. In Simon, the value of revolution is always aligned with its cost.

By setting Reed's account of the Russian Revolution against his narrator's experience of war, Simon 'revolutionizes' his own writing by giving it an added intertextual dimension. Moreover, his experimentation with, and re-ordering of, the original casts light on the absolute veracity of historiography and the documentation of political unrest. By distorting and fragmenting the paradigm of the genre, Simon presents what he would consider to be a more consistent, and thus more revolutionary, description of any revolution. Such a description is necessarily subjective (for no eye-witness can be objective and distanced), incomplete (no reporter can have insights into the whole story) and disjointed chronologically (for no historiographer can give the true and exact order or the logical development of events). Thus Simon does not expunge politics from *Histoire*: he changes the mode of presenting it.

Simon and Orwell

Having learnt in *Histoire* how to manipulate and rework a single intertext for the ends of his own writing, Simon gains confidence and complexity in his intertextual play through *La Bataille de Pharsale,* as the previous chapter on Proust amply demonstrated. In *Les Géorgiques,* his style sews together a patchwork of fragmentary accounts of other documentary genres dealing with conflict. Chapter one dealt with Virgil, and I have written elsewhere about Simon's revolt against biography as epitomized by his use of Strachey (Orr, 1988), which becomes an anti-model and fully integrated intertextual foil complementing his own biography of LSM which he leaves unfinished. The historical fragment from Michelet's *Histoire de la Révolution française* describing LSM is broken off for exactly the same effects: the finished saga, historical or personal, defies definitive articulation. While Simon's use of Reed and Strachey adds political and revolutionary strata to his writing, and the 'archétypes' of documentary and biography to his collage of genres, the Russian Revolution and the Oxford Movement and their intertexts appear only once each in Simon's *œuvre*. The Spanish Civil War, both as event and intertext, is much more pervasive, and this is probably due to the fact that Simon participated in it, and was deeply moved by the experience. His Spanish Civil War novels span most of his *œuvre,* but are intertextually intensified in *Les Géorgiques,* which has embedded in it the very different narrative account of the event, Orwell's *Homage to Catalonia.*

Before turning immediately to Orwell, several important points should be made concerning Simon the PSUC member in Barcelona during the Spanish Civil War, and Simon the writer. Simon always distinguishes between his personal, political views and any mouthpiece of political events found in his novels. In other words, however similar they might appear, Simon is *not* the Georges of his fiction. As was evident from our analysis of Reed, fiction can never, in Simon's view, be an objective documentation of events, just as histories cannot be expunged of subjective opinion. So, even though Simon experienced the Spanish Civil War at first hand, and was both politically involved and aware, he states categorically in 1962, on the publication of *Le Palace*:

> Non, ce n'est pas un livre sur la révolution espagnole... c'est un livre sur ma révolution... J'ai voulu décrire ce qu'a été pour moi la révolution espagnole... Et aussi par goût, c'est ce que j'aime faire, traduire en mots, en langage ce que Samuel Beckett appelle le 'Comment c'est' ou plutôt le 'Comment c'est maintenant', comment c'est désormais dans ma mémoire (Chapsal, 1962, p. 32).

The point is that, in Simon's novels, the historical and political are combined with the imaginary. The purpose is not to idealize war, the writer on war or the genre of war or revolutionary literature, nor even to promote a particular political response: the purpose is rather to describe and paint fictional impressions of the events. This will produce not a history or an autobiographical account, but a feeling of the turmoil and horror of war and revolution in general, through the particular microcosm of the Spanish Civil War. Therefore, despite active involvement on the Republican side in Barcelona and in the 1940 débâcle, Simon portrays action in his novels not as a 'message' but as a medium of language. The events he recounts are never complete entities fitted into an overall unfolding of the war in question. They are always related from the subjective and limited perspective and experience of a narrator who is often remembering what may have happened. Thus, although the motives behind the political struggle in Spain are not necessarily devalued for Simon, historical 'realism', supposedly accurate overviews and naive adventuring are secondary to revolution as pretext for investigating *narrative* as action, as opposed to action as the motor of narration. Simon makes this clear in his derogatory comments on Malraux's *L'Espoir,* which is everything Simon sees as antithetical to his accounts of Spain at the time:

> L'Espoir pour moi est un peu Tintin faisant la révolution. C'est une sorte de roman feuilleton... de roman d'aventures, écrit par... un... aventurier, dans le cadre de la révolution. En plus, il raconte des choses qu'il n'a pas perçues lui-même. C'est le romancier-Dieu, il est partout: au sol, dans les avions, chez les uns, chez les autres... D'alleurs, Malraux parle de la guerre d'Espagne. C'est un guerrier qui décrit des actes de guerre. Mon livre est sur la révolution... *Le Palace* ne mérite que le nom de rêve sur la révolution espagnole (Chapsal, 1962, p. 32).

Simon therefore speaks quite openly of his borrowing of Orwell's *Homage to Catalonia* in *Les Géorgiques* as it dovetails and contrasts with his own experiences whereas the identity of Reed and *Ten Days* are kept as a closely-guarded, literary secret, as the events themselves lie totally outside Simon's own experience:

> When I conceived the (very vague) project of *Les Géorgiques*, I was already thinking of including in it a re-writing of *Homage* which seemed to me (and still seems to me) to strangely reduplicate the story of LSM because of its themes (revolution and war). It does not appear to have been noticed how much the two adventures (LSM and O) in the midst of tumultuous periods of history presented similarities up to and including the decision, taken by both LSM and O, to go back and fight in spite of everything, after the collapse of their illusions (Pugh, 1985, pp. 8-9).

At the time when *Les Géorgiques* appeared, critics noted the rewriting of *Homage* within it, but conducted surprisingly little detailed exploration of the intertextual reverberations between the two, and made next to no reference to the parallels between LSM and O, to which Simon draws attention above. Sykes draws attention to the pun on the title of the novel, referring to Simon's Georges and *George* Orwell (1983, p. 82). It is Britton who analyses in greatest detail the role of Orwell as both protagonist and narrator of *Homage* in Simon's text, comparing him to Simon's O who is in the same position, yet not the central mouthpiece in *Les Géorgiques*: LSM fills this place. Britton also distances Simon's O from the precursor by stating that the intertext is both a documentary source to provide an imaginary reconstruction of O's actions and a foil for the 'proper' vision of events which are the text of *Les Géorgiques* (Britton, 1984, p. 434).

Simon gives reasons for subordinating Orwell on two accounts, the fictional and the personal. Orwell's *text* is coupled with the family papers of LSM and the 'story' of Georges to add another layer of textual experience of revolution and war, 'de façon à donner une image globale, universelle de la vie, ce qui apparente au poème' (Piatier, 1981, p. 13). It is then the superimpositional function of *Homage* which Simon underscores, and can admire as intertextual comparison. However, because of the political and personal stance of its author, Simon reacts strongly against Orwell, and, by extension, treats certain elements of *Homage* ironically within *Les Géorgiques*:

> There is an element of fellow-feeling in my response to Orwell's personality and I have a profound admiration for his personal courage. I would unfortunately not be inclined to go so far regarding his intellectual courage and honesty. Without making too much of it, and mentioning only for the record his idyllic description of Barcelona in November 1936, which is little more than a comic tourist guide, I should point out to these same critics that *Homage* is a work (or rather a piece of special pleading on his own behalf) which is faked from the very first sentence... I shall restrict myself to informing them that one did not just wander casually into Republican Spain at that time and that if there did exist in Barcelona something called the 'Lenin Barracks' (or rather a Cuartel Lenin) there was also, not far away, a 'Cuartel Karl Marx' and another invoking the name of Bakunin. The respective occupants of these various barracks considered each other to be 'counter-revolutionaries', and thought only of the best way of eliminating them (as happened in May 1937 to the benefit of the Stalinists). To give an idea of the idyllic proletarian unanimity which then reigned in Barcelona, it should be recalled that the occupants of the Cuartel Karl Marx called the occupants of the Cuartel Lenin 'hitlero-trotskyites'. Finally, it was not 'by chance' that a foreigner made for one of the cuartels rather than another: thus it was because I had a communist party membership card in my pocket at that period (September 1936) that I went straight to the Hotel Colon, which was then the HQ of the PSUC. All these things (including the motives which led him to the Cuartel Lenin) are carefully suppressed by Orwell, until he gets to the account of the May insurrection, about which the uninformed reader will know very little... (what is more, I did not call my character Orwell but O) (Pugh, 1985, pp. 9-10).

Simon's character assassination of Orwell, here, makes it very clear that he wishes to distinguish his own writing from Orwell's, in particular what he considers to be his own greater honesty in the representation of the events in Barcelona. Simon does not 'romanticize' these from the armchair comfort of later documentation of what happened, whereas Orwell, in fact, admitted that he gave a more sympathetic account in *Homage* than he actually felt (Thomas, 1977, p. 707). Furthermore, while both Simon and Orwell were on the Republican side, and against fascism, their political positions were very different. Simon thus separates himself as PSUC member from Orwell on the side of the POUM who were:

> anti-Stalinist revolutionaries led by Catalan ex-communists... Some joined this party believing that it represented a mean between the indiscipline of the anarchists and the strictness of the PSUC. Foreigners in Barcelona [including Orwell] joined the POUM in the romantic supposition that it embodied a magnificent Utopian aspiration. Franz Borkenau noted the atmosphere of political enthusiasm among these émigrés, who clearly enjoyed the adventure of war and had complete faith in 'absolute success' (ibid. pp. 301-2).

The PSUC, on the other hand, were Communist Party members, and were opposed to revolution. 'All their attitudes were reformist, and conciliatory, in the sense that they were intended to improve conditions within the society that existed; the new society could wait' (ibid., p. 301). Their aim was to win the war, restore the power of the *Generalidad* against the anarchists (Bakuninists) and the POUM, and then help the central government take over the *Generalidad*. While the PSUC was sustained by diplomatic and military help from the USSR, and was guided by a group of experienced international communists, it was, however, no ordinary Communist Party. They 'stood for a disciplined, left-of-Centre, bourgeois régime, capable of winning the war' (ibid. p. 646). With these distinctions in mind, Simon's personal politics, never openly stated, are clarified indirectly by their opposition to Orwell's. Both were 'against' the anarchists, but Simon stood with the official, anti-revolutionary communists, whereas Orwell joined with the POUM, the revolutionary Marxists who were independent of Moscow. Indeed, this distinction also helps to explain some of Simon's prejudice and attitudes to Orwell; the character assassination, then, being simplistic and over-ferocious because it is ideologically based.

An excursion into the historical account of the Spanish Civil War also helps to shed light on the actual rifts and factions of the Left to which Simon is referring in his attack on Orwell, and to overturn Orwell's picture of 'idyllic proletarian unanimity' in *Homage*. It was in fact the tensions between the separate groups which led to the May riots in Barcelona in 1937, at which Simon and Orwell were both present, but on different sides. The POUM had spoken of the PSUC as 'Stalinist Thermidorians', criticizing their centralism (the defence of the democratic 'bourgeois' republic). Because the POUM's leaders were allex-communists, they could be labelled as traitors, and hence the communist line was to remove the POUMists. There were also tensions between the many anarchist groups: the FAI (the Friends of Durruti) and the CNT (anarchist Trades Unions). Barricades were built, and each faction took up its position. The POUM tried to form an alliance with the anarchists against the PSUC and the government: to no avail. The extremists among the anarchists broke out with new acts of violence in the name of the revolution. The PSUC and the POUM were unwilling to collaborate against the anarchists. When the May insurrection ended, the particular tensions in Barcelona and in Catalonia, its wider context, were quelled. The May insurrection also marked the end of revolution in Spain. The republican state was now at war with the nationalist state, rather than the revolution seeking to oust fascism. Gradually, Franco 'nationalized' Spain, by uniting the nationalists, because the individual rivalries among the republicans, seen in the microcosm of Barcelona, prevented them forming a unified front.

The political differences, then, between the two writers, Orwell the anti-communist and Simon the card-carrying member of the Communist Party, may be summed up in the final sentence of the above attack on Orwell: Simon did not call his fictional character Orwell, but O, as a mark of initial equation, but thereafter distinct separation from him. Moreover, from Simon's personal and political reaction to Orwell, it is impossible to endorse such critical statements as Fletcher's conclusion to his study of *Homage* as intertext in *Les Géorgiques*, that Simon's elaborate reworking 'basically admires and respects Orwell's political attitude, which is radical, a shade anarchic, and deeply commited to ideals that are democratic and socialist' (Fletcher in Duncan, 1985, p. 111).

Returning to the intertextual reactions between Simon and Orwell, I wish to show that the relationship is highly complex, a mixture of admiration and contempt. Simon distances O from Orwell because, I suggest, this relationship is not the primary focus of comparison in Simon's text: the reduplication concerns LSM and O, although it has always been the O/Orwell connection that critics have stressed (see Fletcher in Duncan, 1985, pp. 100-12). The parallel between LSM and O occurs even on the level of the initialization of their respective names, a link which Simon himself makes:

> LSM is made of words and images and cannot be a portrait of General Lacombe Saint-Michel, in the same way that O is not Orwell (who in any case was himself not George Orwell, since his real name was Eric Arthur Blair) (New York, 1982, pp. 22-3).

The historical person is thus kept distinct from the fictional in the same manner that the political Simon is not the writer or his writings. Orwell's pseudonym (fictional name) acts as a more overt signal of this same differentiation.

Such notions of disguised identity are paramount to the intertextual complexities of Simon's novel. From a close reading, it is obvious that *Homage* appears throughout, but in diverse ways. From the outset (Part One of *Les Géorgiques*) it quickly follows the history of an eighteenth-century revolutionary, by offering a twentieth-century version. The personal experiences of social and political upheaval undergone by the two protagonists in two separate epochs are intertwined, and interlock textually to form a larger jigsaw: the themes of revolution and war. The unidentified 'Il' who opens the text (and therefore takes first place contextually and in order of importance) only takes on the name LSM much later, when his pieces have been put together. It is exactly this jigsaw-puzzle technique which is mirrored in the secondary figure, whom we later discover to be O. In the process of discovering their identities, the reader focusses more carefully on their actions and compares their experiences of hardship, discomfort and the sufferings of war. What is stressed particularly in Part One *and* Part Two of *Les Géorgiques* is the great physical misery suffered during Winter campaigns.

Nor have critics commented on the breadth of military experience that LSM represents, mirrored by the vast geographical areas he covers in the course of the novel. The O thread is less extensive, because less important, but is no less comprehensive of O's political service and involvement. Simon stretches it by commingling the events of the 1940s debacle experienced by his other twentieth-century narrator-protagonist [Georges] with O(rwell)'s involvement on the Aragon Front during the winter *before* the Barcelona riots in May (specific reference is made on p. 25). The links between LSM and O, established in Part One, do not end there. LSM is seen, long after his involvement in the French revolution and its aftermath, writing up his experience as memoirs, and we have constant documentation of his letters and written directives to his military and personal attendants. There are many striking parallels concerning the activities of O as *write,* early in the text: 'Le soleil éclaire d'un jour frisant la main qui feuillette les cahiers format registre aux pages couvertes d'une écriture régulière' (p. 24). Six pages later, the writings in roman and italic script, to distinguish the writers LSM and O respectively, blend together, mirroring the thematic similarities between them: their lives and writings are variations. The description of O's hand betrays its owner indirectly by the pun on page 24, 'comme du crêpe *georgette*' (my emphasis). This hand, like LSM's, is soon writing letters to officials (page 30) and pleading for supplies for the front (page 32). The only signal we have that this is (O)'s narrative thread is the place name 'Bilbao'.

Where the first section of Part One mainly refers obliquely to Orwell's Aragon days through buried intertexts, the second part of *les Géorgiques* signposts the identity of O and then events in Barcelona, not Aragon. On page 61, we read 'O raconte que... ', and this introduces his first experience of throwing a bomb and his fear in the heat of war. On page 66, we have moved to Barcelona, and to a later period in Orwell's life. This greater specificity, however, does not detract from the force of the Orwell intertext, which is used to paint a vivid background of warfare—fear, fatigue, the noise of fighting—in a twentieth-century key, to complement the whirl of similar experiences in the main LSM narrative. Positive collusion with *Homage* in Part One is therefore established by its juxtaposition with the main body of Simon's text. The suppression of the intertext's origin ensures that the fragments chosen remain a minor theme, but intact, as far as their thematic associativity is concerned.

This is not however the case in Part Four of Simon's novel. I suggest that this is because O's identity must be closely tied to Orwell's. By narrowing the field to twentieth-century comparisons, and by negating the LSM links in doing so, the universalizing elements of O are removed. It is as this point in *Les Géorgiques* that admiration for the intertext is superseded by mockery, exaggerations, criticism, even contempt, as Simon's *text* attacks Orwell and *Homage* directly. It seems no accident, then, that this stage of intertextualizing *Homage* coincides with the many specific episodes from the May riots in Barcelona, and with unmistakably Orwellian turns of phrase. Integration of the intertext (Part One) is replaced here by overt delineation *apart* from Simon's writing. So, while the experiences of Orwell and Simon's O in Barcelona operate in tandem, by spotlighting the former, their foreignness and difference are emphasized, and these produce the necessary forum for criticism and attack. Complete identification of Orwell and

Homage, then, destroys their universal implications. Such shifts in the reusage of this intertext, and the reasons I suggest for them, go some way to explaining why Simon, in Part Four, as Fletcher says, 'quotes or paraphrases less and offers instead a commentary or meditation on Orwell's document' (in Duncan, 1985, p. 105). Fletcher also notes, but does not explain why

> the May troubles are closely annotated, particularly... the actual street fighting... This is covered in two main passages in *Les Géorgiques,* pages 293-308 and 355-60... Finally, the last two chapters, covering Orwell's experiences as a wanted man, his escape to France and return to peaceful England, are retold in some detail in *Les Géorgiques* (particularly on pages 263-80 and 310) (ibid., p. 104).

My reading of the Orwell intertext in its LSM context offers an interpretation for these emphases. The parallels of taking part in action and the later documentation of it are central foci. Simon dwells on these two aspects to make explicit what has been implicit and intertwined with earlier parts of his novel. The explicit particularizes, and therefore contrasts with, Simon's own narrator and writing. Furthermore, because of Simon's own involvement in Barcelona, he can pinpoint particular elements: the May riots occupy the centre position of his text, but they do so as O's and Orwell's experiences. Thus Simon borrows what he would never have employed himself, Orwell's overviews and asides, and his Englishness (the foreign perspective on the Spanish Civil War). This Englishness is epitomized in such things as humour: 'leurs organes virils ce qu'en argot militaire les Anglais appellent avec humour un "D.S.O", entendant par là non le glorieux "Distinguished Service Order" mais le peu enviable "Dickie shot off" ' (p. 282). English institutions such as 'Army and Navy Stores' (p. 284) Penguin Books ('un roman policier intitulé "La disparition de l'usurier" ' p. 302), and his English public school background which includes accent, dress ('col Eton', 'pantalons de flanelle'—pp. 326 and 328 respectively), cricket, insularism and the idealisms which lead him to join the POUM, 'sa secte philosophique' (p. 298).

It again seems to me quite in order that the Barcelona May riots are the balance point (Part Four to page 308) between use of Orwell as mirror and foil in *Les Géorgiques.* Barcelona, as we have discussed in the personal and historical excursions into the PSUC/POUM differences between Simon and Orwell, is the nexus of similarity and difference: two men involved in the same event, but on opposing sides. Textually speaking, Simon's O, and Orwell of *Homage,* react in the same way, Simon's fictionalized narrator elaborating Orwell as narrator of *Homage.*

The rift separating O and Orwell, and Simon and Orwell as *writers* coincides, I maintain, with the break in Part Four at page 308. Because Orwell and his text are identified, and utterly recognizable, Simon's reworking and attack move from the mainly thematic to the scriptural. His writing now examines and challenges *Homage* as an alternative written documentation of personal involvement in the Spanish Civil War. The tinge of personal prejudice evident in Simon's reconstruction and reappraisal of Orwell's involvement as O is much more pronounced when it comes to comments on Orwell as *writer* of *Homage.* The quotation of several long sections from the second section of Part Four underscores, and mirrors in fictionalized form, exactly the same issues for which Simon criticizes Orwell's account in his interview: the presentation of a chronological, apparently logical overview, the suppression of important facts to make the account more coherent, action-packed and self-congratulatory, and the lack of explanation of the factions involved:

> Peut-être espère-t-il qu'en écrivant son aventure il s'en dégagera un sens cohérent. Tout d'abord le fait qu'il va énumérer dans leur ordre chronologique des événements qui se bousculent pêle-mêle dans sa mémoire ou se présentent selon des priorités d'ordre affectif devrait... les expliquer. Il pense aussi peut-être qu'à l'intérieur de cet ordre premier les obligations de la construction syntaxique feront ressortir des rapports de cause à effet. Il y aura cependant des trous dans son récit, des points obscurs, des incohérences même. Soit qu'il suppose certains faits déjà connus (son passé...), soit que pour une raison ou pour une autre il passe sous silence ses véritables motivations...
> Il essaie de faire comprendre cela. Visiblement il écrit... à l'intention d'uncertain public... dont il connaît les penchants, les opinions, peut prévoir les réactions. D'une part son éducation... le préserve de toute vantardise... d'autre part, pour mieux convaincre, il s'efforce (feint?) de se borner aux faits... étayant son récit de juste ce qu'il faut d'images pour que celui-ci n'ait pas la sécheresse d'un simple compte rendu, lui conférant plus de persuasion, de crédibilité... de ces 'choses vues' dont tout bon journaliste sait qu'elles constituent les meilleurs certificats d'authenticité d'un reportage, d'autant qu'elles s'insèrent dans une forme d'écriture qui se présente comme neutre (il recourt des phrases courtes, il évite... les adjectifs de valeur et d'une façon générale tout ce qui pourrait ressembler une interprétation partisane ou tendancieuse des événements, comme s'il n'y avait pas été étroitement mêlé mais en avait été un témoin sans passion...
> Il ne dit pas pour quelles raisons il se rendit à telle caserne des milices...

> Sauf qu'il ne parla pas des cortèges, ni des insidieuses et meurtrières manchettes des journaux, ni des rivalités entre les différentes casernes aux différents parrainages, il raconta tout le reste sur ce même ton rêveur, pensif, qui se voulait neutre, s'appliquant à dissimuler sous une distanciation teintée d'humour ce qu'il y avait de pathétique dans son aventure (pp. 310-11, 314, 328 and 331 respectively).

The narrator of *Les Géorgiques* is now acting as a textual critic. What has previously been suggested by the juxtaposition of the two different narratives in previous sections of the novel is now openly expressed. The criticisms are dressed up as mock hypotheses, the comment of the 'other', what Orwell does *not* say and irony. In turn, the mock reconstruction of Orwell writing his *Homage* through the use of a narrator/writer, O, and intertexts from *Homage*, which involves going back over events we have already read, is a *tour de force* of self-conscious writing and intertextual reflexivity. The complexity of superimposition is increased when we recall that O and Orwell interlock with Georges and LSM and of course overlap with the personal experience of Simon himself.

Both O(rwell) and L(acombe) S(aint-)M(ichel), through their respective revolutionary involvements, to some extent seek to *justify* their actions. This counterpoints Simon's intention throughout *Les Géorgiques* to show instead of tell. Simon also offers insights into the genre of political autobiography by using LSM and O to sum up the distance between the personal experience of revolution and its later documentation. Both O (at the end of Part Four) and LSM (at the end of Part Five) fade out of the narrative, their stories incomplete and incompletable, and thus presenting a challenge to the genre (political autobiography) by offering a 'revolutionary' alternative.

Simon, then, intertextualizes Orwell, not for who he was, but for what he and *Homage* represent. In this sense only is *Les Géorgiques* a paean to *Homage* as exemplum of subjective, and therefore coloured, participation in political activity and its reporting. *Les Géorgiques,* through the parallel of LSM and O and a re-fictionalized *Homage,* opens up the categories of history, political autobiography, biography and documentary, to present a new intertextual freeplay, and a *Catalogne libre.*

Les Géorgiques is also the culmination of an increasingly complex mingling of textual viewpoints on the Spanish Civil War and includes intertexts and episodes from Simon's earlier novels, notably *Le Palace,* all of which can be seen to stem from Simon's personal account in *La Corde raide*. Reference to Orwell, I contend, plays an important role in the plotting of this growing intricacy. This aspect of Orwell has not been studied in detail, and I shall now investigate it across Simon's *œuvre*.

In *Le Sacre du Printemps,* the debate about political idealism is set up by the bipartite juxtaposition of Bernard and his step-father, who reminisces on the Spanish Civil War. Despite its doubled structure of youth and middle-age, 1936 and 1952, the whole narrative is recounted from an authorially distanced standpoint. It is interesting to note the involvement of Ceccaldi, the Italian militiaman, with the stepfather in view of a similar character in *Homage*. It is next in *Le Palace,* that more complex narrative structure mirrors the involvement of the narrators and their intertwined accounts of the action. The Italian, Ceccaldi, of *Le Sacre du printemps* becomes the 'Homme-Fusil', his story occupying Part Two. That his name is replaced by that of an object is indicative of the distancing of his personality from narrative function. Focus is now on the tale and the telling, not the teller. The nickname (as other) is equivalent to the 'otherness' of a penname (as 'Orwell' for Blair). In Part Three, the mouthpiece is the American, the war veteran instructing the student to enable the latter to become the vehicle of narration in Part Four. The omniscience of this American is rather Orwellian in tone. In *Le Palace,* therefore, the narrative angle of *Homage* is mirrored, but without the intertext intruding specifically as Fletcher hinted: '*Le Palace* est revu, réécrit comme par (ou pour) un George Orwell' (1981, p. 1216). Simon is questioning coherent eye-witness reports and retelling of events through the narrative division of *Le Palace,* each actor or embodiment of a viewpoint failing to complete his story before the following one is overlaid. The student's viewpoint is comparable to Simon's own, but the author Simon remains outside his text, which, like *Le Sacre du printemps,* remains a third person narrative.

By *Histoire.* the involvement of first-person narrative intrudes into Spanish Civil War experiences. Thus the directness of eye-witness reports, and the account of them, are introduced into the exploration of history and fiction seen in the earlier novels. These were the preparatory build-up for the introduction of intertexts *incorporating* these genres as textual protagonists in their own right. The 'je' and 'il' of *Histoire* signal more personal narrative involvement, which is developed in Simon's next novel, *La Bataille de Pharsale.* Here a very personal search to recount the past (both historical and individual) occurs. By Part Three, the *writing down* of these viewpoints has now been introduced into the text: O sits alone at his desk. It is the figure of the writer which is important here, and while O is the commingling of the 'je' and 'il' into an anonymous, zero-degree writer who may shift between the two modes of narration, O (as we know in retrospect) can also be seen as a sign for Orwell. The description of him at his desk is repeated in those sections of *Les Géorgiques* where the Orwell intertext is privileged. In *La Bataille de Pharsale,* the text of *Homage* is not included, because, I suggest, the war descriptions from Proust are more important in this battle of precursors. Once Simon's own voice is firmly established, intertexts from all previous writing pose no threat to his textual dominance. Thus the intrusion of a mass of war intertexts in *Les Géorgiques* demonstrates Simon's authorial confidence and subjugation of precursors. Simon can then include not just the Orwell writer figure as model, but also his writing, to criticize such modes of narration and fictional production. To conclude, then, I suggest that Orwell has been a subconscious intertext long before *Les Géorgiques,* traces of this gradually emerging in the course of Simon's development. This suggestion comes certainly with a degree of reader hindsight from *Les Géorgiques,* but is a valid reading nonetheless. Orwell, seen in this light, demonstrates Simon's most deep-rooted fictional concerns and personal prejudices.

*****

Simon is therefore a French revolutionary of writing in more than one sense. He includes the French Revolution, and revolution as an historical and thematic subject, within his works. He reworks the writings of the revolutionaries of prose development such as Proust, Joyce and Faulkner. Despite the strongly political overtones in his writings, as exemplified in his intertextual layering of Reed and Orwell, Simon is seen to be most interested in the revolutionary form of writing itself. Simon, by rewriting *his own work* as well, goes through the same points (words), but with each revolution a new dynamic of writing is produced. The next chapter will investigate how.

In conclusion, therefore, the reopening and reworking of structures of language, be they quotations from writers from one's own or a foreign tradition, and the re-deployment of genres of writing through parody, pastiche or textual juxtaposition, are the deep intertextual processes which constantly rejuvenate and complicate the novels of Claude Simon. His usage of twentieth-century materials incorporates an enormous range of 'architextes' and 'archétypes', the extent and complexity of which have not been fully appreciated. With each succeeding novel, Simon's use of intertexts demonstrates his greater mastery of mixing, intertwining, regenerating and revolutionizing the fragments of previous literature, so that within the 'courbe fermée' of writing he does 'repasse[r] par les mêmes points', but in his own particular way.

Chapter Seven

Simon quoting Simon

Having considered the many and various influences on Claude Simon, this final chapter will consider his latest novel *L'Acacia* in the light of what can be described as *intra-textuality* (Fitch, 1983, p. 85) to distinguish it from *intratextualité* or those processes of linguistic reverberations which operate within one text field. It is the author's use of his or her own *œuvre* as regenerative reference points for which I shall reserve Fitch's term. This self-quotation also revitalises the concept of literary copying, plagiarism, which I discussed in the first chapter. When one quotes oneself, *autocritical* examination is at stake. Dällenbach's conceptualising of *mise en abyme,* 'le retour de l'œuvre sur elle-même' (1977, p. 18) can thus be further complicated when *'œuvre'* is not merely meant as one text but the opus of a writer. For such a self-reflexive and self-conscious novelist as Simon, the 'récit spéculaire' is also superimposed by the *'œuvre spéculaire'*. How and where this happens in his writing will be the point of particular interest. It is clear from our investigations thus far that Simon's borrowings from other writers have diminished as his own inimitable style has emerged; we have suggested disaffiliation from Proust as a crucial threshold. Do *intra-texts* actually become more important? The other key consideration regarding self-centering *mises en abyme* is the autobiographical nature of use of one's own previous work. Such self-referentiality is therefore a marker of development and direction across an *oeuvre*, and serves at the same time to highlight the new elements in a given text. We shall be examining *L'Acacia* for this very pattern. Along the way we shall be discussing the question of autobiography itself, for this text is the most overtly autobiographical account to date of who Simon is in relation to his family. It is however a text which is as problematic as to its generic specificity as it is to its investigation of how self-reference operates. Suffice it to say at this point that the agenda of this novel is a summation of themes and episodes which are quintessentially Simonian hallmarks. By aligning *H/histoire* in both its senses once more as an almost overlapping duality, and to a degree more transparent and yet more paradoxical, the new departures of *L'Acacia* which is its reworking are particularly noticeable.

This chapter also raises a major methodological problem in the study of intertexts in any, but particularly contemporary, writing. I approach this text very differently, say, to someone coming to Simon for the first time, or, indeed, coming with different cultural baggage. I therefore cannot offer a 'naïve' reading. Simon's self-reference is then obvious to me but not to a newcomer. As I have knowledge of the whole of the *œuvre* behind me, the problem of missing allusions or traces is less acute. However, this mix of reader responses merely underlines the fact that no uncovering of allusion, trace or reference is ever exhausted—textual reverberations and reference-spotting depend on the vigilance of multiple readers.

Intra-textuality as regenerative strategy

In the last chapter we discussed revolutionary intertexts in Simon's writing which recharged his own in both form and content. Simon's revolutionizing of his own writing is the intra-textual equivalent of these processes and *L'Acacia* provides their clearest and most complex illustrations. However, while they are most sustained here, intra-textuality is not unique to this novel. Each new revolution produces a new dynamic of writing because total re-quotation with expansion yields automatically a different text. It needs to be said that most of Simon's pre-*La Bataille de Pharsale* novels have within them a kernal from an earlier, published short text. Even a novel as 'mature' as *Les Géorgiques* expands a rewritten fragment of the same name published in the *NRF* in 1978.

Simon's *œuvre* has witnessed more sustained self-regeneration than has been recognised and when the rewriting is a complete novel, not just fragments, this suggests defiant plagiarism for a purpose, marking off crucial points for development and change. *Les Corps conducteurs* takes its core intra-text, *Orion aveugle*, expands and renames it, and removes the pictorial juxtapositions accompanying the earlier work. In turn, a whole phase of densely associative and almost formalistic gaming opens up, this cycle of Simon's novels then closed off by another self-subsuming intra-text, *La Chevelure de Bérénice*. More subtle in its reworking—only the title is changed—this text nonetheless follows the exact patterning of the first of the 'period', *Femmes* (1966). It illustrates scriptorial independence as against pictorial substrata: reproductions of Miró's *Femmes* in Simon's *Femmes* enable the earlier work, even providing its title. The later intra-textual reworking clearly establishes its own dense prose poetry as I have established elsewhere (Orr in Duncan, 1985, pp. 131-9). These texts, then, pave the way for larger-scale intra-textual activity, tantamount to the practices we have examined in Simon's intertextual development. To recap, one major intertext was reworked, such as *Ten Days* in *Histoire,* to provide a practice ground for combinations and complications of intertextual design and usage. The investigations of the Latin texts and Proust in *La Bataille de Pharsale* and Virgil, Orwell (and elsewhere, Strachey) in *Les Géorgiques* have amply proved the point. It is thus the self-inter-referentiality that must be born uppermost in mind in L'*Acacia* as we survey its multiple intra-texts.

The intra-texts in *L'Acacia* have been noted by Sardonak recently and give a helpful list of references to Simon's other novels (1991). I do not intend to cover the same ground but to take Sardonak's research beyond the point of simply listing the references, helpful though this is. What Sardonak fails to do is to analyse the data he has collected; why has Simon chosen certain topoi for example, or lifted sections from earlier novels? Why too does he use, say, a section in *Herbe* where a similar event recurs in *La Route des Flandres*? Sardonak claims intra-texts from the whole of Simon's opus, but makes no reference to the reusage of sections from *Femmes* or *Orion aveugle* in *L'Acacia.* Such omissions I will rectify as they seem highly pertinent in this novel which is, as Sardonak rightly describes it, 'une arborescence intertextuelle' (ibid., p. 229) and hence intra-textual. Other questions arise from his list which again Sardonak does not himself pose. Why does Simon include in this novel his earliest texts like *Le Tricheur* and *Gulliver* when he overtly eschews these as writerly juvinalia in interviews? *La Corde raide* seems also to take up substantial intra-textual space, comparatively speaking, when again it has been largely discounted by Simon and his critics. The obvious question is: why? In addition, some of the fragments which Sardonak attributes to one of the 'middle period' novels could equally well be classified against another, as what is at stake is more a recurrent motif with variations. How should such intra-texts then be classified?

With these multifarious questions in mind, the obvious place to start is the interpretation and analysis of the many intra-texts in *L'Acacia.* The first point to note is their sheer abundance. Hardly a page goes by where there is not some reference to a former work. Obviously the effect is one of 'déjà vu et lu', that self-conscious literary collusion between Simon and his readers at one level and this text as against its forebears on the other. Rather than being seen as a postscript or appendix (Nitsch, 1990, p. 590), *L'Acacia* so incorporates its previous manifestations that it becomes almost a palimpsest or foreword, prefacing a new vision, not a revision. That the reader of Simon's novels is familiar with the earlier materials in no way detracts from the reworking. The superimposition of layers of text is a serious 'représentation' or enactment of the subject in the sense we discussed in chapter two, where we said that drama is the making present of the totally quoted form in a new body. I argue that this is the power of *L'Acacia,* for the reworking prevents the undermining facet of intertextual repetition, travesty or pastiche from occurring. Instead, the former texts become almost the retrospective synecdoches of this one which overarches them all and elucidates them afresh. The familiar then becomes defamiliarised, not only because the new context does this anyway, as in any intertextual operation: the reordering of the narrative pieces automatically adds different and complementary perspectives.

This reordering is further enhanced by what is trully unfamiliar; the totally new episodes which are included in *L'Acacia.* It is these which are not simply the glue pasting the intra-texts together. They have a dynamic of their own and form new lines or link persona in the family tree of Simon's novels. One of the most crucial of these is the opening section of the novel. It is immediately striking to readers of Simon that the first word is 'Elles' (p. 11). Simon is notorious for his male-centred texts, and the designation of narrators always as 'il' or the masked 'je' as male subject. The multiple 'il(s)' linking male protagonists across generations in *Les Géorgiques* is a case in point. Altogether, women occupy little textual space across Simon's *œuvre* and when they do, are often the objects of erotic fantasy or artists' models. Corinne and Tante Marie are exceptions, but even these women are reductions to female archetypes, the lover/whore and the old maid. They are passive, static, the fixed points around which the more important acts of men revolve be these war or sexual exploits. This whole opening section of *L'Acacia* is therefore a new departure. The women are active and involved in war as the protectors of the child who will become the future narrator. Of different generations and ages, they nonetheless fulfil roles normally meted out in Simon's novels to the war heroes; they undergo discomforts and dangers (p. 15); they are constantly on the move, and need to use their resourcefulness to eat and sleep safely; they confront the wreckage and destruction of buildings ravaged by war as the male narrator does in *Leçon de choses* (p. 20). Most importantly, they succeed where male narrators fail. Often the latter are trying to find a location, a past rootedness. The narrator looks unsuccessfully for the site of the Battle of Pharsalus but this is also a paradigm of the activity of this whole cycle of Simon's novels, the abortive verification of events, the suicide of Reixach being the chief of these. Here in *L'Acacia,* the women find the tomb which is the probable depository of the dead father (p. 25). Subsequent sections of the novel which have the 'elle(s)' subject then take a new line into the familiar (male) dramas, filling in previous lacunae and integrating the story of the female side of the family drama with the ancestor/LSM documents. Sections to note are for example pages 113-128, 143-150, 263-279, 309-313. The 'elle' narrative does disappear at this last point as the narrator they have been nurturing grows up and becomes independent. However, his greater involvement with the all-too-familiar war themes is offset by the fact that the 'female' sections I have quoted are all to be found in the material relating to the 1919, 1880-1914, 1910-1914(-1940) strand of historical strata, itself new to Simon's novels. The only other reference to this period of history is through the use of literary intertexts from Proust centring on episodes like the sinking of the Lusitania in *La Bataille de Pharsale* in part three of the text, where, I suggested, the power of the 'father-figure', Proust was conquered by the independent literary 'son'. It seems no accident then that in *L'Acacia,* where the historical interfaces of generations in Simon's family history are at stake, that it is the sections surrounding the death of the actual father and the role of these strong women/mother figures which regenerate the whole text. They are its dynamic, as Simon has openly declared: 'Je n'ai trouvé la composition du livre qu'au mois d'octobre de l'année dernière. Il y avait des années que j'y travaillais,... et cette construction binaire, je n'en ai eu l'idée que l'année dernière alors que presque tout était écrit' (Lebrun, 1989, p. 39). In terms of rather basic feminist readings of male-centred texts, Simon's revelation seems somewhat trite and unspectacular. Given the evermore self-endorsing, and consequently male, viewpoint of the whole, this 'new' device is effectively a breakthrough in regeneration of the *œuvre.* The inclusion of the female subject not as object of male desire (negative 'other'), but as independent principle seriously revitalises not just the 'archive simonienne' in terms of the female forebears. It begs questions concerning the very structuring devices and layering of narrations of the past.

Throughout this book, I have discussed layers of 'il'-centred narratives. As early as *Le Sacre du printemps* the dual twining of times, Bernard's and his step-father's provides contrastive and comparative narrative movement. Later novels complicate this pattern by trebling or multiplying viewpoints culminating in the complex structure of *Les Géorgiques*. What I have hitherto not also spelt out is that all the intertextual layers that highlight and accentuate the historical and literary time strands in Simon's texts are without exception male-authored. Intertextually and intra-textually speaking, Simon is then totally canonical in this respect even though his literary practice seeks to subvert and regenerate more revolutionary and 'authentic' modes of narrative. Only time will tell whether his extensive use of these female subjects who also write copious amounts of letters will produce or accentuate alternative descriptive techniques in Simon's future writing, those often associated with 'écriture féminine'—blanks, non-visual descriptive focus, fluid imagery. A note in passing is revealing of the intertextual potential the women figures harbour in *L'Acacia*. Contents of LSM's library in *Les Géorgiques* revealed again a male canon. The texts ascribed to the mother in *L'Acacia* are notable for their difference to the collected Rousseau, and the Latin Classics: 'les œuvres de la Comtesse de Ségur, d'Andersen, quelques Balzac, Verlaine, Albert Samain, Anatole France' (p. 119). A woman writer, a poet and obvious creators of fictions and fairystories mark an other view of literature generating reverberations which, even by allusion and a degree of dismissal (Balzac's fate sealed in what we discussed in chapter four), nonetheless question the seamless intertextual and intra-textual superstructure of Simon's opus.

I now want to link this new material back to the omissions in Sardonak's catalogue of intra-texts in *L'Acacia*. The chief of these is of course *Femmes* or its later reworking as *La Chevelure de Bérénice*. What is particularly interesting about the fragments which are reworked is that they all appear in the new line, the 'elles' narrative in *L'Acacia*. Indeed the strategy of the feminine pronoun subject can be traced to these much earlier texts. In the latter, the 'elle' is broken off from the surrounding descriptions even when she is joined to the two other women in the text, the narrative overview then encapsulating and controlling the feminine element of the text. In both works, there are three women of different ages, one a young mother with a male child. In *L'Acacia,* there is a marked and major shift of emphasis, in that the female subjects are much more autonomous even though they are always seen in relation to the male narrator(s). The second departure that these intra-texts represent has to do with deep structures and stylistic shifts in Simon's prose, shifts which largely do not occur in the war sections of the novel which lift easily recognisable tropes and segments from Simon's earlier novels. This is perhaps a reason why Sardonak has listed with facility these intra-texts and not seen those from *La Chevelure*. The latter are never direct re-quotations. As we shall see they are associative, interpretative 'reprises' operating on poetic reverberation and peculiarity of image, rather than on direct, *mise en abyme* recognitions. Let us examine what is at work through these intra-texts which are a 'glance' or echo, not repeat performance.

The following comparisons are all linked in *L'Acacia* to references to water. In the final section of part three of the novel, the vision of 'elle' is recorded:

> Elle ne voit pas la foule. Elle voit un confus amas de particules multicolores, claires ou foncées, agglutinées et mouvantes. Autour d'elle les maisons, les quais, les grues dérivent maintenant de plus en plus lentement. Elle peut entendre le timbre d'une sonnerie et sentir les membrures du navire trembler sous la poussée inversée de l'hélice. Elle peut voir l'eau brassée remonter en gros bouillons en même temps que s'en élève une faible odeur de croupissure, de vase... Entre le flanc noir du navire maintenant tout à fait immobile et le quai, il ne reste plus au fond de la profonde tranchée qu'une étroite bande d'eau sale où flottent des détritus (pp. 149-50).

On the deep-structural/compositional levels, compare this to the 'maintenant' marker construction which is the dynamic of movement in *La Chevelure*, the black versus contrasting colours which distinguish one impression and woman from another, the focus on smell and sound, and the wave-like rhythm of the prose itself. Concerning particular details, the following intra-texts from *La Chevelure* illustrate overlapping images:

> Du port arrivait une odeur fade de vase mêlée à celle des caroubes (p. 17)

> une ligne en festons brunâtre faite de détritus algues morceaux de bois flotté doublait la frange d'écume (p. 18).

In part seven of *L'Acacia,* the introit of *La Chevelure* is reworked in the appearance of the woman on the beach:

> au-dessus de la ligne des dunes, entre deux toits de villas, l'ombrelles, puis le chapeau... puis la tête, le buste de la femme tout entière... et arrivée au bord, sans cesser de tenir son ombrelle, sautillant sur une jambe, se déchaussant, lançant l'un après l'autre ses souliers derrière elle, et même sans enlever ses bas entrant elle-même dans l'eau, sa longue jupe retroussée, insoucieuse des éclaboussures, le bas de sa robe déjà trempé... (et dans le fracas des vagues déferlantes, des cris discordants des mouettes...) (*A,* pp. 211-2)

> lourde tout entière vêtue de noir la tête couverte d'un fichu noir elle traversa la plage déserte (*CB,* p. 7)

> elle retira ses bas l'un après l'autre les roulant à mesure ... se leva et entra dans l'eau relevant sa jupe mais pas assez une vague plus haute l'atteignit mouillant une bande ondulée irrégulière (*CB,* p. 8)

> chaque soir les vagues marron sortant l'une après l'autre au fond de la nuit se brisant avançant lentement en lignes parallèles déferlant (*CB,* p. 12)

It is clear that deliberate changes are wrought within a strict set of textual pieces. Collisions and defamiliarisations are produced, but only because the elements are at first familiar and unmistakable. Simon seems here through these intra-texts to be altering previous perspectives not least descriptive techniques themselves recharged from within his own vocabularies. Such transformation of language we saw in operation with the set of Proustian signifier intertexts in chapter five, where Simon transposed each sign into his own tongue. In *L'Acacia,* this process is similar, but intra-textual. As the *'Chevelure'*-like elements are osmosed into the main body of the text and entwined as a strand, the transpositional and accretional factors of association become increasingly visible. The end of part eleven is a case in point. The colours of the sunset, particularly the final pink tone, and the 'plaine sablonneuse' landscape (p. 337) smack of the final, overall impression of the earlier text, which also ends with a narrative focus on the observer, (male) narrator. This 'feel' for the emotive and Simonian poetic of the earlier work is only enhanced as *L'Acacia* reaches its conclusion. The narrator takes a trip to the beach, and sits watching the waves

> couleur de sable, se bousculer, s'écraser dans un assourdissant et vaste fracas. Elles arrivaient... montant l'une sur l'autre, échevelées, galopant comme des chevaux... s'étalant pour finir en longues nappes baveuses

> que buvait le sable, pétillantes... L'hiver vint. Le vent courbait les points effilées des cyprès... Un jour il en abattit sept d'un coup, entraînés les uns par les autres comme des quilles, gisant, semblables à de fabuleux ossements parmi les convulsives chevelures de leurs branches brisées (p. 377).

This passage is an amalgam of key images from *La Chevelure*, the white horses of the waves picking up the descriptions of the constellations, 'la Chevelure de Bérénice Pégase' (p. 12) reflected in the sea where the women are wading, and then rewriting it with a section already used

> longeant la bordure baveuse des vagues...
> la frange d'écume plus loin une seconde encore mais plus imprécise vestige des tempêtes d'hiver parfois un arbre tout entier avec ses racines griffues convulsives (p. 18).

This intercalation of motifs and images culminates in both texts with tree imagery as figure of proliferation into writing. In *La Chevelure,* the narrator sees 'la première étoile ses branches avaient l'air de s'allonger et de se raccourcir tour à tour rétractiles (p. 24), the final word of the text stating a present-tense, uneasy stasis between two opposite forces. *L'Acacia* closes at night also, the branches of the acacia tree being the focus 'comme si l'arbre tout entier ... se secouait, après quoi tout s'apaisait et elles [the branches] reprenaient leur immobilité.' (p. 380). While in no sense can the intra-text be seen as such in conventional terms of a one-to-one relationship, the similarities across *L'Acacia* that I have highlighted, leave the inter-relationship between the two unquestionable. What happens through the proliferations, echoes and decentralisations of the intra-text in the new frame is the reinterpretation of a writing experience through regeneration from the same roots. Simon does not so much plagiarize his own earlier novels in this case as revolutionize their core engendering potential. This is a reason why the family tree is troped back onto the tree-like structure and growth of Simon's *œuvre.* It is the female family line which is the prime mover, not the familiar LSM branch. And it can be argued that it is this new poetic echoing of his previous lyricised descriptive texts which amplify and aerate Simon's writing. The product is a kind of simonian 'écriture féminine', embedded into the more familiar 'écriture masculine'.

The intertwining of the 'male' and 'female' lines of writing in *L'Acacia* allows further latent stylistic features in Simon's writing to surface. One I particularly wish to draw attention to is epitomised in chapter eleven which openly signals the liaison of the two lines by the dates 1910-1914-1940... It closes significantly with four prisoners of war suffering familiar hardships to those of earlier Simon novels. Here, however, they form a quartet using scrap objects as instruments:

> Il remplace parfois le bidon par une gamelle de fer blanc... Les autres instruments consistent en une flûte de roseau au son voilé et deux morceau de bois dont les chocs font entendre un bruit creux, sec, contrastant avec le bruissements d'une boîte à clous. A part la gamelle, l'ensemble (le flanc de la baraque, les musiciens, leurs vêtements, leurs visages) est tout entier composé dans une gamme de couleurs terreuses et les seules notes vives sont apportées par les écussons de laine qui subsistent encore aux cols des vareuses, l'un portant un numéro noir sur fond rouge, l'autre un numéro rouge au font vert (p. 335).

The interplay of colours, the flotsam and jetsam and musicality of prosidy from *La Chevelure* is orchestrated in an alternative male context. In musical terms, this is indeed a 'reprise' of simonian themes with variations. What this 'new' passage does quite stunningly is foreground the tones of Simon's prose, its stylistic colours and musical tonalities. The reader familiar with Simon's *œuvre* need only be made attentive to verbs of sound to see where *L'Acacia* reverberates with a more self-conscious musicality of language by orchestrating afresh its own often visual components. These in turn conduct critical notice back to the fragments of the text which are intra-texts from the 'Georges-cycle' novels, but can now be read musically: the opera episodes in *Les Géorgiques* are repeated in *L'Acacia* (these are associated with the female line, for example p. 120) and elements from *Leçon de choses* ('le son de choses'). These 'reprises' conjoin to illustrate music as topos and verbal structure in Simon's work. In addition, they are parts linked with cameos from each of his preceeding novels. Instead of trying to conceal the identities of the intertexts (as with Reed and Orwell) Simon spotlights individual texts by their distinguishing markers—the postcards from *Histoire*, the 'bonnet phrygien' from *La Bataille de Pharsale,* the *mise en abyme* biscuit tin from *L'Herbe*—and the universal phrases concerning the horse-ride, the conditions of war etc. These can all then be seen to be choric, so that when taken together in *L'Acacia,* they magnify the individual force they enjoyed in earlier manifestations and thus amplify what is quintessential to Simon's prose voice. Such amplification in *L'Acacia,* then, serves retrospectively to accentuate themes, obsessions, tropes and verbal counterpoints across earlier novels. *L'Acacia* is therefore no coda to Simon's *œuvre*, but its symphony.

The intra-text as autobiographeme

Critics have been quick to hail *L'Acacia* as 'le plus autobiographique des livres de Claude Simon' (for example Pobel, 1990, p. 74), and Simon himself has not denied the real-life basis of his fiction over a substantial period of his output: 'Dans *Les Géorgiques*, *L'Invitation* et *L'Acacia*, il n'y a pas un seul élémant fictif. C'est que j'ai fini par comprendre (ou sentir) que "la réalité" dépasse la fiction' (Armel, 1990, p. 98). However, while there are clear autobiographical overlappings in the text, this is not to say that it is an autobiography. It is interesting to glance at the appelations various critics have preferred to use such as 'une régression dans le biographique gommant le narrateur à contre-jour des *Géorgiques*' (Bon, 1989, p. 981). While this is partly true, it is also inadequate because Simon's project has always defied single categorisations as we have seen with the dualities in *Histoire*. Dällenbach makes the useful distinction between the inter(intra-text) as synecdoche and what he sees to be the properly simonien 'archive', a collection of fragments which operate together but which 'ne restitue jamais qu'un morceau d'une totalité bricolée ... qui accuse vides et trous... L'enquêteur simonien s'implique dans son travail de fouille et s'abîme dans ses sondages; en s'adonnant à ceux-ci, c'est sa propre identité qi'il expose, car le document auquel on donne la parole interpelle le sujet au présent condamne une confrontation dont il ne sort jamais tout à fait indemne' (1988, p. 738). Simon himself valorises the fragmented and fragmentary picture, the (bri)collage text in the context of an interview after the publication of *L'Acacia* (Lebrun, 1989, p. 39) quoting the Flaubert 'corrections' which we discussed in chapter four. The particular fragments Simon sees as the foreground of this, his own, novel are his 'histoire familiale' as elsewhere in his *œuvre*, but with the difference of emphasis being on his immediate parentage, 'la mort de mon père m'ont paru de bons prétextes à écrire. Ça permettrait à l'écriture de se développer' (ibid., pp. 39-40). This statement has a surprisingly unmodern focus to it when we look again at writers such as Montaigne. For Simon as for Montaigne, theories of writing are seen to be inseparable from textual production, just as the writer and narrator are inseparable and yet, paradoxically, not the same entity. The 'moy' of Montaigne's *Essais* is thus not Montaigne: the *Essais* are not his autobiography, but they do plot his self-development as a writer. Empirical facts may be used as raw materials, but they are fictionalized and the writer becomes other by his or her writing, as Cave notes of Montaigne:

> The increasingly reflexive movement of the *Essais* has the dual form: comments on the activities of writing and reading converge with the recurrent abd equally self-endorsing theme of the self-portrait... [The duality between them is unstable because] it can never be fully resolved either in unity or in antithesis; also because the is generated wholly by the writing process itself. In that the *Essais* aim to project the image of a self which conforms to the book, they are neither memoirs not autobiography, but rather a surrogate self, an autoperformance which cannot but displace the 'real' Montaigne (1979, p. 273).

This acute summary applies equally well to Simon, although many of his critics have wanted to equate him with his fictional persona, Georges. *Histoire* and *Les Géorgiques* have been seen as autobiographical texts. The title of the former, however, exemplifies the relationship of Georges with Simon the writer. Both are involved in chronological History and achronological fiction, the one never being exactly the replica of the other because of the ambiguities created by reflection as mental and scriptorial processes. In fact, the more 'personal' the detail included in the fiction, the more the fiction itself questions its own authenticity. In our investigations of the *Homage* intertext in the last chapter, this became abundantly clear. The authenticity of Simon's experience in Barcelona was only more apparent by its uncorroborated absence as 'document' in Simon's novel. The actuality of his participation could only be seen through the screen of personal judgement of Orwell's very different written account whose very style and rhetoric decried its 'honesty' to truth.

Chapter Three of this book undertook to compare Rousseau's idealism and belief in Truth as intertexts against which the textual experience of *La Route des Flandres* could be shown up more clearly in its complex and undisclosing modes of narration. Particularly through his *Confessions*, Rousseau brought about evolution in autobiography and the confessional novel as genres. Art was then an important means of divulging truth and attaining reality: self-description (autobiography) was considered to be the most authoritative presentation of a person's life, introspection, then seen as the best path to self-knowledge. Simon has stated openly that, concerning the autobiographical in his novels: 'C'est vrai, je n'invente rien. Ce que l'on écrit est toujours autobiographique (Senlis, 1960, p. 27). However, Simon makes clear distinctions about what he means by autobiography and thereby marks a clear break with Rousseau's model of self-authentication. The 'je' becomes in Montaigne's sense a surrogate self, not the writer but the other ('il') that he wishes to be:

> Nous ne pouvons imaginer que ce que nous avons vécu nous-mêmes: imaginer l'histoire des autres, c'est donc encore se souvenir de soi. Il y a un passage extraordinaire de Buffon, décrivant Adam tel qu'il vient de s'éveiller au monde. Buffon suppose qu' Adam regarde autour de lui, et tout ce qu'il voit, il croit d'abord que c'est lui-même. Ainsi le monde se réflète en nous (Duranteau, 1967, p. 3).

Autobiography is the means of comparing self with others or previous selves and is a present-tense activity allowing no completed picture to emerge. Because mental processes of memory, imagination and fictional production intervene, discrepancies, distortions, inflations and fictionalizations are the inevitable result. Where Rousseau seemed unaware that any retelling becomes a variation, Simon is highly conscious of the fictional element in any histoire. In fact he positively exploits the notion of variation in his *œuvre,* so that, by *L'Acacia,* our very familiarity with certain tropes becomes our undoing for the new is not the same as the old because of its context and reenactment, even as totally quoted form. Thus the drama of the same re-enters our discussion, but as the interlocutions of speaking voices belonging to the one playwright. Of *Histoire,* Simon made its generic standing quite categorical:

> C'est un roman. Sans doute j'utilise mes souvenirs personnels comme premiers materiaux, mais la dynamique de l'écriture et de l'imaginaire les déforme. Il y a des choses que j'ai passées sous silence, d'autres qui ont grossi. Au bout de compte, le narrateur est moi et n'est pas moi (Simon, avril 1967, p. v).

Autobiography, then, for Simon impinges always on the personal, but only in the broadest sense are Rousseau and he interfaces. I have investigated the 'autobiographical' characteristics in *Les Géorgiques* elsewhere, arguing that this text is an unfinished 'autoportrait' (Beaujour, 1980, pp. 10, 22), 'a portrait of the writer through a portrait of the Novel (Orr, 1990, p. 238). Biographies tie in with memoirs, chronicles and personal letters, all vignettes of lives across historical times and literatures linked by family ties to Simon's own fictionalised experiences. What emerged were less his own recognisable reactions to events (as is usual in autobiography) and more his experience of the substance of writing itself.

In *L'Acacia,* given its intricate intra-textual and 'intertextual bridging' (Orr, ibid., p. 231), the question of its status as autobiography arises more forcibly. It is a feature of the autobiography to include the emergence of the writing-self, even to refer to one's works as Sartre does in *Les Mots,* for example. There seems no doubt that by this criterion *L'Acacia,* because of its intra-textuality, is highly autobiographical. However, it, like *Les Géorgiques,* is sub-titled 'roman', and is narrated through third-person perspectives rather than the traditional first-person autobiographical voice. Where *Les Géorgiques* had at least an autoportraitural dynamic, *L'Acacia* lacks this frame, indeed eschews it in preference to writings throughout, intra-texts from earlier works. What these and the new 'biographemes' concerning Simon's parents seem to articulate is the space for the *narrator* of *L'Acacia* to come into being. The growth and development of Simon as writer is merely inferred, his narrative control not showing overtly until the palimpsest blank page at the end of the text. The very fact that the first-person narrator of earlier works is absent may be due to the fact that the cumulative overlapping intra-texts from all of Simon's *œuvre* cancel out any single previous autobiographeme such as those from *la Corde raide* which is often regarded as an autobiography.

Our problem is not actually solved, either, by evading the label 'autobiographical' altogether, for clearly self-quotation must be categorised as such. *L'Acacia* thus presents knotty questions concerning self-representationality. Not even Dällenbach's concept of *mise en abyme* interpreted to include both the writer figured within a text also featuring the previous writings of its author is flexible enough a model to describe the multiplicity of *L'Acacia*'s self-resuming artefacts. A set of inter-reflecting and refracting mirrors such as in a telescope or kaleidoscope again underplay the reverberations and echoing waves in this text which are caused by the intrusion of the self as subject obliquely into the narrative space.

The connection is, I suggest, the tenuously metonymical relationship between the signifier and the signified, so that the subject balances precariously over the abyss between the two. The title of *La Corde raide* actually sums up this position rather aptly, and the concept has been explored recently by Leah Hewitt in her study of women's autobiography called 'Autobiographical Tightropes' (1990). Simon seem to be questioning the traditional autobiography in ways similar to feminists who attempt to carve new forms out of existing materials: the position of the other to the self is what is at stake. By chosing the outsider viewpoint in *La Corde raide*, the fictionalised self overtly expressed, Simon may actually have relegated autobiography to the wings henceforth in his *œuvre*. That this text makes a comeback in *L'Acacia* would then be recognition of this decision and a reiteration of the impossibility of reconciling subject and self in the new fictional space. Too many intervening tightropes have been walked. The self is ever subsumed in the narrative of self-quotation which only underlines the linguistic constructions of writing selves, not the Self behind them (the point at which *L'Acacia* ceases).

The ending of this novel is therefore crucial to our problem of how we redefine this text of autobiographemes/themes. Critics have been quick to note the recharge of this text from *Histoire*, the now-named acacia tree mirroring the family tree being the link. While *L'Acacia* certainly is 'la plus grande innovation consistant à greffer la branche des Thomas à celle du narrateur d'*Histoire* et à celle du garçon-soldat des *Géorgiques*' (Sardonak, 1991, p. 216), the text which most requires highlighting is the other which Sardonak omits, *Orion aveugle*. Simon himself draws attention to this text in an interview and highlights not a straight tightrope, but a convoluted one:

> J'ai effectivement illustré ma petite préface à *Orion aveugle* par le dessin d'une ligne sinueuse revenant sur elle-même, se recoupant plusieurs fois. Sur ce dessin, les deux extrémités de la ligne ne se joingnent pas. J'ai répété un dessin semblable dans la page *manuscrite* de *L'Album d'un amateur* mais là les deux extrémités se rejoignent (Armel, 1990, p. 98 [my emphasis]).

This 'tightrope' is only one ingredient towards a response to the autobiography question. The other, interrelated 'text' which is its double yet other is the first drawing accompanying *Orion aveugle*, Simon's drawing of his hand about to write on a blank piece of paper, an open window and a tree outside in the background. The line traced is then the sinuosities of writing itself, the intermediary between the visual and scriptorial forms. This is precisely the implication behind the reworked ending of *L'Acacia*, which takes up and develops the figure of O in *La Bataille de Pharsale,* writing independently after being released from the intertextual shadow of Proust. This heralded the drawing and the intermeshing of word and image in *Orion aveugle*. The final stage, the narrator of *L'Acacia* as artist turning writer does in some way join the two ends as Simon underlines above. The leaves which are at once the acacia and the blank page are 'comme animées soudain d'un mouvement propre,... après quoi tout s'apaisaient et elles reprenaient leur immobilité (p. 380). This is the very paradox or double movement of *Orion aveugle,* 'immobile à grands pas', the final word of *L'Acacia* working the intra-textual joining link back to the earlier image-and-word text, and uniting the whole *œuvre* here as scriptorial reembodiment only. The subject conducting this orchestra, the writer-Simon, gives a performance of the new musicality of the very language of the joining description of word and image. This then is the 'autobiographical' marker of his presence, a tonal persona brought forth only when the 'écriture féminine' side of the story has been paired with the 'Georges' cycles. The 'moissonneuse-batteuse-lieuse', broken and fragmented in *La Bataille de Pharsale,* is transposed in *L'Acacia* into a 'moi-sonneur' formed from the fragments and realignments of his own narratives.

*****

As essence of Simon's *œuvre spéculaire, L'Acacia* is a virtuoso performance of the regenerative process of writing from self-resuming artefacts. Plagiarism is circumvented on two counts. First, Simon does not quote himself exactly, and rarely in context. Second, as we have seen, many reworkings are in fact transpositions, amplifications and transformations of the earlier materials. This use of 'secondhand' literature as Compagnon elucidates in his book on intertextual procedures, *La Seconde Main* (1979), takes on a new dynamic in Simon's hands, particularly when he includes the work of his own (with illustrations!) in *L'Acacia.* The double act of writing and drawing associations together in new arrangements coupled with the musicality of Simon's mature prose produces a 'symphonie scripturale' an orchestration of what is quintessentially simonian in his novels. The novel is thereby moved closer to autobiography than was the case with *Les Géorgiques,* for more than ever 'le style c'est l'homme'. By combining afresh intertexts from other literatures to establish his own brand of writing in the earlier novels, Simon moves on in *L'Acacia* to experimenting and perfecting the *mise en abyme* effects of self-conscious literary tradition. He does, however, avoid narcissistic or solipsistic self-centredness in his work. A major reason for this is the refusal to adopt a first-person narrative voice. With characteristic modesty, and also within the tradition of experimental autobiography itself, the text closes at the birth of the writer. It is his writings which speak his formation and development. *L'Acacia* takes the codes of narrative from H/histoire, through biography and fictionalised autobiography and is the coda of the ensemble, a coda which is at the same time the distillation of the main themes. Intra-textuality is thus a creative force in Simon's maturity works to be reconsidered as more important than intertextual strategies, if it is also at the same time itself an intertext.

Conclusion

The evidence of the preceding chapters shows conclusively the complexity and variety of Simon's uses of previous literature, including his own, in his interviews and novels. In the main, he mentions other *writers* in the former to expound his own criteria of writing, while it is largely in his novels that he exploits and distorts *writings* from many centuries. The studies of the particular writings of Virgil, Shakespeare, Rousseau, Proust, Faulkner and Reed, to name but a few, demonstrate this, and illustrate the range of Simon's borrowings and reworkings, which include intertextual operations such as imitation, adumbration, antithesis, deep influence, part adoption, distortion amplification and foil. Simon's breadth of intertextual borrowing is not only obviously transhistorical: it is also transcultural. So, while we have seen that he is most conversant with his French literary heritage, epitomized in his absorption of Proust, ample proof of his knowledge of Latin and other literatures also emerges from this book. Indeed, it is often the 'foreign' texts which furnish more interesting intertextual parallels and comparisons than, say, Simon's statements and borrowings from nineteenth-century French literature. Our chapter on the subject offers almost a picture of 'negative intertextuality': the works from his own culture and language (with the exception of Proust), are, interestingly, the ones Simon criticizes with most prejudice, and he does *not* include them in his own writing except as gross caricatures.

From our century-by-century study, it seems beyond dispute, then, that Simon is a major practitioner of intertextuality. Our organization of materials has treated many writings and aspects of intertextual usage, but with the sacrifice of a chronological study of intertextuality as Simon's *œuvre* unfolds. As with the formation of Simon's whole writing practice, this literary technique was formed gradually and may indeed be defined in relation to his increasingly dextrous and complex reworking of intertexts from various literatures with the concommitant increase in intra-textual usage. The stages have in fact been treated, but not highlighted, in the course of this book, and I wish to draw these threads together from various chapters to show the centrality of intertextuality to Simon's development as a writer.

Critics have accorded to the development of Simon's novels certain stages: the early works, the 'middle' novels, the third cycle and the new departure of *Les Géorgiques*. What has gone hitherto unnoticed is that important lessons learnt from *intertextual* and *intra-textual* experimentation at a specific moment of Simon's literary output can be mapped against these phases. Thus, from our analysis of Simon's admiration of Dostoyevsky early in his career, we can see how the psychological ambiguities acknowledged in this Russian novelist helped to shape and complicate Simon's view of characterization: *Le Vent* is regarded as 'Simonian' where *Le Tricheur* is still 'traditional'.

When fictional characters were no longer 'prime movers' in Simon's novels, Dostoyevsky as intertext and model was replaced by a different literary exemplar. In the early 'middle' period, it was Faulkner who became Simon's 'instructor', and his works provided a new storehouse of intertextual materials. The reasons are clear. Faulkner's interest in shifting narrative perspective, expression of the inexpressible through anti-hero mouthpieces like Benjy Compson, and language as a 'character' in its own right caught Simon's attention, for these matched his own preoccupations concerning fictional production. *L'Herbe* and *La Route des Flandres* are cases in point.

By experimenting with the literary techniques gained from Faulkner, Simon then recognized that there was much in him which was contrary to his own prose production, such as the desire to create and sustain a kind of historico-fictional epic. At this point, with language holding Simon's main interest, he rejected the American writer and turned to his most major influence, Proust. Here, Simon found the inspiration required to recharge his work: the use of association and the layering of themes, references and language registers. The density of these operations in the 'middle' period proper (as exemplified by *Histoire* and *La Bataille de Pharsale*) is matched by the extent of Proust's influence, which was explored in some detail in the fifth chapter. In spite of Simon's ultimate rejection of the weight of Proust through his 'remake' of a very different *A la recherche* in Part Three of *La Bataille de Pharsale*, it may be argued that Simon can never be entirely free of this influence, because he and Proust in fact share a very similar fictional practice. Thus, while the so-called 'third' cycle from *Orion aveugle* to *Leçon de choses* is stripped almost bare of intertexts from any literature, and the style is distinctive and Simonian (intra-textual), the motor is still inherently Proustian: the associative power of language to construct text.

The mature and independent Simon appears most forcefully in *Les Géorgiques*. This novel highlights more than any other the culmination of a literary development in general and a virtuoso reworking of intertexts in particular. Materials from every century and tradition are built together within this 'architexte' or architectural frame—Virgil's *Georgics,* Orwell's *Homage,* Strachey's *Eminent Victorians,* to name but a few. It is no accident that this text steals the limelight in both the sixteenth- and twentieth-century chapters and is mentioned frequently elsewhere, for it is the most intertextually rich and regenerative of Simon's novels. Association as fictional principle is rejuvenated from the third cycle: its closed network of associative language is intertwined once more with external referents, these being the intertextual fragments from many other writers and kinds of writing.

The virtuoso revolution of intertextual layerings in *Les Géorgiques* from the mixage of *La Bataille de Pharsale* mirrors the revolutions of intra-textual activity in Simon's *œuvre.* The fulcrum of both inter- and intra-textuality is the crucial breakpoint in the third section of *La Bataille de Pharsale.* This opens the *Orion aveugle* cycle where Simon's *bricolage* of his own materials begins to be more overt. The complete reworking of this novel as *Les Corps conducteurs* then signals the self-engendering nature of the whole of Simon's opus. The principle of building on and expanding his own earlier fragments then becomes increasingly accentuated. *L'Acacia* then demonstrates the full-volume orchestration of intra-texts from both the 'Georges' theme of his works and the formal reworkings of *Femmes/La Chevelure de Bérénice* and *Orion aveugle/Les Corps conducteurs.* Significant for its lack of intertexts—there is one reference to *Lady Chatterley's Lover* (p. 177)—*L'Acacia* nonetheless demonstrates through its intra-textual activities the range of the modes normally associated with intertextual usage, except for parody. Simon is not mocking his own earlier attempts to capture experience in and of writing; he amends, expands and magnifies the intricacies of such a task.

The second area which remains in the background of our chronological approach to Simon's uses of previous literature is a classification of the kinds of intertext Simon uses. A synthesis of these from the findings of each chapter is again illuminating as to the diversity of operation to be found in Simon's works. While a degree of overlapping is unavoidable, two distinct kinds of usage emerge: the *types* of intertext used, and the *functions* at work between the intertext and its host. By summarizing the elements of both, an overall evaluation can be made as to the intertextual simplicity or complexity evident in Simon's writings.

The most slight type of intertext is embellishment, and is found in Simon as literary name-dropping. It is often an indicator of character comparison, and is most frequently identifiable in the early novels, the Sganarelle reference in *Gulliver* being a good example. Embellishment occurs where the intertext is not integrated or developed in the text.

Brief allusion is the second type of intertext, and is more developed. It is best illustrated by Simon's allusions to characters from Molière, Calderón and Shakespeare, again in his early novels. Our seventeenth-century chapter showed how these allusions became alternative character-descriptions to those suggested by Simon's own protagonists. Thus, the new character was amplified and qualified by the illustriousness of its cultural forebear. With further elaboration and evolution, the intertext as character allusion may then act as an antithetical model and mock, deflate, exaggerate or distort its new incumbent. An example is the Arnolphe / Reixach comparison in *La Route des Flandres.*

A less microscopic type of intertext is the shorthand event or situation. The 'story' of Marie in *L'Herbe,* which reworks the experience of Faulkner's Addie Bundren into a whole novel, is a good example. One episode of *As I Lay Dying* is then inflated. The opposite use of intertextual qualification of events, compression of the intertext, comes in the packaging of the span of Reed's *Ten Days* into just one 'chapter' of Simon's *Histoire*. Another variation of this type of intertext is the use of a previous work to provide a complete sub-structure. Virgil's *Georgics* is obviously behind, or straddling, the title to *Les Géorgiques,* the same name not merely allowing direct comparison and contrast with the Classic, but actively encouraging it. The purpose of this, as I suggested, was to show not only the close links between Virgil's work and Simon's, but also the separation caused by the very different conceptions and world-views behind the original and Simon's 'remake'. His *Géorgiques* certainly provoke the reader not just to compare events and plots, but to define modernism *as against* the Classics on all levels: literary, psychological, religious, social, even economic and political.

Of wider parameters again than the category of plot is that of thematic reverberation: this occurs when differing, but collaborating, intertexts are aligned. This type of intertext adds a depth of association to the new context without recourse being had to operations such as those found in the literature of 'signification'—message, myth, parable, allegory or propaganda. The simplest and least successful form of this type of intertext in Simon is again illustrated by an early novel, the use of references to *Hamlet* in *Le Sacre du printemps.* Here, a nexus of ideas about adolescence and Oedipal relationships is grafted directly onto Bernard. More successful, because more carefully chosen, is the combination of intertexts of thematic reverberation revolving round one subject. Thus, assassination and revolution in *Le Palace* are emphasized by implication through the superimposition of the relevant intertexts from Shakespeare's *Richard III* and *Julius Caesar*, which are then knitted together with the fate of the anarchist Durruti during the Spanish Civil War. Interplay of several intertexts of this variety allows explicit intertextual gaming and implicit, but no less pointed, thematic comment to occur. The development and wider implications of this kind of intertext are achieved by addition of relevant materials, again epitomized in *Les Géorgiques.* The temporally diverse experiences of LSM (during the aftermath of the French Revolution) and Orwell (at the time of the Spanish Civil War) are foils and mirrors for Simon's narrator, Georges, and build on layers established in *Le Palace.* This 'Chinese box' effect of melding a complex variety of intertexts round a theme makes much greater demands on the compositional skill of its user, and is therefore visible only in Simon's later works. *L'Acacia* then illustrates the harmony of intra-texts as themes, this self-resuming strategy acting as the double or Sosie of intertextual thematic performance.

While intertexts of 'character', 'plot' and 'theme' provide much of the literary parallelism in Simon, it is obvious from our analyses of specific references that there are types of intertext which relate not to 'fond', but to 'forme'. Awareness of language is intrinsic to Simon's development as a writer, and in tandem, various kinds of linguistic intertexts are evident. These generate new text as Simon's language enters into dialogue and verbal partnership with previous literature and his own.

Our first chapter focussed on intertexts of translation. This type of intertext explores the relationship between words in a foreign language and one's own, both given in the text. Direct, accurate transcription of the Latin into French as embodied in uncle Charles's versions were seen to be unregenerative of new text, whereas the boy-narrator's mistakes and literalisms furnished other linguistic possibilities and bifurcations in the text.

Direct quotation from another work in one's own language (often through the medium of translation) disguises the overt 'foreignness' of the intertext concerned, but this type of intertextuality also operates to disrupt the host text. The intrusions of the Reed intertext in *Histoire* are an example of this category. Reed also illustrates the advantages of leaving the origin unsignalled. By hiding the source, the focus shifts to the words themselves, and therefore, by comparison, to Simon's own. By reproducing quotations, we noted that the repositioning of the words was also underlined, the new context playing against the old. By contrast, specification of the originator, as exemplified in the quotations taken from Strachey, is the other option available with this type of intertext. Then, the author's kind of language—his style—is emphasized, and again compared to Simon's own. By thus varying the degree of obtrusiveness of authorship, Simon indirectly examines the role of the writer as individual wordsmith. Orwell presents a useful model here, for Simon makes manifest his unique style by 'talking' and arguing with Orwell's individual language usage. As our final chapter exposed, Simon's use of his own language to establish and demarcate its essence is the culmination of the movement of translation or transposition across his *œuvre*.

Such linguistic intertexts of direct quotation on this small scale may then be transformed by bowdlerization, pastiche or parody into what may be deemed 'mixed' intertexts (in the sense of mixing sound recordings). There is little evidence in Simon of this type of intertext taken from foreign literatures - language barriers pose an automatic block on such activity for Simon; his reworking of Proust, however, is a cameo of this category. In *La Bataille de Pharsale*, Simon uses direct quotations, paraphrases, parodies, vulgarizations and extensions of Proust's language. The influence of Proust as the major precursor has been discussed fully, particularly his language, which resounds in the deepest linguistic levels of Simon's prose. This type of intertext would seem to be language-specific in Simon, that is, relevant only to intertexts first of one's mother tongue (where the full richness of nuance determines direct linguistic inheritance) and second, linguistic inclination. Thus, Simon shows considerable knowledge of Faulkner, for example, and may have read his novels in English. However, the language barrier still prevents complete interiorization of 'foreign' style. Similarly, although Simon is conversant with the writing of, say, Flaubert or Balzac, it is his literary inclination (*in extremis* prejudice) which again blocks the occurrence of 'mixed' linguistic intertexts.

In the eighteenth-century chapter, citation (not quotation) from other writers was discussed. Intertexts of discourse are the next type to summarize. Here, intertexts are not author-specific, but discourse- or code-specific. *Histoire* provides the greatest number of instances of such intertexts. On the small scale, Simon remodels previous structures such as 'romans à tiroir', in this case by literalization: the drawers of postcards generate new text. In the novel as a whole, however, this type of intertextuality is extended in the constant questioning of the boundaries of language classifications as 'Histoire' and 'histoire'. We considered many variations on the scale between these two extremes. Indeed, in one light, Simon's whole *œuvre* may be seen to illustrate the cross-pollination between the larger codes of History, Fiction, Biography and Autobiography. The osmosis and blurring of code labels prevents any strict categorization from emerging and, in turn, allows for a constantly renewable fluidity to generate ongoing writing.

A further type of intertext, similar to intertexts of discourse but at the same time distinct, is genre. Again this depends on a specific kind of language usage, but the difference lies in the fact that the material chosen is representative and often exemplary of its particular *formal* construct ('l'archétype'). Reed's *Ten Days* offers the paradigm of historical reportage as genre, so it is this which dialogues with *Histoire* which might be defined in contrast as a conglomeration which defies all generic classification. *Les Géorgiques* develops this interplay of intertexts of genre by addition of the biography (LSM's and *Eminent Victorians*), political autobiography (Orwell), and blueprints for a new society (Rousseau and Virgil's *Georgics*). The dramatic nature of genre intertextuality was also considered in the seventeenth-century chapter, where the dialogic force of intertextual activity was given fullest attention. While Simon's writing does have a 'poetic' density of linguistic association, the lyric genre does not play a major role, perhaps because the formal aspects of poetry do not integrate into a prose structure as successfully as, say, those of drama. The nineteenth-century chapter offers a second reason for the lack of poetry in Simon. In the vein of Bakhtin, Simon would consider the novel to be the most adaptable and protean literary form, and therefore prose, and prose intertexts are the most malleable forms from which to fashion new writing. The final chapter, however, shows that the novel may also include operations normally associated with poetry such as musicality, colour and the associativeness of imagery. The title of *L'Acacia* epitomises these operations.

This classification of the types of intertext to be found in Simon must be considered alongside the functions in operation between the new and old writings. All intertexts signal past and completed utterance, and belong to a unique and closed setting, their original context. These properties then make them available to other practitioners. Thus, juxtaposition of writings is the basic structuring principle involved in intertextuality, and is always accompanied by the function of association: there must be some common denominator (thematic or stylistic) between the intertext and its host. At the same time, however, the intertext must keep its distinctiveness—it is recognizably other, 'foreign' to the new text. These essential ingredients, juxtaposition, association and otherness, make the intertext (and intra-text) fundamentally comparative devices, and in every instance of their usage in Simon this is always the implicit reason for employing either or both.

Having established how any intertext operates, let us now draw up a list of specific intertextual functions, as illustrated in Simon's works. By collating these, it will then be possible to suggest ways in which Simon's use of intertexts has its own particular slant. The intertext has the basic function of signalling similarity and difference. The qualification of characters, events or themes by an intertext then asks such questions as: How relevant is the reference? Is the comparison incongruous? In what ways does it amplify the host? As we suggested in the first chapter, the plagiarist may be distinguished from the user of intertexts proper, for the former's construct does not appear very different from the original. It is too relevant, too harmoniously linked, without amplification. Simon, as imitator, again meant in the non-plagiarist sense, always uses intertexts which show some degree of difference in their new reformulation, even when he 'repeats' his own writing. There is always a sense of the antithetical, the mirror or foil in the intertexts he chooses. Concerning his intra-texts, the critical element inherent in the intertext as other refers more to a time gap, otherness related then to the differences between the previous intra-text and its new manifestation in the present.

This leads to another central function of the intertext: it is a commentator. Manifestations of this role are exaggerations: Sabine, for example, is described as a rather grotesque Phèdre. Related to this is deflation—Reixach's prowess as a lover is punctured through intertextual comparison to Arnolphe—and distortion: the Reed intertext as a whole undergoes many chronological and narrative contortions. Frequently, the intertext acts as a commentator because its origins are either compressed, inflated, varied or changed in some way. The reworkings of Orwell's *Homage* are a good illustration. With *L'Acacia*, the intra-text acts as a stylistic commentator which draws attention to its own self-consciousness.

A third function of the intertext is the ludic. Intertextual interplay is often a literary joke, a collusion between reader and writer. Modes of the ludic function are mockery, caricature, parody, pastiche, satire, bowdlerization and vulgarization. Simon's use of Proust's language and the content of *A la recherche* in *La Bataille de Pharsale* exemplifies all of these. Familiarity with the original is essential to this function in order to *deform* its uniqueness, but the success of the literary humour depends on maintaining more than a semblance of the intertext's identity. Intertextual disguise and revelation of true identity also fit into this ludic category of intertextuality. Again the Reed and Strachey intertexts have been discussed in this light and are good examples of the kind of game which texts play with Simon's own, very different, writing. Intra-textuality lies outside these ludic ploys because it is never deflationary. It does however highlight the ludic on a different plane, that of reader response, the collusion between Simon and readers familiar with his whole *œuvre*.

These two compilations of types and functions of intertexts make it abundantly clear that Simon is no simplistic user of intertexts. Admittedly, in Simon's early works 'simple' intertextuality is in operation: this quickly gives way, however, to 'complex' intertextual usage as his writing develops, eventually paving the way to intra-textual virtuosity.

From these syntheses, it is also possible to make some observations on the particular importance of intertextuality as a narrative strategy in Simon, and its place in his writings relative to other narrative problems. Linguistically speaking, intertextuality, in Simon, is a means of reformulating the sentence itself, through the association, superimposition and concentration of multiple discourses, and may add layers and styles of language which have no obvious equivalent in French, such as the borrowings from Swift and Strachey. Simon, furthermore, uses intertexts as commentaries. This stance provides a judgement, but without the need to resort to an omniscient narrator to fill this role. Similarities and differences emerge on many planes, but with the circumvention of authorial interruptions of the plot, or didactic comments to the reader. Simon therefore loses nothing of the 'message' element, or the 'depths' of meaning of so-called 'traditional' fiction, because these are *implied* through their intertextual reappearances. This is particularly pertinent to the political and 'revolutionary' novels. At the same time, Simon never sacrifices his principles of narration. The narrator in his works remains omnipresent, never omniscient. This aspect of intertextuality is then closely related to the general questions of narrative viewpoint and authorial standpoint in fiction. It is at this point that Simon comes closest to 'autobiography', but, as our final chapter on *L'Acacia* shows, this authorial presence with or without intra-textual support in the form of quotations from his own previous works can never *be* Simon himself.

A related issue also emerges from Simon's intertextual usage: authorial control. Again, his collaging of intertexts and intra-texts recognizes authorship (be this suppressed or overtly signposted), but his own authorship is then never *ex nihilo* or 'inspired', but compositional, synthetic and 'artisanal'. Reference to Simon's comments on Balzac or Baudelaire are useful reminders that Simon eschews all that smacks of the overt control of the God-like author/creator. Once more, nothing is lost of the architecture of the overall work. The emphasis, though, is shifted from the universal and expansive Author to the selective and self-conscious *bricoleur*.

The self-consciousness inherent in the choice of intertexts, so that reverberations between the source 'meaning' and the new context occur successfully, opens up questions of representation and reality in fictional production. Intertexts are anti-representational at one level because they demand intellectual appreciation of layers of reality, not the 'realistic' apprehension of reality directly. So, while intertexts in Simon represent the past, their new context makes them anachronistic, and therefore unrepresentational. The same is equally true of the intra-textual dimensions of Simon's work, which redefines the impossibility of capturing 'reality', even at its most personalized.

Another interesting issue provoked by the consideration of Simon's uses of intertexts and intra-texts is the role of the reader. Not only does the writer have to have inherited a considerable wealth of cultural baggage, but the reader must have done the same. Appreciation of literary tradition is therefore essential to both, so that writing and reading can progress or react to what has gone before. Intertextuality thus puts literary history back on the map of fictional production and reader response. The final chapter has also shown that Simon also depends heavily on reader familiarity with his *œuvre*. Otherwise the subtleties of his intra-textual regenerations go unrecognised. Whether this can be seen as an imposition or advantage to the reader is an order of question related to allusive writing in general. What it does clarify is the cultural awareness of the writer who also seeks a place within a highly literary tradition.

*****

Literary history and literary criticism go hand in hand, and while Simon is an ingenious user of intertexts, superimposing and combining them with skill in his novels, one may have major reservations concerning his critical acumen. These have already been suggested in the chapter on nineteenth-century intertexts, which displayed Simon's sweeping generalizations about trends in literary development. His prejudices were reiterated by his constant allusion to, and lambasting of, those writers, such as Stendhal, who do not share his writing criteria (or who he claims do not). As for his all too simplistic comments on Balzac, or his interpretations of Flaubert's habits of writing, we can only endorse Simon's own words:

> I must warn those who have come to listen to me that they have before them just a self-taught writer whose literary knowledge does not go beyond an amateur level (Simon, New York, 1982, p. 14).

As amateur critic, Simon also states: 'As far as I am concerned, my cultural equipment is that of a dilettante' (ibid., p. 14). In one respect this is true, for Simon does not read other writers in depth or immerse himself in one particular literary tradition. He also reads, and incorporates as examples in interviews, what is current at the time. The conclusion can only be that Simon is at his best when not citing writers or movements, or when not trying to theorize on the nature of writing. He is above all a practitioner, and is no dilettente *user* of intertexts. It is through his practice that his theory is implied, and emerges most successfully.

Throughout this book, my study has shown the variety and range of Simon's reading incorporated as intertexts in his works. His historical breadth (from the Classics to contemporary literature), and his cultural diversity (from Calderón to Reed) have not been fully appreciated by previous critics. My survey has attempted to form a more complete inventory than has been made hitherto of the wealth of literary reference at the disposal of this highly self-conscious writer. Some consideration has also had to be made of the types and functions of intertexts in operation in Simon's novels, as well as the theories of intertextuality which place different emphases on the position of the quoted and quoting materials. As I have tried to suggest throughout, Simon's work can be seen as a paradigm of intertextuality in its many guises, on large and small scales and including self-quotation. It amply illustrates the theories touched on in the course of the discussion, be they as diverse as Kristeva and Bloom, Bakhtin and Genette. Any of these could usefully be applied in more detail to Simon's writing, or, indeed, the inverse would add understanding to theories of intertextuality. The field of intra-textual usage is just such a departure which needs to be taken further than space allows in this book.

If one overriding and individual use of intertextuality is to be chosen from this compilation and discussion of previous literature in Simon's works, it is this: language as a tool for communicating a 'message' (or, *à plus forte raison,* propaganda) finds its antithetical formulation in Simon. Language is for him above all an associative network of reverberations, where what is suggested is infinitely richer than what is stated. This is nowhere better illustrated than in his abundantly rich intra-textual self-generative writing as expressed in *L'Acacia*. As my book makes clear, this text offers a coda to the intertextual codes which are its forebears and mainspring. The retrospective dynamics of the whole *œuvre* also become more apparent. The summa which is *L'Acacia* clearly energises study of the intertextual and intra-textual writing processes, both for renewed critical attention to the writings of Claude Simon and to the wider field of intertextuality as postmodern practice.

Bibliography

Place of publication is Paris, unless otherwise stated.

1. Works by Claude Simon

Le Tricheur. Sagittaire, 1945, reissued by Minuit.

La Corde raide. Sagittaire, 1947, reissued by Minuit.

Gulliver. Calmann-Lévy, 1952.

Le Sacre du printemps. Calmann-Lévy, 1954; Poche, 1975.

Le Vent. Minuit, 1957.

L'Herbe. Minuit, 1958.

La Route des Flandres. Minuit, 1960; UGE, 1963, with essay by J. Ricardou; Minuit 'double', 1982, with essay by L. Dällenbach.

Le Palace. Minuit, 1962; UGE, 1971; Methuen, 1972, edited and with an introduction by J. Sturrock.

Femmes. Maeght, 1966. Text by Claude Simon, 23 colour plates by J. Miró.

Histoire. Minuit, 1967; Folio, 1973.

La Bataille de Pharsale. Minuit, 1969.

Orion aveugle. Skira, 'Les Sentiers de la création', Geneva, 1970.

Les Corps conducteurs. Minuit, 1971.

Triptyque. Minuit, 1973.

Leçon de choses. Minuit, 1976.

Les Géorgiques. Minuit, 1981.

La Chevelure de Bérénice. Minuit, 1983 (reprint of *Femmes*).

Discours de Stockholm. Minuit, 1986.

L'Invitation. Minuit, 1987.

Album d'un amateur. Éditions Rommerskirchen, 1988.

L'Acacia. Minuit, 1989.

2. Short texts by Claude Simon

'Babel', *Les Lettres nouvelles*, no. 31 (oct. 1955), pp. 391-413.

'Correspondance', *Tel Quel*, no. 16 (1964), pp. 18-32.

'Les Géorgiques', *NRF*, no. 308 (sept. 1978), pp. 1-27.

3. French fiction consulted

Balzac, *Le Père Goriot* (ed. S.C. Gould). London, Hodder & Stoughton, 1967.

Baudelaire, *Les Fleurs du mal*. Classiques Garnier, 1961.

Beckett, *En attendant Godot*. Minuit, 1952.

Corneille, *Le Cid*. Bordas, 1962.

Corneille, *Horace* Larousse, 1965.

Flaubert, *Madame Bovary*. Livre de Poche, 1972.

Laclos, *Les Liaisons dangéreuses*. Garnier-Flammarion, 1981.

Malraux, *L'Espoir*. Gallimard, 1937.

Molière, *Œuvres complètes*. Classiques Garnier, 1962.

Montaigne, *Essais I, II, III*. Garnier-Flammarion, 1969, 1979, 1979.

Proust, *A la Recherche du temps perdu I, II, III*. Gallimard, Pléiade, 1954.

Rabelais, *Pantagruel*. Gallimard, 1964.

Rabelais, *Gargantua*. Gallimard, 1965.

Racine, *Bérénice*. Bordas, 1963.

Racine, *Phèdre*. Bordas, 1963.

Racine, *Athalie*. Larousse, 1970.

Robbe-Grillet, *La Jalousie*. London, Methuen, 1969.

Rousseau, *Les Confessions I, II*. Garnier-Flammarion, 1968.

Rousseau, *Du contrat social*. Garnier-Flammarion, 1966.

Sartre, *Les Mots*. Gallimard, 1964.

Stendhal, *La Chartreuse de Parme*. Gallimard, 1967.

Stendhal, *Le Rouge et le Noir*. Livre de Poche, 1972.

Stendhal, *Vie de Henry Brulard*. Gallimard, 1973.

Voltaire, *Candide*. ed. J.H. Brumfitt, London, O.U.P., 1968.

4. Other fiction consulted

Apuleius, *The Golden Ass*. Harmondsworth, Penguin, 1950.

Caesar, *The Conquest of Gaul*. Harmondsworth, Penguin, 1951.

Caesar, *The Civil War*. Harmondsworth, Penguin, 1976.

Cervantes, *Don Quixote*. Harmondsworth, Penguin, 1950.

Dostoyevsky, *The Idiot*. Harmondsworth, Penguin, 1955.

Faulkner, *As I lay dying*. Harmondsworth, Penguin, 1963.

Faulkner, *Absalom! Absalom!*. Harmondsworth, Penguin, 1971.

Faulkner, *The Sound and the Fury*. Harmondsworth, Penguin, 1984.

Joyce, *Ulysses*. Harmondsworth, Penguin, 1969.

Orwell, *Homage to Catalonia*. Harmondsworth, 1962.

Plutarch, *Fall of the Roman Republic*. Harmondsworth, Penguin, 1958.

Shakespeare, *Othello*. London, Methuen, Arden Shakespeare, 1958.

Shakespeare, *Julius Caesar*. London, Methuen, Arden Shakespeare, 1965.

Shakespeare, *Romeo and Juliet*. London, Methuen, Arden Shakespeare, 1980.

Shakespeare, *King Richard III*. London, Methuen, Arden Shakespeare, 1981.

Shakespeare, *Hamlet*. London, Methuen, Arden Shakespeare, 1982.

Strachey, *Eminent Victorians*. Harmondsworth, Penguin, 1948.

Swift, *Gulliver's Travels*. Harmondsworth, Penguin, 1967.

Virgil, *The Georgics*. Harmondsworth, Penguin, 1982.

5. Books wholly or in part on Claude Simon

Apeldoorn, J. van, 'Balzac: A la lecture de Claude Simon, divertissement', in Rossum-Guyon, F. van & Brederode, M. van, eds., *Balzac et 'Les Parents pauvres'*. S.E.D.E.S., 1981.

Bertrand, M., *Langue romanesque et parole scripturale*. PUF, 1987.

Birn, R., & Gould, K., eds., *Orion Blinded: Essays on Claude Simon*. Lewisburg, Bucknell UP, 1980. (Bibl. pp. 297-303).

Britton, C., *Claude Simon: Writing the Visible*. London, Cambridge University Press, 1987.

Calí, A., *Pratiques de lecture et d'écriture*. Nizet, 1980.

Carroll, D., *The Subject in Question: the Languages of Theory and the Strategies of Fiction*. Chicago, Chicago U.P., 1982.

Chapsal, M., *Quinze Écrivains*. R.Julliard, 1963. (Interview with Claude Simon).

Dällenbach, L., *Le Récit spéculaire*. Seuil, 1977.

Duncan, A.B., ed., *Claude Simon: New Directions*. Edinburgh, Scottish Academic Press, 1985.

Evans, M., *Claude Simon and the Transgressions of Modern Art* London, MacMillan Press Ltd., 1988.

Fletcher, J., *Claude Simon and Fiction Now*. London, Calder and Boyars, 1975.

Fletcher, J., *Triptych—Claude Simon*. London, Calder & Boyars, 1977.

Gould, K.L., *Claude Simon's Mythic Muse*. Columbia, S.C., French Literature Publications Company, 1979.

Grivel, C., ed. *Écriture de la religion, écriture du roman*. Lille, Presses de Lille, 1979. (Also includes an interview with Claude Simon, 17 avril 1979).

Hollenbeck, J., *Éléments baroques dans les romans de Claude Simon*. La Pensée universelle, 1982. (Bibl. pp. 185-90).

Jiménez-Fajardo, S., *Claude Simon*. Boston, Mass., Twayne, 1975.

Kadish, D.Y., *Practices of the New Novel in Claude Simon's 'L'Herbe' and 'La Route des Flandres'*. Fredericton, N.B., York Press, 1979.

Loubère, J.A.E., *The Novels of Claude Simon*. Ithaca and London, Cornell U.P., 1975. (Bibl. pp. 255-61).

Moncelet, C., *Essai sur le titre—en littérature et dans les arts*. B.O.F., 1972. (Appendice questionnaire by Claude Simon).

Pugh, A.C., *Simon: 'Histoire'*. London, Grant and Cutler, 'Critical Guides to French Texts, 22', 1982.

Reitsma-La Brujeere, C., *Passé et Présent dans 'Les Géorgiques' de Claude Simon*. Amsterdam, Rodopi, 1992.

Ricardou, J., *Nouveau Roman: hier, aujourd'hui*. UGE, 1972. (Vol. I, Problèmes généraux & Vol. II, Pratiques).

Ricardou, J., dir., *Claude Simon:* Colloque de Cerisy. UGE, 1975. (Bibl. pp. 432-43).

Roubichou, G., *Lecture de 'L'Herbe' de Claude Simon.* Lausanne, L'Age d'homme, 1976. (Bibl. pp. 323-34).

Sardonak, R., *Claude Simon: les carrefours du texte.* Toronto, Paratexte, 1986.

Sardonak, R., *Understanding Claude Simon.* Colombia, S. Carolina, Univ. S. Carolina Press, 1990.

Sturrock, J., *The French New Novel.* London, Oxford University Press, 1969.

Sykes, S.W., *Les Romans de Claude Simon.* Minuit, 1979. (Bibl. pp. 190-4).

Tost Planet, M.A., *Claude Simon: novelas españolas de la guerra y la revolución.* Barcelona, Ediciones Península, 'Nexos', 1989.

6. Special numbers of periodicals on Claude Simon

'Claude Simon', *Entretiens,* no. 31 (1972).

'Claude Simon', *Études littéraires,* IX, no. 1 (1976).

'La Terre et la Guerre dans l'œuvre de Claude Simon', *Critique,* no. 414 (1981). [Bibl. pp. 1244-52].

'Claude Simon', *The Review of Contemporary Fiction* (Spring 1985).

'Claude Simon', *Revue des Sciences humaines,* no. 220 (oct-déc. 1990).

7. Articles on Claude Simon

Abirached, R., 'Carnet de Théâtre', *Études,* no. 317 (mai 1963), pp. 231-5.

Albérès, R.-M., 'Claude Simon écrivain "alexandrin"', *Les Nouvelles littéraires,* no. 2100 (30 nov. 1967), pp. 1, 7.

Armel, A., 'Claude Simon: le passé recomposé', *Magazine littéraire*, (mars 1990), pp. 96-103.

Aubarède, G. d', 'Instantané—Claude Simon', *Les Nouvelles littéraires*, no. 1575 (7 nov. 1957), p. 7.

Birn, R., 'Proust, Claude Simon and the art of the novel', *Papers on Language and Literature*, no. 13 (Spring 1977), pp. 168-186.

Biro-Thierbach, K., 'Claude Simon sur les sentiers de la création', *Gazette de Lausanne*, no. 147 (27-28 juin 1970), pp. 32-3.

Blanzat, J., '*Le Sacre du printemps* de Claude Simon', *Le Figaro littéraire*, no. 440 (25 sept. 1954), p. 9.

Bon, F., Claude Simon: Fantastique et Tragédie: Claude Simon, *L'Acacia*', *Critique*, no. 511 (déc. 1989), pp. 980-96.

Bourdet, D., 'Images de Paris', *La Revue de Paris* (janv. 1961), pp. 136-41.

Bourin, A., 'Techniciens du roman—Claude Simon', *Les Nouvelles littéraires*, no. 1739 (29 déc. 1960), p. 4.

Bourin, A., 'Le Roman—jugé par N. Sarraute, M. de Saint Pierre, C. Simon, J. Hugron, J.-R. Huguenin', *Les Nouvelles littéraires*, nos. 1764 (22 juin 1961), p. 7, & 1765 (29 juin 1961), p. 8.

Brewer, M.M., 'An Energetics of reading: intertextuality in Claude Simon', *Romanic Review*, vol. LXXIII, no. 4 (Nov. 1982), pp. 489-504.

Britton, C., 'Diversity of discourse in Claude Simon's *Les Géorgiques*', *French Studies*, vol. XXXVIII, no. 4 (Oct. 1984), pp. 423-41.

Calle Gruber, M., 'Sur les brisées du roman', *Micromégas*, VIII (gennaio-aprile 1981), pp. 108-113.

Carroll, D., 'Diachrony and synchrony in *Histoire*', *Modern Language Notes*, vol. 92, no. 4 (May 1977), pp. 797-824.

Carroll, D., 'For example: psychoanalysis and fiction or the conflict of generation(s)', *Sub-Stance*, no. 21 (1978), pp. 49-67.

Chapsal, M., 'Un idiot', *L'Express*, no. 328 (3 oct. 1957), p. 29.

Chapsal, M., 'Tandis qu'elle agonise', *L'Express*, no. 386 (6 nov. 1958), p. 25.

Chapsal, M., 'Le Jeune Roman', *L'Express*, no. 500 (12 janv. 1961), pp. 31-3.

Chapsal, M., 'Entretien, Claude Simon parle', *L'Express*, no. 564 (5 avril 1962), pp. 32-3.

Culler, J., 'Presupposition and Intertextuality', *Modern Language Notes*, XCI, no. 6 (1976), pp. 1380-96.

Dällenbach, L., 'Intertexte et autotexte', *Poétique*, 27 (1976), pp. 282-96.

Dällenbach, L., 'L'Archive simonienne', *Modern Language Notes*, vol. CIII, no. 4 (Sept. 1988), pp. 736-50.

Duffy, J.H., 'Meaning and Subversion in Claude Simon's *Le Vent:* some structural considerations', *French Studies Bulletin*, no. 15 (Summer 1985), pp. 8-9.

Duncan, A.B., 'Claude Simon and William Faulkner', *Forum for Modern Language Studies*, vol. IX, 3 (July 1973), pp. 235-52.

Duncan, A.B., 'Claude Simon's *Les Géorgiques*: an intertextual adventure', *Romance Studies*, no. 2 (Summer 1983), pp. 90-107.

Duranteau, J., 'Claude Simon, "le roman se fait, je le fais et il me fait"', *Les Lettres françaises*, no. 1178 (13-19 avril 1967), pp. 3-4.

DuVerlie, C., 'Interview with Claude Simon', *Sub-Stance*, no. 8 (Winter 1974), pp. 3-20.

Eribon, D., 'Fragments de Claude Simon', *Libération*, no. 91 (29 août 1981), pp. 20-2.

Evans, M., 'Two Uses of intertextuality: reference to impressionist painting and *Madame Bovary* in Claude Simon's *Leçon de choses*', *Nottingham French Studies*, vol. XIX, no. 1 (May 1980), pp. 33-45.

Fletcher, J., 'Claude Simon: autobiographie et fiction', *Critique*, no. 37 (nov. 1981), pp. 1211-17.

Gosselin, C.H., 'Voices from the past in Claude Simon's *La Bataille de Pharsale*', *New York Literary Forum*, no. 2 (1978), pp. 23-33.

Haroche, C., 'Claude Simon, romancier', *L'Humanité*, no. 11560 (26 oct. 1981), p. 15.

Hassan, I.H., 'The Problem of influence in literary history: notes towards a definition', *Journal of Aesthetics and Art Criticism*, no. 14 (Sept. 1955), pp. 66-76.

Hinkle, D.L., 'The Mystery of significance and the enigma of time: an analysis of the thematic structures of Faulkner's *The Sound and the Fury* and Claude Simon's *L'Herbe*', *DAI*, vol. 32, no. 5, 2689-A - 2690-A (Nov. 1971).

Howard, R., 'Un mot d'un traducteur américain de Claude Simon', *Entretiens*, no. 31 (1972), pp. 163-6.

Isaacs, N.D., 'Faulkner with a vengeance. The Grass is greener', *The South Atlantic Quarterly*, vol. LX no. 4 (Autumn 1961), pp. 427-33.

Jenny, L., 'La Stratégie de la forme', *Poétique*, no. 27 (1976), pp. 257-81.

Joguet, M., 'Dialogue avec Claude Simon: "Le poids des mots"', *Le Figaro*, no. 1559 (3 avril 1976), pp. 13-14.

Juin, H., 'Les Secrets d'un romancier', *Les Lettres françaises*, no. 844 (6-12 oct. 1960), p. 5.

Kanters, R., 'La Difficulté d'être romancier', *La Table ronde*, no. 81 (sept. 1954), pp. 117-25.

Knapp, B.L., 'Interview avec Claude Simon', *Kentucky Romance Quarterly*, vol. XVI no. 2 (1969), pp. 179-90.

Labriolle, J. de, 'De Faulkner à Claude Simon', *Revue de Littérature comparée*, LIII, no. 3 (juillet-sept. 1979), pp. 358-88.

Lebrun, J.-C., 'Visite à Claude Simon: l'atelier de l'artiste', *Révolution*, no. 500 (29 sept-5 oct. 1989), pp. 36-41.

Le Clec'h, G., 'Claude Simon: le jeu de la chose et du mot', *Les Nouvelles littéraires*, no. 2272 (8 avril 1971), p. 6.

Lefere, R., 'Claude Simon et Marcel Proust', *Studi francesi*, 100, anno XXXIV, fasc. 1 (gennaio-aprile 1991), pp. 91-100.

Lemarchand, J., 'Au théâtre de Lutèce, *La Séparation* de Claude Simon', *Le Figaro littéraire*, no. 883 (23 mars 1963), p. 20.

Leonard, D.R., 'Simon's *L'Herbe:* beyond sound and fury', *The French-American Review*, vol. I, 1 (Winter 1976), pp. 13-30.

Levitt, M.P., 'The Burden of history', *Kenyon Review*, no. 123 (1969), pp. 128-34.

Magny, O. de, '*Le Vent* par Claude Simon', *Les Lettres nouvelles*, no. 55 (déc. 1957), pp. 764-6.

Morrissette, B., 'The New Novel in France', *Chicago Review*, vol. 15, no. 3 (Winter-Spring 1962), pp. 1-19.

Nadeau, M., 'La Triste Histoire d'Antoine Montès', *France Observateur*, no. 387 (10 oct. 1957), pp. 17-18.

Nitsch, W., 'Von einer Katastrophe zur anderen: Claude Simon und sein neuer Roman *l'Acacia*', *Merkur*, XLIV, 7 (1990), pp. 588-92.

Orr, M., 'Literary embellishment or functional intertext in Claude Simon's *Les Géorgiques*?', *French Studies Bulletin*, no. 26 (Spring 1988), pp. 14-17.

Orr, M., '*Mot à mot:* Translation as (inter)textual generation in five novels by Claude Simon', *New Comparisons*, Autumn 1989, pp. 66-74.

Orr, M., 'Intertextual bridging: across the genre divide in Claude Simon's *Les Géorgiques*', *Forum for Modern Language Studies*, vol. XXVI, no. 3 (1990), pp. 231-239.

Paulhan, C., 'Claude Simon "J'ai essayé la peinture, la révolution, puis l'écriture"', *Nouvelles*, no. 2922 (15-21 mars 1984), pp. 42-5.

Peyroux, M., 'Claude Simon et Proust', *Bulletin de la Société des amis de Marcel Proust et des amis de Combray*, no. 37 (1987), pp. 23-32.

Piatier, J., 'Claude Simon ouvre *Les Géorgiques*', *Le Monde*, 4 sept. 1981, pp. 11, 13.

Pobel, D., 'Le Son du canon', *La Nouvelle Revue française*, no. 445 (fév. 1990), pp. 73-76.

Poirson, A. & Goux, J.-P., 'Entretien avec Claude Simon—un homme traversé par le travail', *La Nouvelle Critique*, no. 105 (juin-juillet 1977), pp. 32-44.

Poirson, A., 'Avec Claude Simon sur les sables mouvants', *Révolution*, no. 9 (22-28 janv. 1982), pp. 35-9.

Pugh, A.C., 'Du *Tricheur* à *Triptyque* et inversement', *Études littéraires*, no. 9 (avril 1976), pp. 137-60.

Pugh, A.C., 'Interview with Claude Simon: autobiography, the novel, politics', *The Review of Contemporary Fiction*, vol. V, no. 1 (Spring 1985), pp. 4-13.

Reitsma-La Brujeere, C., 'Récit et métarécit, texte et intertexte dans *Les Géorgiques* de Claude Simon', *French Forum*, vol. IX, no. 2 (May 1984), pp. 225-35.

Ricardou, J., 'La Bataillle de la Phrase', *Critique*, no. 26 (mars 1970), pp. 226-56.

Riffaterre, M., 'The self-sufficient text', *Diacritics*, no. 3 (Fall 1973), pp. 39-45.

Riffaterre, M., 'Le Syllepse intertextuelle', *Poétique*, 40 (nov. 1979), pp. 496-501.

Riffaterre, M., 'La Trace de l'intertexte', *La Pensée*, no. 215 (oct. 1980), pp. 4-18.

Rossum-Guyon, F. van, 'De Claude Simon à Proust: un exemple d'intertextualité', *Marche Romane*, no. 21: 1-2 (1971), pp. 71-92.

Sardonak, R, 'Comment fait-on un cocktail simonien? ou *Les Géorgiques* relues et corrigées', *Romanic Review*, vol. LXXXI, no. 2 (March 1990), pp. 236-47.

Sardonak, R., 'Un drôle d'arbre: L'Acacia de Claude Simon', *Romanic Review*, vol. LXXXII, no. 2 (March 1991), pp. 210-32.

Senlis, J., 'Nous avons choisi Claude Simon', *Clarté*, no. 31 (déc. 1960), pp. 27-8.

Sigaux, G., 'Claude Simon: *L'Herbe*', *Preuves*, no. 94 (déc. 1958), pp. 73-4.

Simon, C., 'Je ne peux parler que de moi', *Les Nouvelles littéraires*, no. 1809 (3 mai 1962), p. 2.

Simon, C., 'Débat—le romancier et la politique', *L'Express*, no. 632 (25 juillet 1963), pp. 25-6.

Simon, C., 'Les Écrivains français prennent leur distance: Claude Simon: contre un roman utilitaire', *Le Monde*, 8 mars 1967, p. V.

Simon, C., 'Je ne suis pas un mandarin', *Le Monde*, no. 6932 (26 avril 1967), p. 4.

Simon, C., 'Tradition et révolution', *La Quinzaine littéraire*, no. 27 (1-15 mai 1967), pp. 12-13.

Simon, C., 'Roman, description et action', in *The Feeling for Nature and the Landscape of Man*, ed. P. Hallberg. Proceedings of the 45th Nobel Symposium held 10-12 Sept. 1978 in Göteborg to celebrate the 200th anniversary of the Royal Society of Arts and Sciences of Göteborg (Göteborg, 1980), pp. 78-93.

Simon, C., 'La Voie royale du roman', *Le Nouvel Observateur*, no. 900 (6 fév. 1982), p. 74.

Simon, C., 'Lecture to the colloquium on the New Novel, New York University, October 1982', *Review of Contemporary Fiction*, Spring 1985, pp. 14-23.

Sykes, S.W., '"Mise en abyme" in the novels of Claude Simon', *Forum for Modern Language Studies*, IX, 4 (Oct. 1973), pp. 333-45.

Sykes, S.W., '*Les Géorgiques:* une reconversion totale?', *Romance Studies,* no. 2 (Summer 1983), pp. 80-89.

Sykes, S.W., 'Tintin faisant la révolution? Novel attitudes to the Spanish Civil War', *Romance Studies,* no. 3 (Winter 1983-4), pp. 122-35.

Thiébaut, M., 'Parmi les livres: Claude Simon, *La Route des Flandres*', *Revue de Paris,* no. 67 (déc. 1960), pp. 159-61.

Zumthor, P., 'Le Carrefour des rhétoriqueurs—intertextualité et rhétorique', *Poétique,* 27 (1976), pp. 317-37.

8. Books consulted

Bakhtin, M. & Medvedev, P.N., *The Formal Method in Literary Scholarship.* Baltimore & London, Johns Hopkins U.P., 1978.

Barthes, R., *Essais critiques.* Seuil, 1964.

Barthes, R., *Le Degré zéro de l'écriture.* Seuil, 1972.

Beaujour, M., *Miroirs d'encre.* Seuil, 1980.

Bloom, H., *The Anxiety of Influence.* Oxford, O.U.P., 1973.

Brumfitt, J.H., *Voltaire Historian.* O.U.P., 1970.

Cave, T.C., *The Cornucopian Text.* Oxford, Clarendon Press, 1979.

Compagnon, A., *La Seconde Main.* Seuil, 1979.

Culler, J., *Structuralist Poetics.* London, Routledge & Kegan Paul, 1975.

Derrida, J., *La Carte postale.* Flammarion, 1980.

Genette, G., *Introduction à l'architexte.* Seuil, 1979.

Genette, G., *Palimpsestes.* Seuil, 1982.

Hermerén, G., *Influence in Art and Literature.* Princeton, Princeton U.P., 1975.

Hewitt, L., *Autobiographical tightropes.* Lincoln, Univ. of Nebraska Press, 1990.

Josipovici, G., *Writing and the Body.* Harvester Press Ltd., 1982.

Kristeller, P.O., *Renaissance Thought.* Harper Torchbooks, 1961.

Kristeva, J., *Séméiotiké: recherches pour une sémanalyse.* Seuil, coll. 'Points', 1969.

Lejeune, P., *Je est un autre.* Seuil, coll. 'Poétique', 1980.

May, G., *L'Autobiographie.* PUF, 1979.

Meyer, H., *The Poetics of Quotation in the European Novel.* Princeton, Princeton University Press, 1968.

Mylne, V., *The Eighteenth-Century French Novel.* London,. Cambridge University Press, 1981.

Riffaterre, M., *Semiotics of Poetry.* Bloomington & London, Indiana U.P., 1978.

Robbe-Grillet, A., *Pour un nouveau roman.* Minuit, 1963.

Rousset, J., *La Littérature de l'âge baroque en France.* José Corti, 1954.

Rousset, J., *Narcisse Romancier.* José Corti, 1973.

Schmid, W. & Stempel, W.-D., hergst., *Dialog der Texte: Hamburger Kolloquium zur Intertextualität.* Wien, Wiener Slawistischer Almanach, 11, 1983.

Shergold, N.D., *A History of the Spanish Stage.* Oxford, Clarendon Press, 1967.

Thomas, H., *The Spanish Civil War.* London, Hamish Hamilton, 1977.

Tieghem, P. van, *Les Influences étrangères sur la littérature française 1550-1880.* PUF, 1967.

Todorov, T., *Mikhail Bakhtine: le principe dialogique.* Seuil, 1981.

Weinstein, A.L., *Vision and Response in Modern Fiction.* Ithaca & London, Cornell U.P., 1974.